Palm Beach Palate Cookbook

*Experience the best of
Palm Beach County's
cuisine, culture,
& community*

The **Suncoast High School Foundation** was formed in 2000 to advocate continuation of adequate public and private funding for Suncoast Community High School's four outstanding magnet programs – Computer Science, Interdisciplinary Program, International Baccalaureate, and the Math Science and Engineering Program. The Foundation works to ensure that the school's students and faculty have the materials, equipment, and facilities to pursue the school's challenging curriculum.

The foundation supports the school's outstanding programs by means of fundraising drives, events, and projects. This cookbook represents the first fundraising project of its kind for this dynamic foundation.

First printing 2005

Information on obtaining additional copies of *Palm Beach Palate Cookbook* may be found at www.PalmBeachPalate.com or by contacting:

$\mathcal{P}$alm $\mathcal{B}$each $\mathcal{P}$alate $\mathcal{C}$ookbook
Suncoast High School Foundation
600 West 28th Street
Riviera Beach, FL 33404

International Standard Book Number
0-9770782-0-5

WIMMER
COOKBOOKS

A CONSOLIDATED GRAPHICS COMPANY

800.548.2537   wimmerco.com

Foreword

Two years in the making, this cookbook is the delicious culmination of the efforts of a large group of dedicated Suncoast High School parents. Six hundred contributed recipes demonstrated the enthusiastic involvement of the community in this labor of love. We didn't stop there. We acquired recipes from acclaimed chefs at some of the area's best restaurants and museum cafes, from the elegant Breakers Hotel to the beloved Food Shack. Hundreds of recipes were tested, tasted, and perfected in the kitchens and homes of committee members. The resulting cross section of mouth watering recipes will give you a taste of South Florida's lifestyle. Whether you are a visitor or a resident, dish into this book for inspiration for a seaside barbeque or breakfast on the patio.

The cultural diversity on the campus of Suncoast High School is a microcosm of Palm Beach County's cosmopolitan population. Through our culinary choices, we have endeavored to celebrate these rich cultural influences. Our project grew from a volunteer cookbook to a unique venture when we collaborated with the Palm Beach County Cultural Council. The council's mission is to develop, coordinate, and promote the county's arts and cultural activities.

Palm Beach County offers nationally accredited museums, one of the top rated zoos in the US, and many outdoor art and music festivals. Many of our cities feature historically significant architecture amidst cultural, dining, and shopping districts. Numerous venues around the county host outstanding performances in opera, ballet, theater, dance, and popular and classical music.

In our sidebars, learn about our cultural offerings and our history. Read about our African-American heritage at the S.D. Spady Museum, or the Gilded Age at Whitehall, the home of oil and railroad tycoon, Henry Flagler. Arts and culture in Palm Beach County have all the right ingredients. The Palm Beach Palate Cookbook committee extends our collective gratitude to the Palm Beach County Cultural Council and many of its distinguished members for their participation in this book.

We extend our deepest thanks to the Suncoast High School administration and the many restaurants who shared some of their finest recipes with us. To each and every person who submitted a recipe, a sponsorship, or a wish for success – thank you for all you have done.

Bon appetit!

The Suncoast Community High School Cookbook Committee

Culture has found its place in the sun.

Palm Beach County — Florida's Cultural Capital

Culture in Palm Beach County has all the right ingredients.

 CENTRE for the ARTS AT MIZNER PARK

 BOCA BALLET THEATRE

 HENRY MORRISON FLAGLER MUSEUM PALM BEACH, FLORIDA

 bob lappin & the palm beach POPS

 ZOO

 ArtiGras

 ROOTS CULTURAL FESTIVAL, INC.

 MIAMI CITY BALLET EDWARD VILLELLA ARTISTIC DIRECTOR Florida's Internationally-Acclaimed Dance Company

 KRAVIS CENTER FOR THE PERFORMING ARTS

 STREET PAINTING FESTIVAL

 LIGHTHOUSE CENTER FOR THE ARTS

 SUNFEST OF PALM BEACH COUNTY, INC

 pbcc Palm Beach Community College
Eissey Campus Theatre
Dolly Hand Cultural Arts Center
Duncan Theatre

 LAKE WORTH PLAYHOUSE

 PALM BEACH INTERNATIONAL FILM FESTIVAL

 SOUTH FLORIDA SCIENCE MUSEUM

 THE SOCIETY OF THE FOUR ARTS

 LOXAHATCHEE river HISTORICAL SOCIETY

 DOROTHY F. SCHMIDT COLLEGE OF ARTS & LETTERS

 NORTON MUSEUM OF ART

 The Morikami Museum and Japanese Gardens

 BOCA RATON MUSEUM OF ART

 Old School Square CULTURAL ARTS CENTER

 CALDWELL THEATRE COMPANY Boca Raton Florida

 FLORIDA STAGE

 Boca Raton Historical Society

 ARMORY ART CENTER

 Palm Beach Photographic Centre

 Milagro CENTER

 PALM BEACH OPERA

 HIBEL MUSEUM OF ART

 Ballet Florida Marie Hale, Founder and Artistic Director

For up-to-date information on cultural events log on to www.palmbeachculture.com/fun or call our 24 Hour ArtsLine 800.882.ARTS

Palm Beach County Cultural Council

FLA USA Partner

FLORIDA Arts
Sponsored in part by the State of Florida, Department of State, Division of Cultural Affairs, the Florida Arts Council, and the National Endowment for the Arts.

Palm Beach County Florida
THE BEST OF EVERYTHING®
A TOURIST DEVELOPMENT COUNCIL FUNDED PROJECT

WHAT CAN

BOUILLABAISSE

TEACH US ABOUT

INTEGRATED WEALTH MANAGEMENT?

■

In the right hands, unusual combinations can yield satisfying results.

Managing wealth has never been more challenging. Success depends less on the individual ingredients and more on the recipe that brings them all together. This is why Wachovia Wealth Management supports a coordinated approach built around integrated teams of experienced financial specialists. Collectively, the members of our teams cover the spectrum of wealth management disciplines, including financial planning, investment management, trust and estate administration, and insurance.

A local Relationship Manager provides a single point of contact and assembles the team according to your particular needs. Ultimately, the goal is to bring a highly individualized, comprehensive plan to the table — and execute it flawlessly, so you can savor your success.

• • •

For nearly 200 years, successful individuals and families have turned to Wachovia Wealth Management. Talk to us. Together, we can achieve uncommon results.

Palm Beach: Suzanne Holmes, Relationship Manager, 561-820-1003.

WACHOVIA
WEALTH MANAGEMENT

Uncommon Wisdom

Distinguished Sponsors

Diamond

Sue Archer, NWS, AWS
Kenneth and Barbara Horowitz
Denise and Bill Meyer
Wachovia Wealth Management

Palm Beach County Board of County
Commssioners
Palm Beach County Cultural Council

Platinum

Braman Motorcars

Brown Moving and Storage

The Breakers Palm Beach

Gold

Café Chardonnay
Fidelity Federal Bank and Trust
Keith and Renata Jones
Jack and Kim Lansing

Rinker Materials
Roy Assad, Leila Restaurant
and L'Opera Brasserie
Vive Magazine

Silver

Fredric M. Barr, M.D., Plastic Surgeon
Kenneth R. Beer, M.D., –
Dermatologic Surgery and Cosmetic
Dermatology
Cheney Brothers, Inc.
Rosalind Clarke, Corcoran Group,
Palm Beach
Tony and Gloria Davenport

Curt and Susan Fonger
Dr. and Mrs. Samuel Gordon
Larry and Charlotte Pelton
Publix Super Markets, Inc.
Riverside National Bank
RSM McGladrey
Richard & Katarina Rodman
Suncoast Community High School PTSA

Bronze

Gary and Susan Adkin
ASG Medical Systems
Automated Direct Mail Service Center, Inc.
Balfour
Neville and Maxine Benjamin
Dr. Javier Canasi
The Casey Family
Changes Hair, Nails, and Day Spa
Norman and Carol Erenrich

Miami International Machinery
Paul and Michong Ogden
Palm Beach Dermatology/Dr. Steven
Rosenberg
Pepsi Bottling Company
PFS Advisors, LLC
Mr. and Mrs. Jay Shearouse
Mr. and Mrs. Robert Silvani
Nori and Lorna Trehan

Friends

Ashley Farms, Inc.
Communications by Johnson, Inc.
Ina Garten
Golf Links of Florida
Independent Construction

Deborah Martyn
JK and Stephan McCrea
Mr. and Mrs. Robert Panico
Scott and Jill Rippe
Dr. and Mrs. Lawrence Selinger

Cookbook Committee Members

Co-Chairs/Editors
Barbara Horowitz and Susan Fonger

Development Coordinator	*Charlotte Pelton*
Design/Production Manager	*Carol Erenrich*
Recipe Collection Manager	*Susan Adkin*
Managing Editor	*Melody Powell*
Recipe Testing Coordinator	*Jill Rippe*
Cover Artist	*Sue Archer, NWS, AWS*
Production Committee	*Van Ho*
	Jill Rippe
	Jane Rollins
	Michelle Shearouse
	Lorna Trehan
	Tricia Trimble
	Ingrid Kluth
Treasurer	*Patti Abramson*
Celebrity Chefs Collection	*Frank Eucalitto, Café Chardonnay*
Writers	*Liz Best*
	Susan Fonger
	Barbara Horowitz
	Renata Jones
	Palm Beach County Cultural Council Members
Data/Software	*Rick Filsinger*
	Brian Brugger
Community Liaisons	*Marianne Baker*
	Curt Fonger
	Michong Ogden
	Mary Gordon
	Paige Graddy
	Sally Michel

The committee would like to extend heart-felt thanks to all who contributed to this project – whether by contributing recipes, typing, proofing, or by donating your time, talents, and support. We couldn't have done it without you!

Chef Alex Awad
Chef Daniel Boulud
Chef Fu Chen
Chef Lex Chutintaranond
Chef Tom Costello
Chef Dave DeLisa
Chef Roger Dikon
Chef Frank Eucalitto
Chef Bill Flatley
Chef Ricky Gopeesingh
Chef John Jones
Chef Kai Lermen
Chef Laurent Loupiac
Chef Glen Manfra
Chef Ross Matheson
Chef John Mecoli
Chef David Pantone
Chef Mark Ramsay
Chef Elmer Saravia
Chef Kevin Sawyer
Chef Howard Waugh
Gary Adkin
Adele Aiken
June Aiken
Eden Andes
Richard Andreacchio
Linda Angus
William Annis
Autumn Armstrong
Ellen Arnot
Arthur R. Marshall
    Foundation
Jeff Atwater
Doug & Sonia Augeri
Marta Bacalao
Dedra Battles
Yvonne Beasley
Tiffany Bell
Maxine Benjamin
Dino Benvenuti
Abda Bernardino
Rena Blades

Pat Boyer
Clifford & Saundra Brady
Debbie Brannock
Grace Brown
Tevis R. Brown
Shereen Bryan
Stephanie Bryan
Beth Burr
Yvonne Cabrera
Peggy Campbell
Kay Carnes
Tom Carnes
Dan & Chelie Casey
Myrna Charlot
Leigh E. Clark
Vicki Cohen
Stacy Colella
Frank Compiani
Rayna Creedon
Gloria Crutchfield
Cathy Cullen
Lancey Cunningham
Pia Dandiya
Gloria Mosley Davenport
Lois-Anne Davis
Vicki Davis
Luis & Betty de la Maza
Ann Deluca
Jessica Demos
Jane Diaz
Jessie Dixon-Duncan
Barbara Dubow
Barbara Dunn
Janet Eddinger
Georgene Eisenberg
Liz Elliott
John Engelhardt
Rebecca Erenrich
Cory Eucalitto
Gigi Eucalitto
Peggy Fairchild
Greg Fenlon

Pebbles Fergusan
Cynthia Fontaine
Marie-Josee Fortier
Alicia Foster
D. Frank
Marion Frank
Hermione Franklin
John Fresco
Alexa Garcia
Ronni & Alan Gerstel
Marion Glenn
Lynn Gold
Samuel Gordon II
Sandy Graham
Addie L. Greene
Shelley Greif
Pam Hagen
Eileen Harden
Jana Hartley
Denise Hartman
Linda Hastings
Bob Hatcher
Beth Heister
Romy Hochreutener
Merle Hoher
Suzanne Holmes
Ken Horowitz
Rose Horowitz
Craig Howard
Jackie Iles
Carmen Jaramillo
Lisa Jensen
Barbara Johnson
Cheryl Johnson-Riley
Brian Jones
Robin Kanel
Mary Kattan
Ilene Kaye
Marilyn Kligler
Karen Klotz
Mike Knight
Stewart Knight

Terry Knight
John and Laura Kowal
Nicole Lajeunesse
Vanessa Lajeunesse
Rick Lanier
Susanna Laurenti
Ann Levy
Kimberly Leyendecker
Laura Lloyd
Jeannine Lombardo
Nancy Lorelli
Patti Lucas
Jasmine Lynch
Craig MacKenzie
Joy Madden
Sarajane Marell
Deb Martyn
Marianne Matthews
Tommy Mays
Marianne McCann
Molly McCormick
JK and Stephan McCrea
Karol McCredie Krizka
Jessica Mendez
Jane Merritt
Anne Metzger
Denise Meyer
Ed and Toni Meyer
Juanita Minor
Cina Montoya
Dawn Movic
Carol Murphy
Terry Mynar
Gale Nelson
Bill Nix
Susan Noel

Leigh-Ann Oberg
Julia & Claire O'Ceallaigh
Liana Ogden
Nathan Ogden
Emily O'Manoney
Cindy Orlando
Kathy Orloff
Robert Pagano
William Paty
Lambert and Mary
   Pengelley
Barbara Petterson
Wendy Pierce
Joseph & Thuy Pimentel
Vicki Pollitt
Moisette Porcher
Ave Potente
Joseph Powlis
Barbara Puglisi
Angelo Questo
Annette Rallo
Kristi Rand
Nancy Richter
Cathie Riggs
Katarina Rodman
Edwina Rogers
Susan Rosenberg
Susan Rosenthal
JB & Susan Royal
Catherine Royce
Toody Rusnak
Byron Russell
Linda Schaffer
Valerie Schmedes
Carol Schmidt
Victoria Schmidt

Valerie Scott-Duckrow
Rozanne Sehayik
Elizabeth Semple
Darlene Shaw
Linda Shea
Claudia Shea
Fran Sherman
Michaele Shopbell
Irene Simmons
Vivene Simpson
Diane Somerville
Susie Soverel
Mary Lou Staba
Steve Stinson
Kimberly Stumpf
Beth Lynne Suriano
Joan Taylor
Judy Thomas
Karen Turner
Carolyn Van Meter
Sharon Wacks
Holly Wagner
Ruth Walker
Officer Brian Wallin
Peggy Walsh
Lucile B. Washington
Adrianne Weissman
Beth Wong
Diana Wong
Jacquelyn G. Woodard
Michael and Christina
   Worley
Sarah Zambito
Marcia Ziskal
Tracey Zudans

We have tried to remember everyone. If your name was inadvertently not listed please accept our sincere apologies and contact us so we can be sure to include you in the next edition.

Table of Contents

Appetizers & Beverages 13

Brunch & Breads 47

Condiments & Sauces 65

Salads 73

Soup & Sandwiches 97

Vegetables 119

Entrées
    Poultry 131
    Meat 148
    Seafood 161

Pasta, Rice & Grains 187

Desserts 203
    Cakes & Cookies 215
    Pies 230

Contact List for Cultural Organizations 239

Index 241

October 1, 2005

ADDIE L. GREENE

Commissioner, District VII

■

Palm Beach County
Board of County Commissioners
Governmental Center, 12ᵗʰ Floor
301 North Olive Avenue
West Palm Beach, Florida 33401
(561) 355-2207
Fax: (561) 355-6332

South Office:
Southeast County Complex
345 Congress Avenue
Delray Beach, Florida 33445
(561) 276-1350
Fax: (561) 276-1365

agreene@co.palm-beach.fl.us

"An Equal Opportunity
Affirmative Action Employer"

Suncoast High School
c/o Suncoast High School Foundation
600 West 28th Street
Riviera Beach, FL 33404

Dear students, parents and friends:

On behalf of the Palm Beach County Board of County Commissioners, it gives me great pleasure to congratulate all the Suncoast High School parents and friends who have produced this excellent book, the Palm Beach Palate Cookbook. As the Commissioner in whose district this excellent school resides, I extend my best wishes for continued success to the Suncoast Foundation.

Year after year, Suncoast has proven itself to be the premier academic public high school in Palm Beach County. We as a Commission whole-heartedly agree with the Foundation's mission to financially support the academic and artistic excellence that thrives at Suncoast High School. After all, this book is all about insuring our students' future for generations to come.

As I browse through the pages of this book, I am pleased to see that you have included numerous cultures through the recipes and the eye-catching sidebars. You have succeeded in representing the cultural diversity that is a proud component of the Suncoast campus, and our County.

As representatives of Palm Beach County, we are honored to be counted among your distinguished sponsors of this worthy endeavor. Best wishes for continued success!

Sincerely,

Addie L. Greene

Addie L. Greene, Vice-chairperson
District VII

Appetizers & Beverages

Appetizers & Beverages

Helen's Vidalia Onion Dip
Toasted Almond
  Party Spread
Eggplant Caviar
Moroccan Red Bean Dip
Tapenade with
  Sun-Dried Tomatoes
Olive Tapenade
White Bean Dip
  with Herbs
Hearts of Palm Spread
Sun-Dried Tomato & Goat
  Cheese Spread
  with Pita Chips
Florentine Puffs
Mushrooms de Provence
Mushroom Turnovers
Tom's Garlic
  Chicken Wings
Meat Samosas

Combo Pot Stickers,
  One Thai Restaurant
Pierods – a Latvian Specialty
Sazio Restaurant Stuffed
  Portobello
Spanakopita
Hot Artichoke-Lobster Flowers
Blinis, Café du Parc
Conch Fritters
Blue Crab and Sweet Corn
  Fritters, Café Chardonnay
Jumbo Lump Crab Cakes,
  Carmine's Ocean Grill
Crab Cakes with Mango Salsa
Crab Louie Martini,
  E.R. Bradleys
Steamed Corn Custard
  with Crab
Crab and Artichoke Beignets
Smoked and Fresh Salmon
  Tartar, Bice Restaurant
Floribbean Ceviche of
  Yellowtail Snapper,
  PGA National Resort and Spa
Grilled Bacon Wrapped Shrimp
  with Creole Remoulade
Grilled Margarita Shrimp
T-WA Shrimp, Reef Grill
Pan Seared Scallops with
  Vegetable Aioli
Marshalls' Mussels
A Spa in Your Refrigerator
Hibiscus
Irish Cream Cordial
Kahlua Martini
Sparkling Berry Punch
Singer Island Cosmopolitan
Painkiller
White Sangria, Zaza's Cucina
Sparkling Summer Tea
Strawberry Daiquiri

Helen's Vidalia Onion Dip

This is a family recipe from Sea Island, Georgia that has been used for over 25 years. It is a simple but incredible recipe using their local delicious Vidalia onions.

1 cup minced Vidalia onion　　1 cup mayonnaise
1 cup shredded Gruyère or
　　Swiss cheese

Preheat oven to 350 degrees. Combine all ingredients in an earthenware crock or ovenproof dish and bake 15 to 20 minutes until bubbly and lightly browned on top.

Serve warm with crackers or bread. Multigrain flatbreads are particularly good as they make for a delicious contrast in taste and texture.

Sweet onions are a fine substitution when Vidalia onions are not in season.

Toasted Almond Party Spread

This warm spread has an unexpected taste.

1 (8-ounce) package cream　　⅛ teaspoon nutmeg
　　cheese　　　　　　　　　　⅛ teaspoon pepper
1½ cups Swiss cheese　　　　⅓ cup sliced almonds,
⅓ cup Miracle Whip　　　　　　　toasted
2 tablespoons chopped
　　green onion

Preheat oven to 350 degrees. Combine all ingredients and mix well. Pour into a 9-inch baking dish. Bake 15 minutes, stirring halfway through cooking time.

Top with additional toasted, slivered almonds, if desired. Serve with crackers.

Eggplant Caviar

Serving the dip on Belgian endive pieces makes an especially attractive presentation.

3 medium eggplants
12 garlic cloves, peeled
1 tablespoon coarse salt
6 tablespoons fresh lemon
   juice
1 tablespoon olive oil
1 teaspoon ground pepper
¼ teaspoon salt

¾ cup golden raisins
3 plum tomatoes, finely diced
¾ cup chopped black olives
½ cup toasted pine nuts
½ cup chopped Italian parsley
¼ cup diced red onion
8 heads of Belgian endive

Preheat oven to 400 degrees. Cut eggplants in half. Cut deep slits into flesh side and insert 2 garlic cloves per cut. Sprinkle with salt, cover with foil, and bake for 45 minutes. Let cool.

Scoop out eggplant and mash. Add lemon juice, oil, pepper, and salt. Fold in remaining ingredients. Place by spoonful in endive leaves and arrange on round platter.

Yield: 5 cups

If you don't have endive, you may use Boston lettuce or serve on crackers.

George Sukeji Morikami

Visitors are surprised to discover a century-old connection between Japan and South Florida. It is here that a group of young Japanese farmers created the Yamato Colony intending to revolutionize agriculture. Results were disappointing and the Colony dwindled down to just one settler – George Sukeji Morikami. He continued to cultivate local fruit and vegetable crops. In his 80s, he donated his land to Palm Beach County with the wish to preserve it as a park and to honor the memory of the Yamato Colony. Today, the Morikami Museum and Japanese Gardens are a living monument bridging his two homelands.

Moroccan Red Bean Dip

Try serving this with spicy toasted pita triangles; sprinkle split, quartered pitas with chili powder and bake on a cookie sheet at 350 degrees until crisp.

1 teaspoon olive oil
½ red onion, chopped
1 garlic clove, finely chopped
1 plum tomato, diced
1 tablespoon golden raisins
3 dried apricot halves, chopped
1 tablespoon orange juice

¾ cup canned red kidney beans, rinsed and drained
¼ teaspoon cumin
⅛ teaspoon cinnamon
⅛ teaspoon ground cloves
⅛ teaspoon curry powder
⅛ teaspoon chili powder
⅛ teaspoon salt

Sauté onion and garlic in oil until softened, 2 to 3 minutes. Reduce heat, cover, and simmer 2 to 3 minutes more. Stir in tomato, raisins, apricots, and orange juice. Cook, covered, 2 to 3 minutes. Stir in beans and spices. Remove from heat and cool slightly. Blend or purée, keeping it a bit chunky, then refrigerate.

Peanut Island

Since its formation in 1918 in the Riviera Beach Inlet, two theories have emerged as to the origin of the name Peanut Island, a sand island created from the spoil of dredging the inlet. One story is that a county commissioner referred to the island as "not being worth peanuts". Another version holds that a corporate interest planned to build a peanut processing plant on the island, thus the name Peanut Island. Today Peanut Island Park is home to the Palm Beach Maritime Museum and Kennedy Bunker and offers an array of recreational opportunities, including fishing and camping.

Tapenade with Sun-Dried Tomatoes

1 (14-ounce) can black olives, pitted and drained
2 ounces sun-dried tomatoes
2 tablespoons capers

1 tablespoon green peppercorns
3 tablespoons fresh basil
3-4 tablespoons olive oil
2 garlic cloves, crushed
Salt and pepper, to taste

Finely mince olives, tomatoes, capers, peppercorns, and basil. Add oil, garlic, salt, and pepper.

Olive Tapenade

Tapenade is a delicious spread to serve with fresh crusty French bread and some extra virgin olive oil for dipping.

1 (14-ounce) can pitted
  black olives, drained
½ cup green olives with
  pimento, drained
1 garlic clove, crushed
¼ cup fresh parsley
1 teaspoon fresh thyme or
  ½ teaspoon dried thyme
  (not ground)

2 shallots or 1 teaspoon finely
  chopped red onion
3-4 tablespoons olive oil
Coarse salt, to taste
Freshly ground pepper, to
  taste
1 pinch dried red pepper
  flakes, or more to taste

Finely mince olives, garlic, parsley, thyme, and shallots. Mix in oil, salt, pepper, and red pepper.

White Bean Dip with Herbs

This is better than hummus.

¼ cup olive oil
3 garlic cloves, chopped
  very finely
1 teaspoon finely chopped
  sage
½ teaspoon finely chopped
  rosemary

2 (10-ounce) cans cannelloni
  beans, drained
2 tablespoons water
Salt
Cayenne pepper
2 tablespoons olive oil
Pita chips

Heat ¼ cup oil in a medium skillet until shimmering. Add garlic, sage, and rosemary and cook over moderately high heat, stirring, until fragrant and garlic just begins to brown, about 1 minute. Add beans and toss to coat. Transfer beans to a food processor. Add water, season with salt and cayenne pepper, and process to a fairly smooth purée. Transfer dip to a small serving bowl, drizzle with 2 tablespoons olive oil, and serve with pita chips.

Yield: 3 cups

Palm Beach Maritime Museum

A little piece of history can be found on Peanut Island, where the restored command post used by President John F. Kennedy during the Cuban Missile Crisis is located. The president's compound in Palm Beach, which he frequented during his presidency, is close by. The bunker on Peanut Island was built by SeaBees under the direction of the Secret Service. The bunker was a nuclear war contingency facility during the Cuban Missile Crisis. Today, the bomb shelter and nearby Coast Guard station are open to the public.

Hearts of Palm Spread

1 (14-ounce) can chopped and drained hearts of palm
1 cup shredded mozzarella cheese
½ cup mayonnaise
½ cup grated Parmesan cheese
½ cup sour cream

Preheat oven to 350 degrees. Mix all ingredients together and spoon into a lightly greased 9-inch quiche pan. Bake 30 minutes or until brown and bubbly. Serve with assorted party crackers.

Hearts of Palm

Hearts of palm are the hearts, or cores, of the cabbage palm (Sabal palmetto), a tall, tough-barked palm that is the state tree of Florida. Called "swamp cabbage" by Floridians, it used to be considered nourishment for anyone with a machete - and was actively cut down as a source of food during the Depression. It didn't take long, however, before its tenderness and delicacy were noticed. Shortly thereafter, Florida enacted a state law to protect it from excessive harvesting.

Sun-Dried Tomato and Goat Cheese Spread with Pita Chips

This arranged appetizer makes a beautiful presentation.

4 pitas, lightly brushed with olive oil
12 ounces goat cheese
4 ounces cream cheese
½ cup chopped sun-dried tomatoes, drained
½ cup pitted and chopped kalamata olives
3 tablespoons basil, cut into a fine chiffonade
2 tablespoons olive oil
1 tablespoon balsamic vinegar
Fresh basil, for garnish

Grill pitas over moderate flame 1 minute on each side or until you begin to see grill marks on the pitas. Remove pitas from grill and cut each into 6 pieces.

Combine goat cheese and cream cheese together in a bowl. Form into a ball and place in the center of a large plate. Press cheese mixture down slightly to flatten it. Combine the sun-dried tomatoes, olives, basil, oil, and vinegar. Pour tomato mixture over cheese. Arrange pita chips around cheese mixture and serve immediately. Garnish with fresh basil sprigs.

Yield: 10 to 12 appetizer servings

If you like, the pitas can be sprinkled with coarse salt after grilling.

Florentine Puffs

These tasty spinach and cheese balls can be prepared ahead of time, frozen, and quickly made when guests arrive.

1 (10-ounce) package
    frozen chopped spinach
1 medium chopped yellow
    or white onion
1 stick butter
2 cups herb stuffing crumbs

2 cups grated Parmesan
    cheese
6 eggs, beaten
Salt and freshly ground
    pepper, to taste

Thaw spinach and squeeze out moisture. Sauté chopped onion in butter until transparent. Combine spinach and remaining ingredients in a large mixing bowl and mix well. Shape into walnut-sized balls and freeze quickly on a baking sheet. When the balls are frozen, place them in a freezer storage bag. Bake straight from the freezer for 8 to 10 minutes in a preheated 350-degree oven. Do not overbake.

Mushrooms de Provence

Serve these at any party and watch them quickly disappear.

2 pounds mushrooms

Filling:

1 (8-ounce) package cream
    cheese
1 (1-ounce) package ranch
    dressing (dry)

¼ cup mayonnaise
2 tablespoons minced onion
¾ cup minced parsley
½ cup grated Parmesan cheese

Topping:

2 cups breadcrumbs

1 stick butter, melted

Preheat oven to 350 degrees. Clean mushrooms and remove stems. Combine filling ingredients. Stuff mushrooms with filling and top with breadcrumbs. Pour melted butter over mushrooms. Bake 30 minutes. Serve hot.

Washing Mushrooms

Many people never run a mushroom under water before using it in a recipe, while other people are afraid of eating any sort of vegetable without thoroughly washing it. A good rule of thumb is to inspect the mushroom to be sure there is no separation between the cap and stem and no sand or dirt visible. Then either dust it with a soft brush or rub it gently with a towel. If you do wash the mushroom, swish it in a bowl of cold water four or five seconds and pat dry.

Mushroom Turnovers

Here is another wonderful appetizer that can be prepared in advance and frozen. It has become easier to find delicious gourmet mushrooms in the supermarkets. They add a wonderful touch to this recipe. You need to prepare the dough 4 hours in advance.

Dough:

1 (8-ounce) package cream cheese
2 sticks butter
2¼ cups flour
1 teaspoon salt

Mushroom Filling:

3 tablespoons butter
1 large onion, finely chopped
½ pound mixed wild mushrooms
¼ teaspoon dried thyme
½ teaspoon salt
Freshly ground pepper, to taste
2 tablespoons flour
¼ cup heavy cream
1 egg, slightly beaten

To make dough, mix cream cheese, 2 sticks butter, flour, and salt as you would for a pie crust and roll into a ball. Chill for 4 hours.

Preheat oven to 325 degrees. To make filling, heat 3 tablespoons butter in a skillet and lightly brown onions. Add mushrooms and cook 3 minutes. Add thyme, salt, and pepper and sprinkle with flour. Stir in cream until thickened. Roll out dough on a floured board to ⅛-inch thickness. Cut dough circles with a 2½-inch round cutter. Place 1 small teaspoon filling on half of each circle. Fold over to make a half circle and seal edges with water, pressing together with a fork. Poke a small hole in the top of each. Brush lightly with egg and bake 30 minutes or until brown.

Yield: 36 turnovers

These can be made in advance and frozen before baking, but don't brush them with egg until ready to bake. Place turnovers on a cookie sheet to freeze, then transfer them to plastic bags.

Can also be filled with chopped liver, crab, shrimp, lobster, or chicken.

Pelican

The pelican uses its beak as a dip net to catch fish which are soon swallowed. Brown pelicans seem to be everywhere along Florida coastlines. With their long bill, saggy throat pouch, large size, and lugubrious manner, pelicans attract attention whether they are flying in long lines above the water, diving for fish or just sitting on top of a post. Interestingly, the young pelicans are very noisy but adults are essentially silent.

20

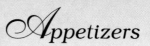
Tom's Garlic Chicken Wings

Great party food. Tom and his wife, Kay live aboard their boat year-round. Doesn't that sound like fun!

1 (4-pound) bag wingettes
¾ cup dry white wine
¼ cup sherry
6 teaspoons minced garlic
   or 1½ tablespoons
   garlic juice

1 tablespoon dry Italian
   seasoning
Oil, for frying

Combine wine, sherry, garlic, and Italian seasoning for marinade. Pour over wings. Marinate in refrigerator overnight, or marinate with vacuum sealer for a minimum of 1 hour.

Fry in deep fryer until cooked, about 20 minutes. Mix in your favorite sauce.

There are several sauces to use on wings and many can be found at your local grocery store. Serve with celery sticks and blue cheese dressing.

Northwood University

Northwood University is a private institution specializing in entrepreneurial education with a defined philosophy about management that guides almost everything it does. Northwood emphasizes the importance of free enterprise and a market-based economy as well as the strong connection between business and the arts in its degree programs. Students come from over 45 countries and 35 states to partake in sixteen different majors of study. Northwood's West Palm Beach campus is located on 90-acres, distinguished by woods, lakes, palm trees, and a unique bell tower and plaza with distinctly Floridian architecture.

Meat Samosas

A fragrant and delicious Indian treat.

¼ pound ground lamb or beef
1 cup water
2 teaspoons chopped onion
1 teaspoon chopped fresh gingerroot
¼-½ teaspoon ground red chili from the Indian market, or cayenne
2 teaspoons butter
2 teaspoons flour

4 ounces peas, cooked and mashed
A few cilantro leaves
2 green chilies, such as jalapeños, seeded and deveined, more or less to taste
1 teaspoon ground allspice
1 teaspoon ground cumin
Salt, to taste
Spring roll pastry squares
Oil, for frying

Cook ground meat with water, onions, ginger, ground red chili, and salt until mixture becomes dry. Melt 2 teaspoons butter, add flour and cook until mixture is very slightly golden brown. Combine with meat mixture, peas, coriander leaves, and remaining spices.

Fill spring roll pastry squares and fold into triangles. Pinch to close. Fry in hot oil on medium heat until golden brown.

Ground red chili is available at Indian markets or at some specialty gourmet markets.

Cayenne pepper may be substituted for the ground red chili. You also may substitute minced vegetables for the meat. To make Vegetable Samosas, sauté peas and carrots together for a traditional flavor.

Hotel Royal Poinciana

The Hotel Royal Poinciana was the largest wooden structure in the world. Henry Flagler constructed the luxurious 1,150-room hotel on the island of Palm Beach near the shore of Lake Worth in 1894. The development of the Hotel Royal Poinciana and later The Breakers, quickly helped establish Palm Beach as a winter resort for the wealthy members of America's Gilded Age. The Hotel Royal Poinciana was razed in 1935 after a hurricane damaged the building beyond repair.

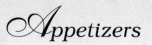

Combo Pot Stickers

This wonderful recipe was contributed by One Thai
restaurant in Palm Beach Gardens.

Filling:

⅓ pound chicken breast,
  minced
⅓ pound shrimp, shelled,
  deveined, and minced
⅓ pound ground pork
½ cup minced Chinese
  celery
3 tablespoons chicken
  broth

½ tablespoon sesame oil
1 tablespoon minced
  gingerroot
1 tablespoon soy sauce
1 teaspoon salt
½ teaspoon sugar
1 pinch white pepper
1 dash rice wine

Dough:

⅔ pound all-purpose flour,
  about 1¼ cups

1 cup boiling water

For Frying:
4 tablespoons cooking oil

Combine chicken and shrimp, then add in other filling
ingredients.

Knead dough ingredients until smooth. Divide dough
into 40 equal-sized portions. Roll each portion into a
flat, round pancake. Place 1 tablespoon of chicken
shrimp filling on half of a round. Wet inside edges of
dough, fold dough in half, enclosing the filling. Pinch
seams together.

Heat cooking oil in a flat-bottomed frying pan. Fry pot
stickers over low heat for 2 minutes. Add water and
cover. Cook over medium heat until water is
evaporated and pot stickers become golden brown at
the bottom. Serve hot.

*To save time, you can use wonton skins instead of
making the dough yourself. They can be found at
most Asian markets or in the produce section of the
grocery store.*

Early Crops

*The 'crops' that the
very first settlers
took to the northern
markets did not come
from their gardens,
but from the beach.
They combed
beaches for wrecked
ships, and salvaged
brass hinges, copper
piping, ship's bells,
and nails. Brass
could fetch 10 cents
a pound, and copper
scraps, 15 cents per
pound. These items
went into their
homes as well.*

Pierods – a Latvian Specialty

This recipe makes a huge quantity – 200 pierods. The assembly time is significant, but they freeze well and are scrumptious.

Filling:

1½ pounds ham	2 large onions
2 pounds bacon	

Dough:

2½ sticks butter	¼ cup warm water
2 cups milk	6 cups flour
5 packages active dry yeast	2 cups flour (approximately,
2 teaspoons sugar	for kneading and rolling
1 tablespoon flour	out dough)
¾ cup warm water	1 egg yolk, beaten

Chop ham, bacon, and onions and fry. Set aside to cool. DO NOT pour off the fat – it is important to the recipe. Set aside to cool.

Mix butter and milk together in a saucepan. Bring to a boil, then set aside to cool until lukewarm.

In a bowl, combine yeast, sugar, 1 tablespoon flour, and ¾ cup warm water. Let rise until bubbly.

In another bowl, combine 6 cups flour, yeast mixture, and butter/milk mixture and mix together. Add ¼ cup warm water. Turn dough out on to floured surface and knead in approximately 2 cups flour, more or less depending on the humidity, until dough is no longer sticky. Do not over-work dough, as it will become tough. Dough should be elastic and your hands should come away clean. Place dough in a lightly oiled bowl and allow to rise for at least 1 hour.

Roll out dough to ¼-inch thick. Cut circles from dough using an upturned wine goblet. Put a generous spoonful of filling in the center of each circle, fold in half, pinch edges closed, tuck ends under, and place seam side down on a cookie sheet. Brush with beaten egg yolk and let rise for 20 minutes.

Preheat oven to 400 degrees. Bake 10 minutes or until golden brown.

Yield: 200 pierods

Trapper Nelson

A classic figure in local history, Trapper Nelson moved here as a young man, living in a cabin, and hunting in the then untamed area around Jupiter. His huge physique earned him the name "Tarzan of the Loxahatchee". His "Zoo and Jungle Garden" was a popular tourist site where everyone including the celebrities of the day, came to watch him wrestle wild animals – alligators most notably. Today you can visit his cabin in Jonathan Dickinson State Park.

Sazio Stuffed Portobello

Portobello mushrooms, roasted red peppers, fresh spinach, and Gorgonzola cheese in a Madeira wine sauce from Chef Dave DeLisa of Sazio, located on Atlantic Avenue in Delray Beach – exquisite!

Marinade:

6 ounces balsamic vinegar
4 ounces sugar

2 cups water

Stuffed Portobello:

2 large marinated
    Portobello caps
1 ounce extra virgin olive oil
1 teaspoon sliced fresh garlic
3 ounces roasted red
    peppers
4 ounces fresh spinach

3 ounces Gorgonzola cheese
1 ounce butter
1 teaspoon diced shallots
2 ounces Madeira wine
1 ounce butter
5 ounces demi-glace
    (commercial or homemade)
2 ounces butter

Pour balsamic vinegar into a bowl and mix in sugar. Add water. Place Portobello caps in marinade. Cover bowl, place in refrigerator, and let sit overnight.

Heat olive oil in pan. When hot, add garlic and lightly brown. Add spinach and sauté 1 to 2 minutes. Place Portobello caps upside-down in oiled pan. In one cap, place red peppers and sautéed spinach. Place Gorgonzola cheese in the other cap. Place entire pan in a 375-degree oven for 8 to 10 minutes.

In a separate pan, heat 1 ounce butter and sauté shallots until soft (approximately 2 to 3 minutes). Add Madeira wine and wait 15 seconds, then add 1 ounce butter and demi-glace. Wait until reduced by ½ to ¾. Remove pan from oven and place Portobello cap with red peppers and spinach in plate with cap down. Gently flip second Portobello cap on top of the first and pour reduction over top; serve.

Yield: 2 servings

Demi-glace is a slowly cooked reduction of beef broth and espagnole sauce. It can take as much as 24 hours to reduce this mixture to a thick and richly flavored sauce, so it might be best to buy a commercially prepared product.

Misunderstood Mainstays

There's not a cook anywhere who doesn't have ample salt and pepper in the kitchen, but many experts advise you to rethink the way you use these popular ingredients. First, throw out your salt and pepper shakers. Replace them with a dish of sea salt and a pepper mill. Using your fingers to add salt helps you control the amount better than the shaking method. Freshly ground black pepper is easy to accomplish and you'll love its brightness of flavor and aroma.

Spanakopita – Greek Spinach Pie

This savory pie is of Greek origin and consists of phyllo dough crusts and a filling of sautéed spinach and onions mixed with feta cheese, eggs, and seasonings.

Sea Gull Cottage

Robert R. McCormick, a railroad and land developer from Denver, Colorado built a home in Palm Beach in 1886, one of the finest in South Florida at the time. When Henry Flagler decided to extend his Florida East Coast Railway and build two luxury hotels in Palm Beach, he purchased McCormick's property. Flagler used the cottage, which featured Georgia marble, stained glass windows, a mahogany staircase, and a three story tower, as his winter residence in Palm Beach until he completed Whitehall in 1902. Today, Sea Gull Cottage is owned by the Royal Poinciana Chapel and is located near Whitehall.

3 tablespoons oil
1 onion, chopped
½ cup chopped green onions, white and green parts
3 garlic cloves, minced
2 pounds fresh baby spinach, trimmed, washed, and roughly chopped
Salt and pepper, to taste
Juice of ½ lemon
2 eggs, lightly beaten

12 ounces crumbled feta cheese
1 tablespoon coriander seeds, toasted and ground
½ teaspoon freshly grated nutmeg
½ pound unsalted butter, melted
1 pound phyllo pastry sheets
¼ cup finely chopped fresh oregano
¼ cup finely chopped chives
½ cup grated Parmesan cheese

Heat olive oil in a large skillet and place over medium heat. Sauté onions and garlic 3 minutes until soft. Add spinach, season with salt and pepper, and continue to sauté until spinach is limp, about 2 minutes. Add lemon juice. Remove from heat and place in a colander. Squeeze out excess liquid and set aside to cool; filling needs to be cool and dry to prevent phyllo dough from becoming soggy.

Preheat oven to 350 degrees. In a medium bowl, beat eggs with feta cheese, coriander seeds, and nutmeg. Season, then fold in cooled spinach mixture until well-blended.

Brush two baking sheets with melted butter. Unroll phyllo dough and lay a sheet flat on a work surface; keep phyllo covered with a damp (not wet) towel as you work to prevent it from drying out and becoming brittle. Brush sheet with melted butter, then sprinkle evenly with some oregano and chives. Repeat with two more sheets of phyllo, stacking each on top of the other.

continued

Spanakopita – Greek Spinach Pie continued

With a sharp knife or pizza cutter, cut sheets lengthwise into thirds to form 2½-inch strips; do this with all sheets of dough. Place a heaping teaspoon of filling near one corner of the layered phyllo strip. Fold the end at an angle over the filling to form a triangle. Continue to fold triangle along strip until you reach the end, like folding up a flag. Brush top with butter and dust with Parmesan cheese; place on prepared baking sheet and cover while preparing remaining pastries. Repeat until all the filling and phyllo strips are used. Bake 20 to 30 minutes until triangles are crisp and golden. Serve hot, warm, or cold.

Hot Artichoke-Lobster Flowers

2 large artichokes	Salt and pepper, to taste
2 lobster tails	1 pinch marjoram
1 small onion	Mayonnaise

Cook artichokes in boiling salted water until tender, 20 to 35 minutes. Remove leaves and reserve hearts for another use.

Add lobster tails to same water and bring to boil. Cook for 5 minutes, then reduce heat and simmer 8 to 10 minutes. Grind cooked meat with onion in a food processor. Add salt and pepper. Add marjoram and enough mayonnaise to make a spread. Mix well.

Place ½ teaspoon lobster mixture on each leaf and top with dab of mayonnaise. Arrange in a circular pattern on a serving dish that can be placed under broiler. Broil just before serving until barely brown.

Yield: 10 to 12 servings

The Barefoot Mailman

At the turn of the last century, the easiest way to get mail around in South Florida was by foot. That's by foot on the sandy beach, hence barefoot. It was about a 3 day walk to get from Jupiter to Miami.

Blinis

This delicious recipe comes from Café du Parc *in Lake Park.*

1 ounce active yeast	2 whole eggs, separated
2 ounces whole wheat flour	2 cups milk
1 cup whole milk	6 ounces sour cream
8 ounces all-purpose flour	4 tablespoons caviar

Combine and mix yeast, whole wheat flour, and milk in a small bowl. Put in a warm place to activate yeast. Mixture is ready when it begins to foam.

In a large bowl, combine all-purpose flour, egg yolks, and milk. Beat well with a whisk. Mix this mixture with the activated starter.

Using an electric mixer, beat egg whites until they form soft peaks. Fold egg whites into other mixture until homogenous. Add half of the sour cream and mix again.

Heat a small nonstick fry pan (or blini pan, if you have one) to medium-high heat. Using a ladle, fill pan until bottom is completely covered with a thin layer. Cook blini on one side until batter becomes dry on the top with a lot of holes. With a small spatula, flip blini over and cook for anther minute. Set aside on a sheet of parchment paper and repeat for remaining blinis.

Serve each blini filled and rolled with 1 tablespoon caviar and sour cream.

As a variation, make 2-inch portions to be used as a base to present finger foods. This size will cook quickly, so be sure not to overcook. Small rounds are especially good with caviar with sour cream or smoked salmon.

Yield: Approximately 24 2-inch rounds or 4 6-inch rounds

A Traditional Time for Blinis

As the Season of Lent is a season of fasting, the day before – Shrove Tuesday, or Mardi Gras, is a traditional time to enjoy a last feast including things like eggs, butter, rich sauces, and dairy products. In North America among religious and non-religious alike it has been a custom to have communal pancake suppers on Shrove Tuesday. The consumption of pancakes, or 'blini' (crêpes) just before Lent begins is also found in the European and Eastern Orthodox traditions. Pancakes or Blinis, tend to use up all those rich products forbidden during fasting.

Conch Fritters

There's nothing like a good conch fritter to make you feel like it's a beautiful tropical day and the world is happy. They're wonderful served with Lime Mayonnaise or another hot dipping sauce.

Fritters:

1 large egg
½ cup milk
1¼ cups flour
½ teaspoon salt
2 tablespoons baking powder
1 pound conch meat, ground in a meat grinder or food processor
2 tablespoons finely diced sweet red pepper

2 tablespoons finely chopped onion
2 tablespoons finely diced celery
1 teaspoon lemon zest (optional)
½ minced habanero or jalapeño pepper
¼ cup beer
Few drops Tabasco sauce
Oil for frying

Lime Mayonnaise:

4 garlic cloves, crushed
Zest and juice of 2 limes
2 egg yolks

1 cup extra virgin olive oil
Few drops Tabasco sauce
Salt and pepper, to taste

Beat egg and milk together in a medium bowl. Sift in flour, salt, and baking powder and mix well. Add conch, peppers, onions, celery, lemon zest, habanero or jalapeño pepper, beer, and Tabasco sauce and mix well; refrigerate.

Add tablespoons of batter to 360-degree oil and fry 6 to 8 minutes until deep brown; drain on paper towels.

For Lime Mayonnaise, combine garlic, lime juice, and egg yolks in food processor or blender. With machine running, add olive oil in a steady stream until mixture forms a thick cream. Pour into a bowl and add zest, Tabasco sauce, salt, and pepper.

Jupiter's Name

Local Indians first called the Jupiter area "Hobe" pronounced HO-bay. Spaniards thought they were saying 'Jove,' pronounced HO-vay – the Spanish pronunciation of a Roman name for the Greek god Zeus. The English equivalent is Jupiter.

Blue Crab and Sweet Corn Fritters

From Chef Frank Eucalitto of Café Chardonnay *in Palm Beach Gardens.*

Military Trail

This north-south artery had originally been known as the Capron Trail at the turn of the century. It was named for Captain Louis P. Capron of the Second Seminole War. The narrow road hand-hewn from the wilderness was used to carry army supplies from Fort Pierce to Fort Lauderdale.

2 ounces sweet red pepper, finely diced
2 ounces yellow pepper, finely diced
2 green onions, cut into thin rounds
6 chives, finely chopped
2 eggs
2 ounces mayonnaise
1 teaspoon Old Bay seasoning
Corn kernels from 1 ear of corn, roasted in foil with butter and salt at 350 degrees for 15-20 minutes until tender
4 ounces crabmeat – lump or claw
4 tablespoons flour
1 teaspoon baking powder
2 tablespoons cornmeal
Peanut oil, for frying
Lime wedges, for garnish

Blend peppers, green onions, chives, eggs, mayonnaise, Old Bay seasoning, and corn in a mixing bowl. Fold in crabmeat and add flour, baking powder, and cornmeal, mixing with a rubber spatula until just blended. The consistency should be slightly runny.

Heat peanut oil for frying in a tabletop fryer or a pot on the stove to 350 degrees. Spoon a tablespoon of batter for each fritter into oil and fry for 2 minutes until golden brown. Turn and continue frying for 1 minute. Remove from oil and place on a paper towel to drain any excess oil. Keep warm while frying the rest of the batter.

Serve hot with lime wedges and rémoulade sauce for dipping (see Index for our Easy Rémoulade Sauce recipe).

Yield: 4 servings

Jumbo Lump Crab Cakes

From Chef Glen Manfra of Carmine's Ocean Grill in Palm Beach Gardens. This crab cake recipe is simplicity at its best.

½ cup fresh mayonnaise
¼ cup whole grain mustard
1 spicy Italian pepper
Coarse salt, to taste
1 cup fresh basil, shredded

1 (16-ounce) can jumbo lump
   crabmeat
Fresh breadcrumbs, enough to
   coat crab cakes
Butter, for frying

Mix all ingredients except crabmeat. Gently fold in crabmeat without squeezing out excess moisture. Dip in fresh breadcrumbs. Fry in skillet with butter until golden brown. Serve immediately with your choice of condiments.

Yield: 4 to 5 crab cakes

Raymond F. Kravis

Visitors to the Kravis Center often wonder about the man for whom the magnificent building is named. Mr. Kravis is one of the country's leading oil and gas consultants and a major philanthropist in his native Tulsa, Oklahoma and in Palm Beach where he and his wife, Bessie, have wintered for more than 30 years. Because of his outstanding philanthropy and generosity, a consortium of his friends, spearheaded by Kravis Center Chairman Alexander Dreyfoos, Jr., donated more than $7 million to the fledgling arts center in Mr. Kravis' name. In 1987, the center was officially named for him.

31

Crab Cakes
with Mango Salsa

Finely chopped ingredients help the crab cakes adhere together better.

Mango Salsa:

1 large mango, peeled and diced

2 tablespoons olive oil

¼ red onion, minced

½ teaspoon salt

¼ cayenne pepper

½ teaspoon pepper

½ jalapeño pepper

¼ lime, juiced

¼ bunch cilantro, chopped

Crab Cakes:

3 tablespoons butter

⅓ cup finely chopped red onion

⅓ cup finely chopped yellow pepper

⅓ cup finely diced sweet red pepper

1 teaspoon dry mustard

½ teaspoon salt

1 tablespoon sherry wine

½ teaspoon white pepper

1 cup fine breadcrumbs

1 cup mayonnaise

½ ounce extra virgin olive oil

2 ounces finely chopped dill

1½ teaspoons Old Bay seasoning

1-1¼ pounds lump crabmeat

Combine Mango Salsa ingredients and chill.

Melt butter in a sauté pan. Add onions and peppers. Reserve and put in refrigerator to cool down.

Mix remaining crab cake ingredients except for crabmeat. Add crabmeat to mixture and check for texture; add more breadcrumbs if too wet. Form mixture into individual crab cake patties and reserve.

Heat oil in a sauté pan. Place crab cakes in pan and cook until golden brown on each side. Top with Mango Salsa and serve.

Currie Park

Currie Park on Flagler Drive in downtown West Palm Beach is named after one of West Palm Beach's first mayors, George Graham Currie. He served as mayor from 1901 to 1904. Currie was a lawyer, a poet, and a developer with a colorful and varied background. He was known as the poet laureate of Florida. His works include How I Once Felt: Songs of Love and Travel.

Crab Louie Martini

From John Mecoli, chef at E.R. Bradley's Saloon,
a restaurant in downtown West Palm Beach
overlooking the Intracoastal Waterway. E.R. Bradley
is a famous character from Palm Beach history.
Tangy Louie Sauce has been popular from his
days to the present.

Louie Sauce:

2 cups mayonnaise
2 tablespoons minced
    shallots
¼ cup chopped pickle
2 ounces chopped capers

Juice of ½ lime
Juice of ½ lemon
½ cup cocktail sauce
1 pinch each salt and pepper

For Assembly (per serving):

1 martini glass, chilled
Chopped field greens

1 ounce Louie Sauce
3 ounces lump crabmeat

Garnish:

Freshly ground pepper
Green onions, julienned
    extremely thin

Carrots, cut in extremely thin
    wisps or ribbons
Lemon wedge
Lime wedge

Combine all Louie Sauce ingredients together and mix
well. Fill each martini glass ¾ full with field greens.
Add 1 ounce Louie sauce then 3 ounces crabmeat.
Sprinkle with a pinch of pepper. Lay garnish of green
onions and carrots on top of crabmeat. Finish with
lemon and lime wedge on side of glass. Serve with a
cocktail fork.

E.R. Bradley

A notorious gambler
and horseman,
Bradley founded Palm
Beach's early high
rolling gambling
saloon. It was known
for being the first
establishment of its
type to allow women
to gamble which was,
without a doubt, one
of the secrets to its
success. All that is left
of the original saloon
now is the old
fireplace in Bradley
Park at the foot of the
Flagler Bridge in Palm
Beach.

Steamed Corn Custard with Crab

Consider serving this with a salad for lunch or a light dinner.

1 cup fresh corn kernels (from 2 ears) or thawed frozen
⅓ cup whole milk
1 large egg, lightly beaten
¼ teaspoon salt, rounded
2 cups lump crabmeat
1 tablespoon unsalted butter
1 tablespoon chopped fresh chives

Cook corn in a 1-quart saucepan of boiling salted water for 3 to 5 minutes; drain well. Purée milk and hot corn in a blender until almost smooth, then force through a very fine sieve into a bowl, discarding solids. Whisk in egg and salt and divide among four 2-ounce ceramic ramekins. (Recipe may be made to this point, covered with plastic wrap, and chilled. Bring to room temperature before continuing.)

Steam custards in a steamer set 1 inch above simmering water, covered with lid, until centers are set and a thin knife inserted into center of one comes out clean, 6 to 8 minutes. Remove from steamer and cool custards slightly.

Break up crab. Heat butter in a small skillet over moderate heat until foam subsides, and then cook crab, stirring constantly, until heated through, about 2 minutes. Stir in chives. Serve custards topped with crab.

Yield: 4 servings

Mounts Botanical Garden

This urban oasis is located just west of the Palm Beach International Airport. Mounts Botanical Garden is Palm Beach County's oldest and largest botanical garden. Its 14 acres contain over 2000 species of tropical and subtropical plants, both native and exotic. There are flowering trees and shrubs, tropical fruit trees, bromeliads, palms, roses, a vegetable garden, herbs and other specialty plants. The Mounts welcomes over 50,000 visitors a year and is an excellent source of gardening information. It offers tropical gardening classes, lectures and workshops, botanical tours, plant sales, fun family festivals and a myriad of other events throughout the year.

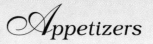

Crab and Artichoke Beignets

This recipe is great served with Rémoulade Sauce for dipping (see Index for our Easy Rémoulade Sauce recipe).

2 whole artichokes
½ teaspoon salt
Bay leaf
1 lemon, halved
½ teaspoon liquid crab boil
1 tablespoon oil
½ cup chopped onions
Salt, to taste
Cayenne pepper, to taste
1 teaspoon minced garlic
½ pound lump crabmeat
3 eggs, beaten
1½ cups milk
2 teaspoons baking powder
3¼ cups flour
¼ teaspoon Worcestershire sauce
¼ teaspoon hot sauce
1 tablespoon minced parsley
Oil, for frying

Trim artichokes and cover with water. Add ½ teaspoon salt, bay leaf, lemon, and crab boil. Bring to boil over high heat. Reduce to medium heat and simmer until tender. Remove artichokes and drain well. Cool slightly, cut in half, and remove choke. Remove artichoke leaves and reserve for another use. Slice heart into thin pieces and set aside.

Heat 1 tablespoon oil over medium-high heat and add chopped onions. Season with salt and cayenne pepper. Sauté until soft, about 2 to 3 minutes. Add artichokes and garlic; sauté 1 minute. Add crabmeat and sauté 1 minute. Remove from heat and set aside.

Make a batter with eggs, milk, and baking powder. Mix well. Add flour, ¼ cup at a time, beating each addition in until all the flour is used and mixture is smooth. Season with salt, cayenne, Worcestershire sauce, and hot sauce. Stir well and add parsley. Add artichoke and crab mixture and fold to mix.

Heat 3 inches of oil to 360 degrees. Drop batter, a heaping tablespoon at a time, into hot oil. When beignets pop to surface, turn them and continue to brown evenly. Remove and drain on paper towels.

Blighia sapida

Commonly known as akee or ackee, this plant is an important ingredient in Caribbean cuisine. The arils (fleshy seed coating) from ripe fruit are separated from the seeds and used to make the Jamaican delicacy, akee and salt-cod. It's important that the arils are harvested at exactly the right time—those harvested from either under-ripe or over-ripe fruit are deadly poisonous!

Smoked and Fresh Salmon Tartar
with Caviar and Cucumber Gazpacho
(Tartara di Due Salmoni con Caviale e Gaspacio di Cetrioli)

This elegant stacked salad is from Chef Elmer Saravia at Bice restaurant in Palm Beach.

Salmon Tartar:

4 ounces fresh salmon

4 ounces smoked salmon

3 stems chives, chopped

1 tablespoon olive oil

Salt and pepper, to taste

4 tablespoons orange tobico caviar

Gazpacho:

1 cucumber

2 garlic cloves

10 cilantro leaves

4 tablespoons lime juice

1 pinch crushed red pepper

2 pinches salt

½ cup olive oil

Chop salmon very thin and mix with chives and oil. Add salt and pepper. Put tartar in a cylinder-shaped object, layering with salmon on the bottom and caviar on the top. Remove cylinder; tartar should have cylindrical shape.

Blend cucumber with garlic, cilantro, lime juice, crushed red pepper, salt, and oil. Put gazpacho on a plate around tartar.

Yield: 4 servings

Armory Art Center

Located in the heart of West Palm Beach's historic neighborhoods, the Armory Art Center campus is an architectural and educational treasure. The original Armory building is an Art Deco gem, built by William Manly King in 1939 and is now on the National Register of Historic Places. Since its founding as a not-for-profit visual arts school in 1986, the Armory Art Center has offered quality studio art education programs for youth and adults in ceramics, drawing and pastels, jewelry and metals, painting, sculpture, photography, digital imaging and printmaking. Offering Master Artists Workshops, lectures, demonstrations, exhibitions, special events and tours they're much more than meets the eye!

Floribbean Ceviche of Yellowtail Snapper
Complemented with Avocado, Hearts of Palm, and Tomatoes

Contributed by Chef Roger Dikon, Executive Chef of PGA National Resort & Spa, Palm Beach Gardens. Fresh fish is the mainstay of diners in Florida and the Caribbean. One of the best ways to appreciate fresh fish is to "cook" it in an acid marinade, which retains the texture and flavor of the fish and cuts its natural oiliness. This recipe calls for yellowtail snapper, but any firm white-fleshed fish may be substituted. The natural sweetness of the Key limes adds that extra-special touch.

Cypress Trees

The largest tree in North America east of the Rockies, the cypress tree can be found in the Loxahatchee National Wildlife Refuge. A quarter mile long boardwalk leads the visitor to the interior of a cypress dome. The "dome" is created as larger cypress trees grow in the center of the dome and the trees become progressively smaller as they expand out from the center. Cypress trees can live for hundreds of years.

Marinade:

¾ cup fresh Key lime juice
2 tablespoons fresh orange juice
1 tablespoon olive oil
2 garlic cloves, minced
Freshly chopped chili pepper or jalapeño, to taste

1 tablespoon fresh cilantro, chopped
¼ teaspoon salt
¼ teaspoon freshly ground pepper

Ceviche:

1 pound fresh snapper, cut into ¼-inch dice
1 avocado, cut into ¼-inch dice
2 medium vine ripe tomatoes, peeled, seeded and cut into ¼-inch dice

2 hearts of palm, ¼-inch dice
2 tablespoons fresh cilantro, chopped
Salt and freshly ground pepper, to taste
Key lime slices, for garnish

Thoroughly mix all marinade ingredients in a medium bowl. Fold in fish, making sure all pieces are coated with marinade. Cover with plastic wrap and marinate in the refrigerator for at least 2 hours.

Just before serving, fold in avocado, tomatoes, hearts of palm, and cilantro. Season with salt and pepper and adjust seasoning, adding more chili peppers or jalapeño if necessary. Serve garnished with Key lime slices.

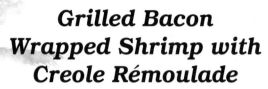

Grilled Bacon Wrapped Shrimp with Creole Rémoulade

The shrimp in this recipe needs to marinate overnight, so remember to start the night before.

8 jumbo shrimp
½ teaspoon chopped garlic
1 teaspoon chopped shallots
¼ cup olive oil
¼ teaspoon oregano
¼ teaspoon thyme
¼ teaspoon basil
Salt and pepper, to taste
4 slices bacon

Creole Rémoulade:

1 egg yolk
1 whole egg
1 teaspoon Creole mustard
Juice of ½ lemon
1 cup olive oil
1 teaspoon horseradish
1 tablespoon paprika
1 teaspoon champagne vinegar
1 hard-boiled egg, finely chopped
2 tablespoons finely chopped red onion
1 teaspoon capers, finely chopped
1 teaspoon Essence or similar seasoning, preferably salt-free
½ teaspoon Tabasco sauce
Salt and pepper, to taste
1 tablespoon chopped parsley

Peel and devein shrimp, leaving last section of tail intact. Combine garlic, shallots, oil, oregano, thyme, basil, salt, and pepper in a bowl. Add shrimp and marinate overnight in the refrigerator.

Cook bacon in a 350-degree oven until slightly rendered but still pliable, about 4 to 6 minutes. Wrap each shrimp with ½ piece of bacon and secure with a toothpick. Refrigerate until ready to serve.

To make the rémoulade sauce, place egg yolk and whole egg in a food processor and blend. Add mustard and lemon juice. With the machine running, slowly add oil until a mayonnaise-like consistency is reached. Add remaining ingredients and refrigerate.

To serve, cook shrimp on a medium-hot grill until bacon is crisp and shrimp are cooked through, about 3 minutes per side. Transfer to appetizer plates and garnish with a dollop of sauce, heart greens of your choice, lemon sections, and parsley.

Yield: 4 servings

Cheeseburger in Paradise

*But at night
I'd had these
wonderful dreams*

*Some kind of
sensuous treat*

*Not zuchinni,
fettucini or
bulghar wheat*

*But a big warm
bun and a huge
hunk of meat*

~Jimmy Buffett

Grilled Margarita Shrimp

A margarita glass rimmed in salt is a nice way to serve this to guests.

1 tablespoon chopped
   cilantro
1 teaspoon minced garlic
¼ cup prepared margarita
   mix

2 tablespoons tequila
1 dozen large shrimp, shelled
   and deveined, tails on

Combine cilantro, garlic, margarita mix, and tequila in a plastic bag. Let rest 1 hour to allow flavors to bloom.

Add shrimp and marinate another hour, depending on size of shrimp.

Soak bamboo skewers in water for 30 minutes so they won't burn. Place shrimp on skewers and grill outdoors about 4 to 6 inches away from heat; also may be cooked in broiler 4 to 6 inches away from heat source or on an indoor grill. Cook shrimp 5 to 7 minutes or until shrimp turn pink. Turn shrimp several times while cooking.

These are fantastic and easy and could also be done with chicken, lobster, or some kind of substantial fish (snapper, grouper, dolphin, cobia, etc.). This recipe can be easily doubled, tripled, or quadrupled.

Putting Out The Fire

Flare ups are a problem any time you fire up the grill. Try to avoid them by trimming excess fat from foods prior to cooking. Also keep a close eye on fatty foods and move them around on the grill as they cook. Closing the grill lid reduces the amount of oxygen in the grill and can help to prevent flare ups. Finally, keep a spray bottle full of water or even a water pistol handy to extinguish flames that get out of control. Careful: if you douse the flame too vigorously you could cause ashes from the fire to be tossed onto your food.

T-WA Shrimp

From Chef Ross Matheson at Reef Grill in Juno and Jupiter. You'll just have to go to the restaurant to find out who "T-WA" is.

Chili Oil:

Red chili flakes, to taste · 1 teaspoon vegetable oil

Shrimp:

1 ounce butter, melted · 2 ounces dark brown sugar
1 teaspoon puréed garlic · 1 leaf Bibb lettuce
Chili oil · (as a serving "cup")
1 pinch pepper · Radicchio, chopped, as
5 ounces fresh rock shrimp · garnish

Place red chili flakes in vegetable oil and marinate 24 hours in advance.

Heat heavy skillet over medium-high heat; add butter, garlic purée, chili oil, pepper, and shrimp. Stir until shrimp turn from translucent to white; add brown sugar. When brown sugar has melted, remove from heat. Pour shrimp mixture into lettuce cup and garnish with radicchio.

Yield: 1 serving

Mother of the Everglades

A dynamic woman, Marjory Stoneman Douglas, came to Florida in 1915 and became a reporter for The Miami Herald. In mid-life she fell in love with one of the nations most forbidding and unexplored wild places: the Everglades. She understood what scientists now know – that the Everglades are not simply a breathtaking natural wonder, but also the key to South Florida's drinking water and environmental health. In 1947 Marjory wrote "River of Grass", a book widely considered the defining description of the 'Glades'. She led environmental causes in support of the Everglades until close to her death in 1998.

Pan Seared Scallops with Vegetable Aïoli

Simple, elegant starter.

Vegetable Aïoli:

1 cup green vegetables
  (any combination of
  asparagus, peas,
  broccoli, etc.)
1 egg yolk
1 tablespoon lemon juice
1 teaspoon minced garlic

½ cup olive oil
Salt and pepper, to taste
2 tablespoons basil, finely
  chopped
1 tablespoon green onions,
  thinly sliced

Scallops:

8 large scallops

⅛ cup olive oil

Garnish:

8 large potato chips

4 ounces baby greens

Drop vegetables, separately, into boiling water and cook each until tender. Drop into ice water to stop cooking. Pat dry, chop, and peel as needed. Set aside.

Whisk egg yolk with lemon juice and garlic in a stainless steel or glass bowl. Pour in ½ cup oil and whisk vigorously to emulsify. Add drops of water if mixture becomes too thick. Season with salt and pepper and stir in vegetables, basil, and green onions. Set aside or refrigerate for up to 3 days.

Season scallops with salt and pepper. Heat remaining ⅛ cup oil in a large nonstick skillet over high heat. When oil begins to smoke, carefully place scallops in pan, one at a time. When a golden brown crust is visible (2 to 3 minutes), flip each with a spatula or tongs. Cook 2 minutes more or until done. Move to plates, 2 scallops per plate. Spoon aïoli onto each scallop. Garnish with potato chips and sprinkle with small baby greens.

Yield: 4 servings

Art Deco Society of the Palm Beaches

This non-profit organization is dedicated to the preservation and awareness of Art Deco and twentieth century art, architecture and design found in the Palm Beaches.

Did you know that...

• *Palm Beach County is home to over 200 Art Deco buildings, most located east of I-95?*

• *Belford Shoumate, Palm Beach's most influential Art Deco architect was part Shawnee American Indian?*

• *The Lake Worth Playhouse, built in 1925, is the oldest building on the historic Art Deco Registry?*

• *Boca Raton has basically no art deco structures?*

Marshalls' Mussels

Submitted by the Arthur R. Marshall Foundation.

3 garlic cloves, minced
2 tablespoons extra virgin
   olive oil
½ cup Gorgonzola cheese
2 cans low-sodium chicken
   broth

1½ cups cooking sherry
Dried basil, oregano, and
   chili pepper flakes, to
   taste
2 pounds mussels

Sauté garlic in olive oil until lightly browned. Add Gorgonzola cheese and cook until cheese is melted. Add broth, sherry, basil, oregano, and chili pepper flakes.

Clean mussels thoroughly. Add mussels to pan with sauce and cook 3 to 5 minutes until they open. Serve in a bowl accompanied with lightly toasted Italian bread.

Yield: 8 servings

Arthur R. Marshall Foundation

The Arthur R. Marshall Foundation was founded in 1998 to restore and preserve the Florida Everglades. In one three year period, the non-profit, West Palm Beach-based organization planted more than 66,000 native wetland trees. The foundation is named after noted conservationist Art Marshall who, in the 1960's and 70's, worked side-by-side with his friend and colleague Marjory Stoneman Douglas to protect the Everglades. In addition to its tree-planting efforts, the Marshall Foundation has a growing environmental education program that includes a curriculum for school-aged children and an award-winning internship for college-aged students.

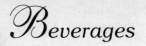

A Spa in Your Refrigerator

Looking for a light drink without added sugar? Keep a pitcher of iced water in your refrigerator and put some cut up fruit in it. You'll be surprised about how much flavor you'll get.

Try combinations of the following:

Sliced strawberries

Whole raspberries

Sliced lemons or oranges

Chunks of melon or
    honeydew

Wedges of pineapple

Cucumber slices and sprigs
    of mint

Egg Safety

According to the American Egg Board, "There is a small possibility of eggs being contaminated with the bacteria Salmonella." Cooking eggs kills the bacteria. The risk of Salmonella poisoning is very small in healthy people, however the pregnant, the very young, the elderly, and those with medical problems such as impaired immune systems should avoid all uncooked animal products. Be sure to keep eggs refrigerated until you are ready to use them.

Hibiscus

A touch of the tropics.

2 ounces cranberry juice

1 ounce light rum

Crushed ice

1 ounce champagne

Hibiscus flower, for garnish

Shake cranberry juice, rum, and ice together. Stir in champagne and garnish with hibiscus flower.

Yield: 1 serving

Irish Cream Cordial

This recipe calls for raw eggs – see the sidebar for safety concerns about raw eggs.

1 cup condensed milk

1⅓ cups Irish or Scotch
    whiskey

½ pint whipping cream

¼ teaspoon coconut flavoring

2 heaping tablespoons Nestle
    Quik

3 eggs, slightly beaten

Place all ingredients in a blender or food processor. Mix thoroughly and refrigerate. Also may be served over ice.

Kahlúa Martini

Give this one a try. It also goes by the name "Barbie and Ken." Just the tiniest hint of sweetness makes it refreshing.

1 jigger good vodka   4 drops Kahlúa

Pour vodka over a generous glass of ice and add Kahlúa.

Yield: 1 serving

Singer Island

This once undeveloped tropical island was to be the site for Paris Singer's "Breakers Hotel". No one ever got to stay there, though. The project went broke as one of many victims of tough times in the Great Depression. The unfinished structure was torn down in the 1940s.

Sparkling Berry Punch

Try this at your next party or brunch.

1 (6-ounce) can frozen
    lemonade concentrate
½ cup water
1 (10-ounce) package
    quick-thaw raspberries
    or strawberries in syrup
1 (1-liter) bottle 7UP, chilled

1 (750-ml) chilled bottle
    champagne or sparkling
    apple cider
Raspberry or lemon sherbet,
    for garnish
Fresh mint (optional)

In a punch bowl, combine lemonade and water. Add raspberries or strawberries, 7UP, and champagne. Garnish with sherbet and fresh mint, if desired. Serve in punch cups.

Yield: 3 quarts or 24 servings. Recipe can be doubled.

Singer Island Cosmopolitan

1 ounce vodka
½ ounce Cointreau
1 tablespoon lime juice

1 splash cranberry juice
1 cup ice cubes
Lime peel, for garnish

Pour vodka, Cointreau, lime juice, and cranberry juice into a cocktail shaker. Add ice and shake gently. Strain into a chilled martini glass and float lime peel in center.

Yield: 1 serving

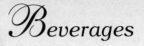

Painkiller

This recipe comes from the British Virgin Islands and is a favorite of sailors and landlubbers alike. Comes in three strengths: mild, medium, and prescription only.

2-4 ounces dark rum
4 ounces pineapple juice
1 ounce cream of coconut

1 ounce orange juice
Fresh nutmeg, grated, for
   garnish

Stir ingredients together and serve over crushed ice. Garnish with a little nutmeg.

Yield: 1 serving

Klein Dance

The Klein Dance School, home of the Demetrius Klein Dance Company, offers the highest quality, multi-disciplinary dance training available in South Florida to students and professionals at all levels. Each student is challenged and encouraged to reach their highest potential while developing a respect and joy for dance in all its forms. The dance company is a center for creative dance with studios in Lake Worth, founded in 1987. The company believes dance is a vital art form whose presence in the community enhances the quality of life for people of all ages.

White Sangría

This recipe was contributed by Lex Chutintaranond of Zaza's Cucina in Ithaca, New York.

Simple Syrup:
1 part sugar

1 part water

Sangría:
1 squeeze simple syrup
1 squeeze lemon juice
4 ounces white wine

1 ounce Mathilde peach
1 ounce orange juice

For simple syrup, mix equal amounts sugar and water together in a pan and heat until sugar dissolves. Cool and store in refrigerator for use where sweetness is desired but sugar granules are not.

To make sangría, shake all ingredients together and strain onto ice.

Yield: 1 serving – recipe can be multiplied

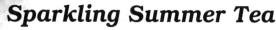

Sparkling Summer Tea

This light, refreshing drink is perfect for an afternoon garden party.

1 quart boiling water
2 family-sized tea bags
½ cup sugar
1 (12-ounce) container
    frozen lemonade
    concentrate

1 quart water
Molded ice rings
1 liter ginger ale
Mint leaves and lemon slices,
    for garnish

Steep boiling water and tea bags for 15 minutes.
Stir in sugar, lemonade concentrate, and water; chill.
Just before serving, put ice rings into punch bowl
and pour in chilled tea/lemonade mixture and ginger
ale. Garnish with mint leaves and lemon slices
and serve.

*When making your molded ice rings, consider putting
in mint leaves and sliced lemons for a decorative
touch. This needs to do be done in stages. Begin by
partially freezing a small layer of water in the
container. Arrange fruit and greenery over frozen
layer and cover the decoration with enough very cold
water just to cover. Return mold to the freezer so that
with renewed freezing the decoration is completely
encased in ice. Repeat as space permits. Allow
contents to become thoroughly frozen. This is so
simple to do yet adds an impressive touch.*

Loggerhead Sea Turtle

*Loggerhead turtles
are named for their
large heads. They
are graceful
swimmers even
though they may
weigh as much as
500 pounds. Our
beaches provide one
of the most important
breeding grounds for
this threatened
species. From May to
September the eggs,
which are about the
size of ping pong
balls, must be
protected from
poachers. During
late night beach
walks in the summer,
you may encounter
females laying their
eggs. When wildlife
officials find these
nests, they will be
marked. Be careful
not to disturb them.*

Strawberry Daiquiri

Try this with mangoes or peaches in season.

1 (6-ounce) can frozen
    limeade
25 large strawberries

2 tablespoons sugar
12½ ounces rum
3 cups cracked ice

Blend all ingredients together in a blender until
smooth. Pour mixture into a pitcher half filled
with ice.

Yield: 4 servings

Brunch & Breads

Brunch & Breads

Crustless Spinach Quiche
Spicy Scrambled Eggs
L'Opera Brasserie
  Quiche Lorraine
Smoked Salmon
  Cheesecake
Swedish Salmon Mousse
Zucchini Carrot
  Dutch Pancake
Irish Soda Bread
Joy's Apple Bread
Mango Bread
Pumpkin Bread
Traditional Scones
  with Cranberries
  & Clotted Cream,
  Flagler Museum's
  Pavilion Cafe
Strawberry Bread
Southern Cornbread
Apple Pancake,
  Café L'Europe
Blueberry Breakfast
  Popover
Granola Cereal
Blueberry Coffee Cake
Fruit Salad
Baked Egg Frittata
Grandma's Lazy Day
  Coffee Cake
Overnight Orange
  French Toast

Crustless Spinach Quiche

Low carb or not, this easy to prepare dish is delicious and satisfying.

1 large onion, diced
1 tablespoon olive oil
1 (10-ounce) package frozen
    chopped spinach,
    thawed and drained dry
5 eggs

1 cup Munster cheese, grated
1 cup Cheddar cheese,
    grated
Salt and freshly ground
    pepper, to taste

Preheat oven to 350 degrees. Butter a 9-inch pie plate or quiche dish. Sauté onion in oil over medium heat until transparent. Add spinach and cook until excess moisture has evaporated. Cool. Beat eggs in a medium bowl. Add cheese. Stir into spinach and onion mixture. Season to taste with salt and pepper. Pour into prepared dish and spread evenly. Bake 40 to 45 minutes until nicely browned.

Yield: 6 servings

Spicy Scrambled Eggs

A flavorful twist on the classic.

3 tablespoons butter or
    canola oil
1 small onion, peeled and
    finely chopped
1 teaspoon grated
    gingerroot
1 small green chili or
    jalapeño pepper, finely
    chopped

1 tablespoon cilantro, finely
    chopped
⅛ teaspoon turmeric
½ teaspoon ground cumin
1 tomato, seeded and
    chopped
8 eggs, beaten
Salt and freshly ground
    pepper, to taste

Heat butter or oil on medium heat in nonstick frying pan. Sauté onion in until soft. Add ginger, chili, cilantro, turmeric, cumin, and tomato. Cook until tomato is soft. Pour in eggs; add salt and pepper. Cook until desired consistency while stirring gently.

Yield: 4 servings

L'Opera Brasserie
Quiche Lorraine

This wonderful rendition is one of many classic dishes that are done to perfection at L'Opera Brasserie in West Palm Beach.

4 large eggs
1½ cups heavy cream
1 sheet puff pastry
1 tablespoon unsalted butter

1 yellow onion, thinly sliced
3 slices smoked bacon, cut
    into half-inch pieces

Preheat oven to 400 degrees. Roll out the puff pastry into a buttered 9-inch tart mold. Cut off excess. Set aside in the refrigerator while you prepare the filling. In a nonstick skillet, melt butter and add the thinly sliced onion. Cook until butter is melted, and the onion is translucent. Set aside in the refrigerator to cool. Place the slices of bacon in a small saucepan, and add cold water to cover. Bring it to a boil, and cool right away by straining immediately while running cold water over it.

Beat the eggs with salt and pepper to taste, and add the heavy cream, stirring until well combined.

Remove the tart mold from the refrigerator. Distribute the onion and bacon evenly over the bottom of the puff pastry shell. Add the cream mixture, making sure to pour evenly, and bake for 20 minutes or until a knife, inserted in the center, comes out clean.

Yield: 4 servings

Palm Beach Photographic Centre

Dedicated to the preservation and promotion of the art of photography and digital imaging, the Centre operates the only museum solely dedicated to photography in the county. This Delray Beach facility holds over 200 masters photographic and digital imaging classes year 'round. It also hosts evening and weekend programs, and provides a number of programs solely dedicated to the youth of our community like the "The Picture My World" program and a summer camp program. Some of the world's best photographers are on exhibit, including Margaret Bourke-White, Linda McCartney, Arnold Newman, Vincent Versace and Stephen Marc.

Smoked Salmon Cheesecake

A savory treat for a special occasion.

Buttery Cracker Crust:

1 cup (approximately 24) crushed buttery crackers

3 tablespoons butter, melted

Salmon Cheesecake:

2 (8-ounce) packages cream cheese, softened

¼ cup heavy whipping cream

2 eggs

¼ teaspoon salt

1½ cups (about 6 ounces) shredded Gouda cheese

¼ cup green onions, sliced, including a bit of green

1 pound smoked salmon, minced

4 medium green onions, sliced (about 2 tablespoons)

2 tablespoons red caviar

Crackers, crostini, etc.

Preheat oven to 375 degrees. Mix crackers and butter until well blended. Press evenly in bottom of 9x3-inch springform pan. Bake 8 minutes or until golden brown.

Reduce oven temperature to 325 degrees. Beat cream cheese in large bowl with electric mixer on medium speed until smooth. Add whipping cream, eggs, and salt; beat until smooth. Stir in Gouda cheese, ¼ cup green onions, and salmon until well blended. Spoon evenly over crust in pan.

Bake 45 to 50 minutes or until center is set. Run knife around edge of cheesecake to loosen. Cool completely at room temperature. Cover and refrigerate at least 2 hours but no longer than 48 hours.

Remove side of pan. Place cheesecake on serving platter. Top decoratively with 2 tablespoons green onions and caviar.

Shell Mounds

The large shell mound upon which the DuBois house rests is the most prominent surface feature of the Jupiter Inlet. It is one of the last remnant coastal shell mounds in southeastern Florida. The large shell mounds found along coasts, rivers and estuaries accumulated over years of consumption of shellfish, fish and turtles by Native Americans.

Swedish Salmon Mousse

This traditional Swedish mousse can be served as an appetizer on toasted bread or served cold as a main course with warm boiled potatoes. It may be prepared in a Bundt pan or fish-shaped mold for a special presentation. Note that for the best flavor you may want to begin this the day before it is to be served.

Salmon:

2 to 3 quarts water
2 tablespoons salt
10 white peppercorns
2 leeks, coarsely chopped
1 handful dill
2 tablespoons vinegar
4 pounds salmon

Mousse:

Salmon cooked in broth
    (see above)
1 can lobster bisque soup
2 cups mayonnaise ½ cup
    bottled chili sauce
1 cup chopped dill
1 tablespoon Italian seasoning
1 pound cooked shrimp; keep
    20 whole, peel and chop
    the rest
Salt and pepper, to taste
3 teaspoons gelatin powder
Lemon wheels, for garnish

Add salt, peppercorns, leeks, dill, and vinegar to water and boil. Reduce heat, add salmon, and continue to cook at a low boil for 30 to 40 minutes. Let fish cool in the water. (Preferably prepare the day before and let salmon sit in the broth overnight in refrigerator. Salmon will stay very moist.)

Remove fish from broth and remove bones. Chop fish meat finely with a fork. Mix salmon with cold lobster soup, mayonnaise, chili sauce, dill, and chopped shrimp. Add salt and pepper. Stir vigorously to make the mixture airy. Mix the gelatin with ¼ to ½ cup hot water and pour into salmon mixture while stirring. Pour into bowl or mold that has been rinsed in cold water. Let stand in refrigerator at least 6 hours

To remove from mold, place base in warm water to loosen, or insert a knife around the edge of the bowl to loosen the mousse; invert bowl onto a serving platter. Garnish with lemon wheels and shrimp.

Yield: 6 to 8 servings

Dutch Zucchini Carrot Pancake

This flavorful dish combines the sweetness of carrots and pairs it with the unassuming flavor of zucchini. Warm Gouda cheese pulls all the flavors together.

2 eggs
½ cup flour
½ cup half & half
¼ teaspoon salt
1 tablespoon butter
1 pound mushrooms, quartered
1 medium zucchini, cut into ¼-inch slices

½ pound carrots, cut into ¼-inch slices
2 tablespoons butter
½ cup sliced pimiento-stuffed olives
2 teaspoons fresh dill
¼ pound Gouda cheese, grated

Preheat oven to 450 degrees. Place a 9-inch ovenproof skillet in the oven. In a small bowl, mix eggs, flour, half & half, and salt. Beat until smooth, about 3 minutes. Carefully remove skillet from oven. Add 1 tablespoon butter and rotate pan until butter melts and coats pan. Add batter immediately. Bake on lowest oven shelf, about 10 minutes. Reduce heat to 350 degrees and bake until golden, about 10 minutes. Remove from oven.

Sauté mushrooms, zucchini, and carrots in 2 tablespoons butter in large skillet until liquid evaporates, about 5 minutes. Add olives and dill. Reduce heat to medium and stir in Gouda cheese. Cook, stirring constantly, until cheese melts and coats vegetables, approximately 2 minutes.

Heat broiler to high. Spoon vegetable mixture onto pancake and broil until light brown. Cut into wedges and serve immediately.

Yield: 4 to 6 servings

Flamingo

Like the palm tree and the sunset, flamingos have become a symbol of Florida. With their large bodies, long legs, long necks, small heads and pink plumage, they are conspicuous and unmistakable. The color is produced by the carotenoid pigments in the algae and various seafood they eat. The long-lived birds, 50 years in the wild, are highly gregarious and their colonies are noisy affairs.

Irish Soda Bread

2 cups all-purpose flour
2 tablespoons sugar
2 teaspoons baking powder
1 teaspoon baking soda

½ teaspoon salt
3 tablespoons butter or
    margarine, softened
1 cup buttermilk

Preheat oven to 375 degrees. Lightly grease a small cookie sheet. In a large bowl, sift flour, sugar, baking powder, baking soda, and salt. Cut in softened butter with a pastry blender or fork until mixture looks like fine crumbs. Add buttermilk and mix in with a fork just until dry ingredients are moistened. Turn out onto lightly floured pastry board and knead gently until smooth. Shape into a ball.

Place on prepared cookie sheet and flatten into a 7-inch circle, ½-inch thick. Press a large floured knife into center of loaf almost through to bottom and repeat at a right angle to divide dough into fourths.

Bake 30 to 40 minutes or until top is golden brown. Loaf should sound hollow when tapped. Remove to a wire rack to cool; brush top with melted butter. If desired, brush with flour.

Yield: 4 servings

Schoolhouse Children's Museum

Boynton Elementary School opened in 1913 with 81 students. The two-story six-classroom building was the pride of the community. Although it had indoor plumbing, electricity would not arrive until the 1920s. The schoolhouse was also the hub of activity for the community. It was closed in 1990, restored in 1997, and is now listed on the National Register of Historic Places. In 2001 it opened as the Schoolhouse Children's Museum. The museum's mission is to encourage children and families in the area to learn about themselves and the history of Boynton Beach and Palm Beach County through a stimulating array of interactive exhibitions, programs, activities, and special events.

Joy's Apple Bread

This tastes even better the next day.

Bread:

3 eggs, slightly beaten
2 cups sugar
1 cup vegetable oil
1 tablespoon vanilla
3 cups all-purpose flour
1 teaspoon salt

1 teaspoon baking soda
1 teaspoon ground cinnamon
4 cups chopped, peeled apples (Granny Smith or Gala)
1 cup chopped pecans

Topping:

1 tablespoon sugar

½ teaspoon ground cinnamon

Preheat oven to 325 degrees. Grease two 8x4-inch loaf pans. Beat eggs, sugar, oil, and vanilla together in a large bowl and set aside. Combine flour, salt, baking soda, and cinnamon in another bowl and set aside.

Add dry ingredients to wet ingredients and mix well. Stir in apples and pecans. Bake for 70 minutes, until toothpick inserted in center comes out clean. Cool 10 to 20 minutes in pan, then finish cooling on cake rack.

Once the loaves have cooled, combine topping ingredients and sprinkle on top.

Yield: 2 loaves

The Everglades

South Florida is home to North America's only subtropical preserve, the Everglades National Park. Famous for its sawgrass prairies, mangrove and cypress swamps, pinelands, and hardwood hammocks, the Everglades is also home to marine environments. Tourists flock each year to observe the park's exquisite bird life which includes large wading birds, such as the Roseate Spoonbill, Wood Stork, Great Blue Heron, and a variety of egrets.

Mango Bread

3 cups all-purpose flour	2 cups sugar
2 teaspoons ground cinnamon	2 cups mango, crushed
1 teaspoon baking soda	½ cup cooking oil
½ teaspoon baking powder	2 eggs
½ teaspoon salt	½ teaspoon lime zest
½ teaspoon ground nutmeg	1 cup chopped walnuts

Preheat oven to 350 degrees. Grease two 8x4-inch loaf pans. In a medium mixing bowl, combine flour, cinnamon, baking soda, baking powder, salt, and nutmeg. Set aside.

In another mixing bowl combine sugar, mango, oil, eggs, and lime zest; mix well. Add dry ingredients to mango mixture and stir until just moistened (batter should be lumpy). Fold in nuts. Spoon batter into prepared pans. Bake 55 to 60 minutes, until toothpick inserted comes out clean. Cool in pan for 10 minutes. Remove from pan and finish cooling on rack.

Yield: 2 loaves

Allspice

Allspice is the pea-sized berry of the evergreen pimento tree native to the West Indies and South America. Jamaica provides most of the world's supply. The spice is so named because it tastes like a combination of cinnamon, nutmeg and cloves.

Pumpkin Bread

1 teaspoon baking powder	3½ cups flour
2 teaspoons baking soda	1 cup butter
2 teaspoons salt	3 cups sugar
1 teaspoon ground cinnamon	4 eggs
1 teaspoon ground allspice	2 cups pumpkin
½ teaspoon ground cloves	⅔ cup water
1 teaspoon nutmeg	1½ cups pecans
	Raisins (optional)

Preheat oven to 350 degrees. Grease three 5x3-inch loaf pans. Sift together baking powder, baking soda, salt, cinnamon, allspice, cloves, nutmeg, and flour. Cream butter and sugar together. Add eggs and pumpkin. Add dry ingredients and water alternately. Bake 50 minutes or until toothpick comes out clean.

Yield: 3 loaves

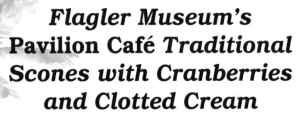

Flagler Museum's Pavilion Café Traditional Scones with Cranberries and Clotted Cream

Henry Flagler and his wife entertained at Whitehall frequently, often serving tea to their guests. In keeping with this tradition, the Flagler Museum's Pavilion Café seasonally serves a Gilded Age Tea featuring the Museum's own special blend of tea. The café serves the scones with clotted cream, strawberry preserves, and lemon curd.

Whitehall – The Flagler Museum

Whitehall, completed in 1902, was the winter home of Standard Oil founding partner and Florida developer Henry Morrison Flagler. Henry Flagler commissioned architects John Carrère and Thomas Hastings to design Whitehall, a 55-room Beaux Arts estate in Palm Beach, as not only a wedding present for his wife, but also as Florida's first museum.

Scones:

4 cups all-purpose flour	2 sticks unsalted butter
¾ cup sugar	Dried cranberries
1½ teaspoons baking soda	2 large eggs, beaten
3 teaspoons cream of tartar	Buttermilk

Clotted Cream:

1 pint heavy cream, whipped	3 ounces cream cheese, softened
2 tablespoons sour cream	2 teaspoons sugar

Preheat oven to 425 degrees. Sift together flour, sugar, baking soda, and cream of tartar, then sift again. Cut in butter. Add a handful of dried cranberries and beaten eggs; blend well. Add buttermilk a little at a time until a stiff dough has formed.

Roll out dough on a flat surface to a thickness of 1½ inches, then cut out 2-inch rounds. Place on parchment paper and brush with beaten egg. Bake about 18 to 20 minutes until golden brown.

Whip heavy cream; add sour cream, cream cheese, and sugar. Serve chilled with preserves to spread on scones.

Strawberry Bread

Make these in mini aluminum pans and give them as gifts.

3 cups sifted flour
1 teaspoon baking soda
1 teaspoon salt
1 tablespoon cinnamon
2 cups sugar
4 eggs, beaten

1¼ cups vegetable oil
2 cups thawed frozen
   strawberries
1¼ cups chopped pecans
   (optional)

Preheat oven to 350 degrees. Grease two 8x4-inch loaf pans. In a large mixing bowl, sift together flour, baking soda, salt, cinnamon, and sugar. In a separate bowl, combine eggs, oil, and strawberries; add pecans, if desired. Make a well in center of dry ingredients, and add liquid mixture stirring until blended. Divide mixture between two loaf pans. Bake 40 minutes, until a toothpick inserted in center comes out clean.

Yield: 2 small loaves

Whitehall – The Flagler Museum continued

Guests of the Flaglers entered Whitehall through large bronze doors flanked by uniformed doormen. Once inside, guests found themselves in the 4,400-square foot Grand Hall, the largest room in any Gilded Age estate. Fourteen guest chambers and the latest in American technology, including indoor plumbing, central heat, and electric lighting, made Whitehall the benchmark of gracious living. Today, Whitehall is a National Historic Landmark and is open to the public as the Flagler Museum.

Southern Cornbread

This dish is great with chili or served southern-style with homemade macaroni and cheese and turnip greens. Leftovers can be eaten as dessert, with butter and pure cane syrup.

Vegetable oil	¾ teaspoon salt
1½ cups course yellow cornmeal	⅛ teaspoon baking soda
¾ cup flour	2 eggs
1½ teaspoons baking powder	Buttermilk (about 2 cups)

Preheat oven to 425 degrees. Add enough oil to cover the bottom of a 10-inch cast iron skillet and place skillet in the oven as it heats. Combine cornmeal, flour, baking powder, salt, and baking soda in a mixing bowl. In a 4-cup measuring cup, beat eggs, then add enough buttermilk to make 2¼ cups of liquid. Add buttermilk/egg mixture to dry ingredients and stir until well mixed.

Carefully remove hot skillet from oven and pour in cornbread mixture. Batter should sizzle when it hits the oil in the pan. Bake 20 minutes, until golden brown. Turn cooked cornbread onto a plate immediately after removing from the oven. Slice into wedges and serve.

Yield: 6 servings

Palm Beach Opera

Gallant sword fights and sopranos holding high C's as every member of the audience gasps for breath; enthralling lifelike sets and dashing tenors who rescue damsels in distress; lavish costumes and world-renowned conductors who draw melodious tunes from orchestras with the slightest dips of their batons; passionate arias and booming basses who can make the house tremble; valiant deaths and stunning altos who speak for us all; magnificent French Horns and The Great Poochini, a dog who sings opera for children; just some of the magic created by the Palm Beach Opera since 1961.

Apple Pancake
Café L'Europe

This fabulous recipe was contributed by Café
L'Europe *in Palm Beach.*

2 cups all-purpose flour
½ teaspoon salt
1 cup milk
6 eggs
1 dash vanilla
2 red delicious apples,
    peeled, cored, and sliced

4 ounces clarified butter, to
    cook
2 tablespoons cinnamon sugar
    (1 tablespoon cinnamon
    mixed with 2 tablespoons
    sugar)

Preheat oven to 475 degrees. Place flour and salt in a
bowl. Add milk and mix with an electric mixer until a
paste forms. Add 2 eggs and mix until smooth. Turn
off mixer and add remaining eggs and vanilla. Let sit
for 20 minutes.

You will need either two 10-inch sauté pans or you will
have to make one pancake at a time, using half the
batter and half the apples. For each pancake, place
2 ounces clarified butter in the pan and sauté sliced
apples for 1 minute. Blend batter for 10 seconds with
mixer, just enough to mix. Add half of the batter per
pan. Tilt pan in a circular motion; using a rubber
spatula, build up the sides of the pan by smoothing
excess batter around sides of pan.

Once pancake is brown on the bottom, flip the
pancake. Sprinkle 1 tablespoon of cinnamon sugar on
pancake and put in preheated oven for approximately
10 minutes or until puffed and golden brown.

Yield: 2 servings

Serve with lingonberries, preserves, or honey.

Blueberry Breakfast Popover

This is a favorite in Lake George, upstate New York. Your grandmother's old well-seasoned cast iron skillet is perfect for making this treat.

1¼ cups milk
3 large eggs
1 cup flour

1 pinch salt
1 tablespoon butter, melted
½ cup blueberries

Preheat oven to 450 degrees. Butter an 8-inch nonstick sauté pan with an ovenproof handle. Place pan in oven to heat.

In a blender, combine milk, eggs, flour, salt, and butter. Blend on high speed for 2 minutes until batter is thoroughly mixed and well aerated. Pour batter into heated pan and sprinkle blueberries over the batter. Bake 35 to 40 minutes, resisting the temptation to peek for at least 20 minutes.

The popover is done when the top is slightly crispy and a knife inserted into the center comes out clean. It should slide out of the pan. Serve immediately with maple syrup.

Yield: 4 servings

Granola Cereal

Better than store-bought.

½-¾ cup honey
½ cup oil
1 tablespoon vanilla
½ teaspoon salt
½ cup sesame seeds
1 cup wheat germ

1 cup chopped almonds,
   walnuts, or pecans
2 cups unsweetened coconut,
   grated
7 cups old-fashioned oatmeal
1-2 cups chopped dried
   apricots or raisins

Heat honey, oil, and vanilla in microwave until mixture is thin. Add remaining ingredients, except for apricots/raisins, and mix well. Place mixture in a jelly-roll pan and bake; it will begin to toast in about 15 minutes. Once it begins to brown, stir every 5 to 10 minutes. Toast according to your preference. Remove from oven and cool before adding raisins or apricots.

Store in an airtight container or freezer to maintain freshness.

Blueberry Coffee Cake

This is wonderful served slightly cooled with whipped cream.

Batter:

4 tablespoons butter, softened	1 cup all-purpose flour
½ cup sugar	1 teaspoon baking powder
1 egg	¼ teaspoon salt
½ teaspoon vanilla	⅓ cup milk
	1 pint fresh blueberries

Topping:

½ cup sugar	¼ teaspoon nutmeg
⅓ cup flour	4 tablespoons butter
½ teaspoon ground cardamom	

Preheat oven to 375 degrees. Cream together butter and sugar. Beat in egg and vanilla. In a separate bowl, sift together flour, baking powder, and salt. Add dry ingredients alternately with milk to creamed mixture, starting and ending with dry ingredients. Pour into greased 9x9-inch pan. Top with blueberries.

For the topping, combine sugar, flour, cardamom, and nutmeg. Using a pastry blender or two knives, cut in remaining butter until texture is like crumb cake topping. Sprinkle topping over blueberries. Bake 40 to 45 minutes.

The Boca Raton Historical Society

In 1925 the Boca Raton town council commissioned noted society architect Addison Mizner to plan a world-class resort community. His exclusive hotel continues its reign as the Boca Raton Resort and Club. Although many of Mizner's plans for the young community were squelched by the demise of the land boom in 1926, a few survive today. One of Mizner's projects was a design for a city hall. Completed in 1927, Old Town Hall still bears the original footprint of the Mizner design, and was constructed using ironwork, tile, and woodwork supplied by Mizner Industries. Today the restored Town Hall is the home of the Boca Raton Historical Society.

Fruit Salad

1 large watermelon
2 cantaloupes
2 honeydew melons
½ cup sugar
½ cup lime juice

¼ cup lemon juice
2 teaspoons lime zest
3 cups sliced strawberries
2 cups green or red seedless
   grapes, halved

Place watermelon on a damp dish towel on a firm surface. Using a water soluble marker, draw an outline of a basket. Cut along outline with a sharp knife to make a basket shape. Scoop out flesh with a melon baller and put in a bowl. Set aside.

Use melon baller to scoop out insides of cantaloupes and honeydews and add to bowl with watermelon. In a large bowl, combine sugar, lime juice, lemon juice, and lime zest. Add all fruit, mix well, and chill 30 minutes. Before serving, place fruit mixture into watermelon basket.

Yield: 10 to 12 servings

Baked Egg Frittata

1 garlic clove, minced
1 onion, chopped
2 pounds combined
   zucchini and yellow
   squash, julienned
1 sweet red pepper,
   chopped
2 tablespoons olive oil
10 eggs

2 teaspoons fresh dill
2 teaspoons fresh basil
2 teaspoons fresh oregano or
   tarragon
2 tablespoons pesto
3 cups grated Monterey Jack
   or Swiss cheese Parmesan
   cheese, for topping

Preheat oven to 350 degrees. Sauté garlic, onion, squashes, and red pepper in oil until soft. Drain and let cool.

In a large bowl, beat eggs well. Add dill, basil, oregano or tarragon, pesto, and Monterey Jack or Swiss cheese. Add cooled vegetables; mix everything together, and pour into a greased 9x13-inch pan. Sprinkle with Parmesan cheese. Bake 40 to 50 minutes until slightly browned around the edges.

Yield: 8 to 10 servings

Grandma's Lazy Day Coffee Cake

Cake:

1 stick butter	2 cups flour
⅓ cup whipping cream	2 teaspoons baking powder
1¼ cups sugar	½ teaspoon salt
3 eggs	

Frosting:

1 cup firmly packed dark brown sugar	6 tablespoons butter, melted
1 cup chopped pecans	¼ cup whipping cream

Preheat oven to 350 degrees. Grease and flour a 13x9-inch baking pan. In a 1-quart saucepan, combine butter and whipping cream. Cook over low heat, stirring occasionally until butter melts (7 to 8 minutes). Set aside.

In a large mixing bowl, combine sugar and eggs. Beat at medium speed, scraping bowl often until creamy (1 to 2 minutes). Add butter mixture, flour, baking powder, and salt. Continue beating until well mixed. Spread batter into baking pan. Bake 25 to 30 minutes or until toothpick inserted in center comes out clean.

Heat broiler. In a small bowl, stir together all frosting ingredients until well-mixed. Spread over warm cake. Broil 2 to 4 inches from heat until bubbly. Serve warm or cool.

Long Before Starbucks

By the 1870's there were a handful of settlers around Lake Worth. They were resilient and resourceful. When provisions of tea and coffee ran out they made tea from dried green leaves of the native wild coffee plant. 'Coffee' was made from sweet potatoes cut into small chunks, baked to a crisp dark brown and ground in a coffee mill. The brew looked exactly like coffee and tasted fairly good.

Overnight Orange French Toast

This is great for Christmas morning. Put it together the night before and simply pop it in the oven in the morning. When the presents are opened, breakfast is ready.

4 eggs
⅔ cup orange juice
½ cup milk
¼ cup sugar
½ teaspoon vanilla
¼ teaspoon nutmeg
¼ teaspoon orange extract

1 loaf French bread, sliced 1-inch thick
⅓ cup butter, melted
½ cup pecans, chopped
Confectioners' sugar and maple syrup, to serve

Spray a 9x13-inch pan with cooking spray. Whisk together eggs, orange juice, milk, sugar, vanilla, orange extract, and nutmeg. Place a single tight-fitting layer of bread slices into pan. Pour egg mixture over bread. Cover and refrigerate overnight, turning once.

In the morning, preheat oven to 400 degrees. Pour melted butter evenly over bread and sprinkle with pecans. Bake 20 to 25 minutes or until golden brown. Cut into pieces and serve sprinkled with confectioners' sugar.

To increase the orange taste, melt orange marmalade in microwave. Brush on a layer of marmalade before serving, then sprinkle with confectioners' sugar and extra pecans.

Yield: 8 servings

Orange Blossom

The blossoms of the orange tree are among the most fragrant flowers in Florida. Millions of these white flowers perfume the atmosphere throughout central and south Florida during orange blossom time. It is no wonder that this sweetest of blooms is Florida's State Flower.

Condiments & Sauces

Condiments & Sauces

Blueberry Chutney
Coconut Chutney
Cranberry Sauce,
  Finton's Landing
Dill Caper Sauce
Cilantro Dressing
Mango Chutney
Classic Aioli with
  Variations
Oriental Ginger
  Dressing
Aged Sherry
  Vinaigrette
Easy Remoulade Sauce
Cheney's Superb
  BBQ Marinade
Whiskey Barbeque
  Sauce
Citrus & Olives
  for Fish

Blueberry Chutney

Sweet, tart, and complex in flavor, serve chutneys with roasted meats, poultry, in omelets, with cheese and crackers, or over rice.

1½ cups apple juice
3 tablespoons cider vinegar
2 teaspoons sugar
1 cinnamon stick
1½ teaspoons ground ginger

½ teaspoon cayenne pepper
1 cup chopped dried apricots
½ cup chopped walnuts
1½ cups fresh blueberries

Palm Beach

The island of Palm Beach had no coconut palms before the wreck of the Providencia spilled its load of about 20,000 coconuts on the shores of the island in 1878. Early settlers wasted no time and planted most of them. They officially dubbed the island "Palm Beach" nine years later.

Mix apple juice, vinegar, sugar, cinnamon stick, ginger, and cayenne pepper in a saucepan and boil 2 minutes over high heat. Add apricots and walnuts. Cook uncovered until thick and syrupy, about 10 minutes or more. Remove from heat and fold in blueberries. Refrigerate overnight.

Coconut Chutney

Fantastically spicy and sweet. Curry leaves can be found at an Indian grocery store; they also can be grown locally.

1½ cups grated coconut
5 green chili peppers
1 onion, finely chopped
1 tablespoon roasted
   peanuts

1 pinch salt
2 teaspoons cooking oil
¼ teaspoon spicy mustard
   seeds
3 fresh curry leaves

Grind coconut, peppers, onion, peanuts, and salt to a fine paste; set aside. Heat oil and fry mustard seeds. When seeds start to crackle, add coconut mixture and curry leaves. Combine well. Remove curry leaves before serving.

Cranberry Sauce

This recipe is served at Finton's Landing Bed & Breakfast *on Keuka Lake in upstate New York.*

1 bag whole cranberries   ¼ cup bourbon
2 cups sugar

Preheat oven to 350 degrees. Mix ingredients together and bake 1 hour in a casserole dish. Serve warm or cold.

This can spill over in the oven, so be sure to use a large casserole dish.

Dill Caper Sauce

Tangy, pungent sauce to complement any seafood dish.

3 cups mayonnaise   2 teaspoons fresh lemon juice
2 ounces capers, drained   ½ teaspoon cayenne pepper
¼ cup diced red onions   ½ teaspoon coarse salt
4 ounces dill pickles, drained   1 teaspoon dill weed
1 teaspoon fresh chopped
    garlic

Combine all ingredients in a food processor. Process until all ingredients are incorporated. Taste for flavor and adjust as needed.

Yield: 1 quart

Manatee

The manatee, also called a sea cow, is a gray, plant-eating mammal that can weigh more than a ton. Manatees are an endangered species but humans are responsible for about half of their deaths. The most common cause of death for manatees is being struck by boat propellers. So boaters – slow down in those manatee zones and protect these gentle giants.

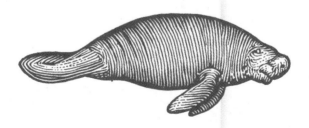

Cilantro Dressing

This recipe should be made ahead of time to allow time to chill. Marvelous, simply marvelous.

1¼ cups coarsely chopped fresh cilantro, well-packed
1 cup extra virgin olive oil
5 tablespoons champagne vinegar
2 garlic cloves, peeled
1 teaspoon ground cumin
1 teaspoon minced seeded jalapeño pepper
Salt and pepper, to taste

Place all ingredients in a food processor. Blend until smooth; season with salt and pepper. Chill before serving.

Yield: 1⅔ cups

Great with a seafood dinner, as a marinade sauce, or on greens.

Mango Chutney

This recipe makes a large amount. Make to use some today and freeze the rest to have ready for your next party.

2 pounds mangoes, sliced
2 tablespoons salt
2 pints vinegar
1 pound currants or golden raisins
6 ounces fresh ginger or 2-3 tablespoons powdered ginger
1 tablespoon white mustard seed
1 cup chopped onion
½-1 tablespoon dehydrated hot pepper
1½ pounds light brown sugar
½ pound sliced almonds

Combine mangoes, salt, vinegar, currants or raisins, ginger, mustard seed, onion, and hot pepper; cook 30 minutes. Add sugar and almonds. Boil 30 minutes until done; add more mango if needed in last 30 minutes.

Serve over cream cheese with crackers.

Classic Aïoli

This is a strongly-flavored garlic mayonnaise from the Provence region of southern France. It's a popular accompaniment for fish, meats, and vegetables.

2 or 3 fresh garlic cloves,
    peeled and chopped
1 large pinch coarse salt
1 egg yolk, at room
    temperature

½ lemon, juiced
1 cup light olive oil
Freshly ground pepper

Place garlic and salt in a food processor fitted with a metal blade or in a blender. Pulse for 2 seconds. Add egg yolk and lemon juice and pulse on and off until blended. Turn on processor and begin adding oil in a thin stream. If mixture becomes too thick, thin with some room-temperature water and continue adding oil until all has been used. Finish with pepper and, if necessary, a bit more salt.

For variations, consider adding the following to the finished sauce and process until smooth:

Roasted Red Pepper Aïoli *– add ¼ to ½ cup roasted red bell peppers, drained, patted dry;*

Fresh Herb Aïoli *– add 1 tablespoon Dijon mustard and 1 teaspoon each minced fresh sage leaves, minced thyme leaves, and minced rosemary leaves;*

Wasabi Aïoli *– add 1 to 2 tablespoons wasabi paste;*

Saffron Aïoli *– add ¼ teaspoon saffron threads, 1 tablespoon chopped orange zest, and a pinch of cayenne;*

Chipotle Aïoli *– add 2 to 3 tablespoons chipotle sauce;*

Rosemary Aïoli *– add 1 teaspoon chopped rosemary;*

Lemon Aïoli *– add 1 more tablespoon freshly squeezed lemon juice and a pinch of cayenne;*

Toasted Paprika Aïoli *– add 2 teaspoons Spanish paprika, toasted;*

Sage Aïoli *– add 1 tablespoon minced fresh sage.*

Palm Beach International Airport

Formerly known as Morrison Field, the airport is dedicated to Grace Morrison, an enthusiastic pilot who believed that more visitors would come if we had a large public airport. She enjoyed her flying lessons and worked tirelessly to get the funding necessary to build a new airport.

Oriental Ginger Dressing

Need a different "salad experience"? Try this dressing for a change from the usual oil and vinegar.

½ cup soy sauce
½ cup white vinegar
½ cup cold water
⅓ cup canola oil
1 medium onion, chopped
1 garlic clove

1 (1-inch) piece fresh ginger, peeled
½ carrot
1 tablespoon ketchup, or more to taste
Salt and pepper, to taste

Blend all ingredients in a blender. Shake before using.

Aged Sherry Vinaigrette

Try this with your favorite salad ingredients. This recipe makes a large quantity, so store any unused portion in refrigerator for later use.

3 garlic cloves
3 shallots
2 tablespoons Dijon mustard
1 egg yolk, whisked
12 ounces good aged sherry vinegar

48 ounces of a blend of 25% extra virgin olive oil and 75% canola oil
½ bunch chives, chopped
2 tablespoons honey
1 dash coarse salt
1 dash freshly ground pepper

Place garlic and shallots in blender and purée. Add mustard and egg yolk; blend. Add vinegar and purée. Slowly add oil to create an emulsion and blend until all oil is slowly incorporated. Add chives and honey; season with salt and pepper.

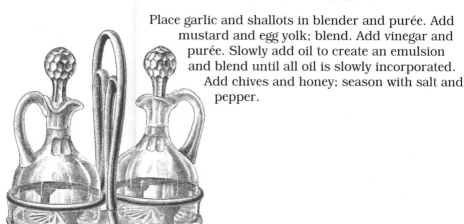

Easy Rémoulade Sauce

Fabulous and cook-friendly for all kinds of seafood. Great with cold boiled shrimp or with any seafood (cold or hot), and also can be used as a dip.

1 tablespoon Creole mustard	¼ cup prepared horseradish
2 tablespoons grated sweet onion	¼ teaspoon salt
	1 tablespoon lemon juice
1 pint light mayonnaise	¼ teaspoon Tabasco or red pepper sauce

Combine ingredients and mix well; refrigerate. Sauce is best after 24 hours.

Yield: 2½ cups

Cheney's Superb Barbecue Marinade

Marinade for poultry, beef, or pork.

8 ounces orange juice	½ cup honey
8 ounces grapefruit juice	Everglades seasoning, to taste
8 ounces pineapple juice	Lawry's seasoning, to taste
⅓ cup white vinegar	3-4 pounds meat of choice

Combine all ingredients in a large container. Refrigerate and marinate meat for 24 hours. Cook as desired.

Yield: Approximately 3¾ cups marinade

Bougainvillea

This vibrant, Brazilian vine transforms any yard into a tropical paradise. It can endure full sun and long, hot summer, making it the perfect accent for South Florida patios and yards. Cascades of showy papery leaves, surrounding tiny white flowers, come in an array of colors from orange and purple to pink, red, and white. Their roots will grow down deep into the earth to seek water, enabling them to withstand our occasional droughts.

Whiskey Barbecue Sauce

A great sauce for pork, chicken, beef, or turkey burgers.

3 slices cooked bacon, crumbled
1½ cups ketchup
¼ cup molasses
2 tablespoons cider vinegar

2 tablespoons Worcestershire sauce
2 tablespoons whiskey
2 tablespoons brewed coffee
1 teaspoon dry mustard
1 teaspoon hot pepper sauce

Combine sauce ingredients and simmer about 30 minutes.

Yield: 2 cups

Citrus and Olives for Fish

Grapefruit is superb with fish as it adds a bittersweet taste sensation.

2 oranges, segmented, membrane and pith removed, cut in half
1 pink grapefruit, same as above
½ teaspoon ground cumin
½ teaspoon paprika

12 kalamata olives, pitted and chopped (about ¼ cup)
2 tablespoons fresh parsley, minced
Cayenne pepper, to taste
Sea salt, to taste

Combine all ingredients in a non-metallic bowl. Serve at room temperature over grilled fish.

For fast preparation, buy already prepared citrus in your grocer's produce section.

Tequesta

In 1955 Charles Martyn heard the area that is now Tequesta described as "just a jungle". As he explored the area by boat, Martyn was intrigued by its beauty and potential. He bought 86 acres on Jupiter Island where he developed the Jupiter Inlet Colony. While excavating the site, Martyn's crew unearthed an Indian mound filled with artifacts. Later speculation was that the mound belonged to an encampment of Tequesta Indians encroaching on the native Jega Indians. Martyn then named an area he was developing after the Tequesta tribe. Two of Charles Martyn's grandchildren attended Suncoast High School.

Salads

Salads

Theory of Knowledge
  Bean Salad
Gorgonzola Pear Salad,
  The Breakers Palm Beach
Walnut and Pear Green Salad
Marinated Grilled Fennel Salad,
  Off the Vine
Nantucket Island Salad
Summer Salad with
  Balsamic Vinaigrette
Casa de Leon House Salad
Currant Coleslaw
Curt's Tall Salad
Armenian Broccoli Salad
Green Bean and Tomato Salad
Kohlrabi Salad
Red Cabbage & Walnut Salad
Tabouleh
Indonesian Rice Salad
Chicken Fruit Salad
Curried Chicken Salad,
  Café 1451 at the
  Norton Museum
Chicken-Melon Salad
Aegean Seafood Salad
Crab and Avocado Salad Louis
Lobster and Pink
  Grapefruit Salad
Melon Salad with
  Lemongrass Shrimp,
  Café Boulud
Mandarin Salad

Theory of Knowledge Bean Salad

This recipe comes from one of Suncoast High School's favorite "thinkers." It is an old family recipe from the Hunter family of Long Island who were known collectively as the biggest thinkers on the island.

1 (15-ounce) can small white beans	1 tablespoon sesame seeds
1 (15-ounce) can black beans	2 tablespoons balsamic vinegar
1 (10-ounce) package shelled edamame soybeans	1 tablespoon safflower oil
1 ripe tomato	Parsley, chopped, to taste
1 ripe avocado	Salt and pepper, to taste
	Garlic powder, to taste
	Cilantro, chopped, to taste

1) Observe the can of small white beans and the can of black beans. Think to yourself: "What is a good bean and what is not a good bean, and need we ask anyone to tell us these things?"

2) Drain and rinse beans and place in a large mixing bowl.

3) Mix in shelled edamame soybeans. Think to yourself: "Does a bean exist outside my own imagination?"

4) Slice tomato and avocado into small sections; mix with the beans. Consider the classic and romantic platforms of the tomato and the avocado.

5) Mix in sesame seeds. Ask yourself: "What is the sound of one hand mixing?"

6) Add Balsamic vinegar and safflower oil.

7) Add parsley, salt, pepper, garlic powder, and cilantro to taste. Ask yourself: "How do I know that I taste?"

8) Mix and allow to chill. Repeat to yourself: "This is QUALITY!" Eat and enjoy. Consume with family and friends. Eat enough, and soon you'll be known as the biggest thinkers in the neighborhood!

Successful completion of Theory of Knowledge Bean Salad makes for great peace of mind!

Gorgonzola Pear Salad from The Breakers, Palm Beach

Pinot Grigio Vinaigrette:

4 whole shallots
4 garlic cloves
2 tablespoons fresh
  rosemary
2 tablespoons fresh thyme
1 ounce olive oil
1 tablespoon shallots, small
  dice

1 tablespoon Pommery
  mustard
2 tablespoons Dijon mustard
3 tablespoons honey
½ cup sherry vinegar
1½ cups canola oil
¼ cup Pinot Grigio wine
Salt and pepper, to taste

Salad:

¾ pound mixed greens or
  salad greens of your
  choice
1 cup Bosc pears, peeled,
  medium dice
1 cup crumbled Gorgonzola
  cheese

1 red onion, thinly sliced,
  sautéed, and cooled
18 slices ripe tomatoes
⅓ cup almonds, toasted
⅓ cup walnuts, toasted

To make the vinaigrette, wrap whole shallots, garlic, rosemary, thyme, and olive oil in a foil package. Roast 1 hour in a 400-degree oven; cool. In a blender, purée roasted shallots and garlic with the diced raw shallots. Add mustards, honey, and vinegar. With blender running, slowly stream in canola oil until mixture is emulsified. Add wine, salt, and pepper.

Toss greens, pears, and Gorgonzola cheese with ½ cup Pinot Grigio vinaigrette and place in the center of a plate. Garnish with red onions, tomatoes, and toasted nuts.

Wild Parrots

A flock of wild parrots enjoys their free nests at The Breakers. A cacophony of chatter accompanies their forays around the island of Palm Beach. The colorful wild parrots that live in the Australian pines along the southeast side of The Breakers property were rumored to have been introduced to the area as escaped pets. Recent research indicates that the endangered Green-cheeked Amazon parrot is native to northeast Mexico and, contrary to popular belief, their true introduction to our area is unknown.

75

Walnut and Pear Green Salad

Pomegranates are seasonal and can be found in October and November in the U.S. They are rich in potassium and vitamin C.

Salad:

1 bunch arugula

3 large bunches watercress

4 ripe, firm pears

Juice of 1 lemon

Seeds of 1 fresh pomegranate (optional)

1½ cups walnut halves, broken into small pieces

½ pound feta cheese, crumbled

Dressing:

3 tablespoons honey

1 teaspoon thyme

½ cup extra virgin olive oil

Freshly ground pepper, to taste

Wash and trim arugula and watercress, then dry well. Peel, quarter, and core pears. Cut quarters in lengthwise slices, put in bowl, and sprinkle with lemon juice. Toss carefully.

Arrange greens on salad plates and top with pear slices and pomegranate seeds (optional). Scatter walnut pieces and feta cheese over the top of each.

Whisk dressing ingredients in small bowl, then drizzle lightly over each salad.

Palm Beach Zoo

The Palm Beach Zoo at Dreher Park features over 1000 animals from Florida, Central and South America, Asia, and Australia in 23 acres of lush tropical landscaped habitats. The new Harriet W. and George D. Cornell Tropics of the Americas is a multi-exhibit showcase of Mayan culture, animals, and horticulture. At the Black Bear Habitat visitors can get up close to the four hundred pound bear brothers from Maine. Enjoy a carousel ride, refreshments at the air-conditioned Tropics Café, a splash in the Interactive Fountain, and a visit to the Zoo Gift Shop.

Marinated Grilled Fennel Salad

Perfect picnic fare with any kind of grilled meat or fish. This recipe was contributed from Off the Vine *restaurant in Palm Beach Gardens.*

1 large head fresh fennel, tops reserved
¼ cup olive oil
½ teaspoon coarse salt
¼ teaspoon freshly ground pepper
1 sweet red pepper, roasted, peeled, and julienned
1 tablespoon chopped fresh Italian parsley
1 tablespoon chopped fresh basil
½ cup extra virgin olive oil
2 tablespoons capers
3 tablespoons balsamic vinegar
1 garlic clove, minced
Radicchio, for garnish

Bring a large pot of water to boil. Have a bowl of ice water ready. Trim fennel, cut in half, and add to boiling water; blanch for 5 minutes. Drain fennel well and add to ice water to stop cooking process. Cut fennel into ½-inch wedges and lightly brush with oil. Sprinkle with salt and pepper. Heat grill to medium-high and grill fennel on both sides until soft and nicely browned. Do not allow to char.

After removing fennel from grill, cut out hard center and toss with remaining ingredients. Season with additional salt and pepper if needed. Place in a shallow bowl and garnish with radicchio. Sprinkle with some of the chopped fennel tops. Serve warm or at room temperature.

The Florida Panther

The official state animal of Florida, this beautiful animal now is largely limited to the Florida Panther National Wildlife Refuge near the Everglades. Also known as the cougar or the puma, these animals need a large territory of approximately 165 square miles. Try to come up with a piece of land for yourself nowadays in South Florida and you can readily see the problem! Habitat loss is a primary threat putting these creatures in imminent danger of extinction. Thankfully, The Preserve measures 30,000 acres. In 1993 the panther population was estimated to be only 30 to 50 animals.

Nantucket Island Salad

Pecans and blue cheese give this salad zip and pizzazz.

Railcar No. 91

Henry Flagler's private railcar, No. 91, was built by the Jackson & Sharp Company in 1886. The railcar was described in a contemporary account as "a palace on wheels". Flagler traveled by this car in 1912 to Key West to celebrate the completion of the Over-Sea Railroad, the most ambitious engineering feat ever undertaken by an individual. The fully restored Railcar No. 91 is on exhibit in the Flagler Kenan Pavilion, a 19th century style railway palace, at the Flagler Museum in Palm Beach.

1 medium shallot, finely chopped
1 tablespoon Dijon mustard
2 garlic cloves, crushed
½ teaspoon salt
½ teaspoon pepper
¼ cup balsamic vinegar
¾ cup olive oil
2 tablespoons butter
1 rounded tablespoon brown sugar
½-¾ cup pecans, coarsely chopped
4 cups lettuce (romaine or leaf), washed and dried
2 Granny Smith apples, sliced thinly or chopped
4 ounces Stilton or blue cheese, crumbled

Whisk together shallot, mustard, garlic, salt, pepper, and vinegar. Slowly add oil while whisking until blended. Dressing will separate upon standing; to recombine, whisk again before mixing with greens.

Melt butter in skillet over low heat. Add brown sugar and stir. Sauté pecans in butter and sugar and mix until golden. Drain on wax paper.

Toss lettuce, pecans, apples, and cheese with dressing and serve.

Summer Salad with Balsamic Vinaigrette

Each cook will want to determine his or her amounts for the salad ingredients.

Balsamic Vinaigrette:

¾ cup olive oil
¼ cup balsamic vinegar
1 shallot, finely chopped

¼ teaspoon salt
¼ teaspoon freshly ground
    pepper

Spiced Pecans:

½ cup pecan pieces
2 tablespoons sugar
1 teaspoon cinnamon

1 teaspoon ginger
1 tablespoon water

Salad:

1 bowl salad greens
1 cup asparagus, blanched
    and cut into 1-inch
    pieces

1 cup sliced strawberries
½ cup spiced pecans
¼ cup Gorgonzola cheese

Combine vinaigrette ingredients in a jar, cover tightly, and shake vigorously. Store in refrigerator until ready to use.

Sauté ingredients for spiced pecans in a saucepan until sugar has coated nuts and turned light brown. Remove onto wax paper and let cool. Just before adding to salad, break up into pieces.

Just before serving, combine salad ingredients, pecans, and vinaigrette; toss.

Extra Virgin Olive Oil

Renowned Italian Chef Mario Batali is serious about extra virgin olive oil and he believes every kitchen should have two bottles. One should be an expensive Tuscan version for drizzling both raw and cooked foods prior to serving, and the other, a less expensive version for everything else including frying.

Casa de Leon House Salad

A perfect dinner for those hot summer nights.

Dressing:

5 ounces mayonnaise
¼ cup oil
¼ cup honey
2 tablespoons Dijon mustard
2 tablespoons onion, finely chopped

¼ teaspoon fresh parsley, chopped
Juice of ½ lemon
¼ teaspoon salt
⅛ teaspoon Tabasco sauce

Salad:

6 cups salad greens (romaine lettuce, escarole, watercress, spinach, and Bibb lettuce)
6 large button mushrooms, sliced

2 tomatoes, cut into wedges
2 tablespoons chives
1 cup chopped cooked shrimp
1 can Mandarin oranges, drained

Blend dressing ingredients. Toss salad greens with dressing to coat. Add remaining salad ingredients and toss gently.

Currant Coleslaw

Coleslaw comes from the Dutch word "koolsla," meaning "cool cabbage." This can be prepared in minutes using a food processor.

Salad:

3 cups shredded cabbage
½ cup currants

½ cup shredded carrots
¼ cup green onion, chopped

Dressing:

⅓ cup plain lowfat yogurt
1 tablespoon mayonnaise
1 teaspoon Dijon mustard

¼ teaspoon dried dill weed
Salt and pepper, to taste

Combine salad ingredients in a bowl. Combine dressing ingredients and blend well. Pour dressing over salad. Season with salt and pepper; toss and serve.

Yield: 4 servings

Curt's Tall Salad

This salad can be made a day in advance, covered, and refrigerated. This is local News 12 anchorman Curt Fonger's favorite salad.

Salad:

1 medium head iceberg lettuce, rinsed, dried, and torn into small pieces

½ pound crumbled crisp bacon

1 (10-ounce) package frozen small English peas, thawed

1 small purple onion, finely chopped

1 medium bag specialty dark green lettuce mix, torn into smaller pieces

1 sweet red pepper, cleaned and chopped

1 (8-ounce) can sliced water chestnuts, drained and chopped

6 ounces feta cheese or goat cheese, crumbled

Dressing:

1 cup mayonnaise

1 cup yogurt

1 tablespoon Worcestershire sauce

1 tablespoon prepared horseradish

2 teaspoons Tabasco or hot sauce, or more if you prefer

Sweet red pepper rings, for garnish

Pepper, to taste

Layer salad ingredients in order they are listed into a large, preferably clear bowl to display the colorful ingredients.

Mix dressing ingredients well and spread over salad to edge of bowl to create an airtight seal. Toss immediately before serving.

Yield: 12 servings

Artists Showcase of the Palm Beaches

You do not want to miss this wonderful experience when visiting the greater Palm Beach area. The Showcase is a multicultural art center located in the heart of West Palm Beach. Come experience the elegant beauty of high quality ethnic art in the great historic Jenkins House. Artists Showcase of the Palm Beaches' mission is to promote & display the creative works of Artists of Color, for the educational enrichment of children and adults through multicultural diversity. "Art is Fun—Come Be A Part Of Greatness."

Armenian Broccoli Salad

This family recipe came to America from Armenia in the early 20th century. It often was served as part of a Sunday dinner.

Dressing:

¾ cup Greek olives

¼ cup fresh or
   2 tablespoons dried oregano

2 tablespoons slivered garlic

1 cup olive oil

2 tablespoons red wine vinegar

2 tablespoons white wine vinegar

2 tablespoons tarragon vinegar

2 tablespoons lemon juice

Salt and pepper, to taste

Salad:

1 head fresh broccoli

1 cup onions, thinly sliced, sprinkled with salt to wilt for 15 minutes and then rinsed

3 large vine-ripened tomatoes, thinly sliced

Drop olives in boiling water. Remove olives from water as soon as water begins to boil again. Drain and cool to lukewarm. In a jar, layer olives with oregano and garlic. Fill jar with olive oil, vinegars, and lemon juice. Shake well and taste. Add more oil if needed to cover. Season with salt and pepper. Refrigerate until ready to use. Keeps well for up to 1 week.

Cook broccoli in boiling water until tender-crisp. Drain and cool. Arrange on a serving platter. Cover with onion, tomato, and olives. Drizzle with dressing.

Yield: 4 to 6 servings

Green Bean and Tomato Salad

This can be served at room temperature or slightly chilled.

6 ounces green beans (small French beans [*"haricot vert"*] are appealing)

3 ripe tomatoes, peeled and seeded (or 1 [14-ounce] can diced tomatoes, drained)

3 tablespoons chopped fresh basil, or 1 teaspoon dried

1 tablespoon extra virgin olive oil

3 tablespoons chicken broth

2 garlic cloves, minced

¼ teaspoon salt

⅛ teaspoon pepper

Trim green beans and cut in 1½-inch pieces. Cook in a medium saucepan for 3 to 5 minutes or microwave in a small amount of water until just tender. Drain and add tomatoes.

In a small bowl, mix basil, oil, broth, garlic, salt, and pepper. Whisk together and add to vegetables. Toss gently and serve.

Yield: 4 servings

Caldwell Theatre Company

Founded in 1975, the Caldwell is the only professional theater in Boca Raton and the oldest, not-for-profit regional theater in South Florida. Caldwell presents a wide variety of productions each season, including the latest Broadway and Off Broadway hits, classics and revivals as well as original plays and musicals. Caldwell also offers community-based outreach initiatives, including its critically acclaimed Play Reading Series and its Theater for Schools program, where one show per season is presented free of charge to thousands of local middle and high school students. Caldwell productions of new or original plays often lead to New York productions.

83

Kohlrabi Salad

Kohlrabi is a member of the turnip family tasting like a mild, sweet turnip. Choose one that is heavy for its size with deeply colored green leaves.

6 kohlrabi bulbs, peeled and julienned (about 3 cups)

Dressing:

¼ cup rice wine vinegar
  or white wine vinegar
2 tablespoons red wine
  vinegar
2 tablespoons olive oil
2 teaspoons minced fresh
  ginger
¼ teaspoon crushed red
  pepper flakes
½ teaspoon salt, or to taste
1 tablespoon fresh chopped
  tarragon (or 1 teaspoon
  dried)
½ cup chopped red onion

Steam kohlrabi until crisp tender, about 2 minutes. Drain and rinse under cold water. Set aside in a medium bowl.

Whisk together vinegars, oil, ginger, pepper, tarragon, and salt. Add onion to kohlrabi. Pour dressing over kohlrabi and onion mixture; toss well. Cover and refrigerate. Allow flavors to meld at least 2 hours.

Yield: 6 to 8 servings

The Great Horned Owl

You can visit "Merlin" and "Lucas" at the Palm Beach Zoo. No, they can't turn their heads 360 degrees – only 270 degrees. They accomplish this by having twice as many neck vertebrae as humans. One ear is higher than the other to improve their hearing, and their eyesight is extraordinary. If humans had eyes in proportion to the owls', our eyes would have to be the size of grapefruit! Maybe these special gifts give the owl the mythical reputation for being a 'wise old owl.'

Red Cabbage and Walnut Salad

Even those who dislike coleslaw enjoy this recipe. It keeps for about 5 days, covered and refrigerated.

Salad:

1 cup chopped, dried cranberries

1 cup walnuts, coarsely chopped

2 cups red cabbage, finely sliced

2 cups green cabbage, finely sliced

¼ cup thinly sliced red onion

Dressing:

⅓ cup cider vinegar

⅓ cup canola oil

⅓ cup sugar

1 teaspoon celery seed

Combine salad ingredients in a large bowl. Combine dressing ingredients and toss into salad. Cover and refrigerate about 3 hours. Drain off liquid.

Yield: 6 servings

Tabouleh

A light and refreshing Mediterranean salad.

1 bunch fresh parsley, washed, dried, and chopped

1 bunch fresh mint, washed, dried, and chopped

½ cup #2 bulgur wheat, washed and soaked 30 minutes in cold water

3 green onions, chopped

¼ head of lettuce (preferably dark leafy green), chopped

2 cucumbers, finely chopped

4 tomatoes, chopped

Juice of 1½ lemons

¼ cup olive oil

Salt and pepper, to taste

Using equal parts of parsley and mint, combine all ingredients. Serve cold.

The Name 'Boca Raton'

The meaning of the name Boca Raton has always aroused curiosity. Many people wrongly assume the name is simply Rat's Mouth. The Spanish word boca (mouth) often described an inlet, while raton (mouse) may have been a term for "cowardly thief". But the "Thieves Inlet", Boca de Ratones, appeared on eighteenth century maps associated with an inlet in Biscayne Bay. By the beginning of the nineteenth century, the term was mistakenly applied to Lake Boca Raton, whose inlet was closed at the time. The "s" and later "e" were dropped from this title by the 1920s, yet the correct pronunciation remains Rah-tone.

Indonesian Rice Salad

A tasty side dish, wonderful for potluck dinners too.

2 cups brown rice
3 cups water
⅓ cup canola oil
2 tablespoons sesame oil
½ cup orange juice
1-2 medium garlic cloves, minced
3 tablespoons soy sauce
1 teaspoon grated fresh ginger

3 scallions, thinly sliced on the diagonal
1 stalk celery, finely sliced on the diagonal
1 (8-ounce) can sliced water chestnuts, drained
½ cup golden raisins
½ cup coarsely chopped cashews, lightly toasted
Fresh snow peas (optional)

Place rice and water in a saucepan. Bring to a boil, lower heat, cover, and simmer until tender, 35 to 45 minutes.

While rice cooks, in a large bowl combine oils, orange juice, garlic, soy sauce, and ginger.

When rice has finished cooking, add hot rice directly to bowlful of dressing. Mix well. When cooled to room temperature, cover bowl tightly and refrigerate. Chill at least 4 hours or preferably overnight.

Shortly before serving, stir in scallions, celery, water chestnuts, raisins, cashews, and snow peas.

Boca Ballet Theatre

The Boca Ballet Theatre is the 6th largest dance company in Florida and one of the top ten civic companies in the United States. The company has perfected a unique performance tradition: "Where the Stars of Tomorrow Join the Greatest Stars of Today". Boca Ballet Theatre is unique as the only civic ballet company with this intentional double focus: the public performance of classic and contemporary ballet works featuring world class dancers, and a school for young dancers that enables them to perform with and learn from these professionals.

Chicken Fruit Salad

Going to a picnic and not sure what to bring? This is sure to be a hit.

Salad:

3 cups cooked elbow macaroni, cooled

3 cups cubed cooked chicken, cooled

2 cups cubed peeled fresh peaches

1 cup sliced celery

1 cup halved strawberries

1 (8-ounce) can pineapple tidbits, drained

1 (11-ounce) can Mandarin oranges

1 (8-ounce) can sliced water chestnuts, drained (optional)

½ cup golden raisins

½ cup chopped pecans

1 head lettuce, washed and dried well

Dressing:

1 cup mayonnaise

¼ cup orange juice

2 tablespoons sugar

½ teaspoon ground ginger

⅛ teaspoon pepper

In a large bowl, combine salad ingredients. In a small bowl, combine dressing ingredients. Right before serving, pour dressing over salad and toss. Serve on a bed of lettuce.

Yield: 12 servings

Mr. U.B. Kinsey

Renowned school principal, Ulysses Bradshaw Kinsey (1918-2005) was an ardent civil rights advocate. As a teacher, Kinsey and his supporters challenged the school board over racial discrimination in teacher salaries. With the help of then-attorney Thurgood Marshall, they won. That was 1942. Fighting against local harvesters' efforts to shorten the academic year for minority schools, Kinsey and others successfully returned those schools to 9-month schedules in 1944. Always insisting on the title "Mr.", he threw away mail that omitted that title in the address. Upon his retirement in 1989, Palmview was renamed U.B. Kinsey-Palmview Elementary.

Curried Chicken Salad

This beautifully composed salad served at Café 1451 at the Norton Museum of Art in West Palm Beach is a work of art. The bulgur for the tabouleh must soak overnight, so you need to start a day in advance.

Curry Chicken Salad:

1 pound cooked boneless roasted chicken breast, small dice
1 cup chopped walnuts
½ cup golden raisins

½ cup Major Grey's Mango chutney
1 cup mayonnaise
¼ cup curry powder
½ cup water
Salt and pepper, to taste

Lemon Soaked Tabouleh:

6 ounces dry bulgur (cracked wheat)
½ cup lemon juice (enough to cover bulgur)
2 medium tomatoes, small dice

1 bunch mint, chopped
1 bunch Italian parsley, chopped
Salt and pepper, to taste

Dijon Dressing:

4 ounces Dijon mustard
⅓ cup red wine vinegar
2 tablespoons water

1 cup extra virgin olive oil
Salt and pepper, to taste

For Assembly:

1 cup lemon-soaked tabouleh
2 cups marinated curry chicken salad
2 cups salad greens

1 Granny Smith apple, sliced
8 grape tomatoes, sliced
½ cup Dijon dressing
Curry powder

In a large bowl, combine chicken, walnuts, and raisins. In a smaller bowl, whisk together chutney, mayonnaise, curry powder, and water; season with salt and pepper. Pour dressing over chicken and toss to coat. Refrigerate.

Soak bulgur overnight in lemon juice in the refrigerator. Next day, flake with a fork and mix in remaining tabouleh ingredients.

continued

Norton Museum of Art

The Norton Museum of Art is one of the Southeast's premier art museums – a 60-year-old flagship institution known for the quality of its permanent collection, traveling special exhibitions, and innovative educational programming. Founded in 1941 by Ralph and Elizabeth Norton, the museum has expanded over the years. The recently opened Nessel Wing increased the gallery space by 75%, including a glass ceiling installation commissioned from Dale Chihuly. The Museum has an internationally renowned permanent collection of over 5,500 works concentrated in European, American, Chinese, and Contemporary art and photography.

Curried Chicken Salad continued

In a medium bowl, combine mustard, vinegar, and water. Slowly whisk in oil and season with salt and pepper.

Using a ring mold, place ¼ cup tabouleh in the center of a plate. Shape sides up to resemble a bowl. Put ½ cup chicken salad in mold and level top. Remove mold from plate. Toss greens with dressing and top chicken salad with small handful of greens. Garnish with 4 slices tomato and 4 slices apple around salad and drizzle with Dijon dressing. Sprinkle curry powder on outer edges of plate for presentation.

Yield: 4 servings

Persian Sea-Life Ceiling

Dale Chihuly's installation is a dazzling array of 693 individual pieces of blown glass sea life forms in aquatic blues and greens, suggestive of a Baroque grotto. Shells, starfish, sea urchins, sharks, and cuttlefish are interwoven with ribbons of sea grass and Baroque putti riding on the backs of dolphins. Chihuly calls his ceiling installations Pergolas. "There's something about putting the glass pieces overhead, on top of the plate of glass, that makes you think of the sea—the reverse of having the glass underwater. There's a feeling of water, at least there is to me. I suppose somebody else could think it's something they might have seen in the sky or in a dream".

Chicken Melon Salad

Perfect for lunch.

½ cup large walnut pieces
¾ cup chopped mint leaves, separated into 3 (¼-cup) portions
¼ cup lemon juice
⅔ cup olive oil
2 tablespoons red wine vinegar
½ teaspoon sugar
Salt and pepper, to taste
2 tablespoons vegetable oil

3 whole skinless, boneless chicken breasts, halved and flattened to ½-inch thick
1 large ripe cantaloupe, peeled, sliced into thin pieces, and cut into thirds
¾ pound feta cheese, crumbled
4 bunches of watercress, cleaned and stems removed

Roast walnuts in a 325-degree oven for 10 minutes or until lightly browned. Cool and coarsely chop.

In a saucepan, cook ¼ cup chopped mint in lemon juice until wilted, about 1 minute. Remove from heat and let stand 10 minutes. Strain juice into small bowl and discard mint. Whisk olive oil, vinegar, and sugar into lemon juice and season with salt and pepper.

Heat 1 tablespoon vegetable oil in each of two large skillets. Season chicken breast halves with salt and pepper; add three to each skillet and cook over moderately high heat until golden and just cooked through, about 3 minutes per side. Transfer chicken to a cutting board and let cool.

Thinly slice chicken across the grain and transfer to a large bowl. Add cantaloupe, feta cheese, and ¼ cup mint leaves. Whisk vinaigrette, add half to the chicken, and toss gently. Put watercress into another large bowl. Add remaining ¼ cup mint leaves and vinaigrette and toss gently to coat. Season with salt and pepper.

Arrange watercress on six plates or a large platter. Top with chicken salad and serve immediately.

Yield: 6 servings

Gardenia

A favorite landscape shrub in Florida, the gardenia has glossy dark-green leaves and very fragrant, creamy-white flowers. The gardenia is considered to have one of the most delightful fragrances of any flower on earth. Its showy flowers are popular for corsages and bridal bouquets. Although the gardenia originated in China and is a member of the coffee family, it is named after Alexander Garden, an 18th century American botanist and naturalist.

Aegean Seafood Salad

A Greek specialty.

Vinaigrette:

1 tablespoon Dijon mustard
2 tablespoons fresh lemon
   juice
½ teaspoon minced garlic

½ teaspoon salt
½ teaspoon pepper
¼ cup olive oil

Seafood Salad:

1½ pounds shrimp, peeled
1 pound squid, cleaned, cut
   into small pieces
1 dozen clams, rinsed
2 large tomatoes, cut into
   large chunks

1 can garbanzo beans
16 sliced, pitted Kalamata
   olives
½ small red onion, minced
½ cup fresh basil, julienned
Salt and pepper, to taste

Combine mustard, lemon juice, garlic, ½ teaspoon salt, and ½ teaspoon pepper in a food processor. Continue to process while drizzling in oil until emulsified.

Boil shrimp in salted water, approximately 3 minutes. Remove shrimp, add squid, and cook 2 minutes. Remove squid; adjust water to leave a small amount in bottom of pan. Add clams; cover and steam 5 minutes until clams open.

Combine shrimp, squid, tomatoes, beans, olives, onion, and basil. Season with salt and pepper. Toss with vinaigrette.

When ready to serve, divide salad among plates and add clams.

Words to live by

"The pleasures of table – that lovely old-fashioned phrase – depict food as an art form, as a delightful part of civilized life. In spite of food fads, fitness programs, and health concerns, we must never lose sight of a beautifully conceived meal."

~Julia Child
1912-2004

Crab and Avocado Salad Louis

Louis Dressing:

1 cup mayonnaise
¼ cup chili sauce
2 tablespoons chopped
   parsley
1 tablespoon finely chopped
   onion
1 tablespoon chives
⅛ teaspoon cayenne pepper
¼ cup heavy cream, whipped

Salad:

2 medium avocados
1 pound lump crabmeat
¼ cup finely chopped celery
¼ cup thinly sliced
   radishes
⅛ cup lemon juice
⅛ cup vinegar
1½ tablespoons olive oil
1 tablespoon finely chopped
   shallots
⅛ teaspoon cayenne pepper
¼ teaspoon salt
Lettuce hearts, tomato
   quarters, and lemon
   slices, for garnish

To make Louis Dressing, mix mayonnaise, chili sauce, parsley, onion, chives, and cayenne pepper; fold in whipped cream.

Cut avocados into 1-inch cubes, combine with remaining salad ingredients, and toss gently. Mound on platter and garnish with lettuce hearts, tomato quarters, and lemon slices. Top with Louis Dressing.

Yield: 4 servings

Florida Avocado Tree

South Florida produces approximately eight popular varieties of avocados, including Brogdon, Choquette, Hall, Pumpkin, and Simmonds. Californians claim their avocados taste better than ours, but Florida avocados are much larger and grow year 'round. The number one predator to the Florida Avocado Tree is the pesky backyard squirrel who nibbles the young fruit then throws it onto the ground to ruin.

Lobster and Pink Grapefruit Salad

Floribbean is an infused cuisine of Florida and Caribbean styles, and this recipe is definitely Floribbean.

4 (8-ounce) Florida (spiny) lobster tails

Citrus Vinaigrette:

2 tablespoons freshly squeezed orange juice

2 tablespoons freshly squeezed lemon juice

Pulp of a vanilla bean

Pepper, to taste

1 cup olive oil

Other Ingredients:

½ pound unsalted butter

2 pink grapefruits, peeled and sectioned

¼ teaspoon sea salt

1 bunch watercress, washed and trimmed

Place lobster tails in a heatproof container. Cover with boiling water and allow to steep for 3 minutes. Remove tails from water. Separate lobster meat from shells and slice into medallions.

To make Citrus Vinaigrette, combine orange juice, lemon juice, vanilla bean pulp, and pepper in a stainless steel bowl. While whisking, slowly drizzle in oil. Whisk until well blended and set aside.

Heat butter in a saucepan on low heat. Add lobster and sauté 2 to 3 minutes. Remove lobster from butter and keep warm.

To serve, divide and arrange grapefruit sections on four plates. Top each plate with lobster medallions. Spoon vinaigrette over lobster, then sprinkle with sea salt and garnish with watercress. Serve at room temperature.

Yield: 4 servings

Melon Salad with Lemongrass Shrimp

Café Boulud in Palm Beach shares this recipe reprinted with permission from Daniel's Dish: Entertaining at Home with a Four Star Chef, *Daniel Boulud, Filipacchi Publishing, 2003.*

1½ pounds large shrimp, peeled and deveined
6 tablespoons extra virgin olive oil
2 teaspoons finely grated peeled ginger
2 teaspoons finely chopped lemongrass
Finely grated zest of 1 lime
Freshly squeezed juice of 2 limes

⅛ teaspoon Tabasco sauce
Salt and freshly ground white pepper, to taste
1 ripe, small red watermelon
1 ripe honeydew melon
1 tablespoon finely chopped purple basil leaves, plus additional small leaves
1 tablespoon finely chopped cilantro leaves, plus additional small leaves

Cook shrimp in a medium saucepan of boiling salted water for 3 to 5 minutes; drain. When shrimp are cool enough to handle, slice each lengthwise in half.

In a small bowl, whisk together oil, ginger, lemongrass, lime zest and juice, and Tabasco sauce. Season with salt and pepper. Set aside.

Cut watermelon and honeydew in half, cut away rind, and remove seeds. Cut melons into ⅛-inch thick slices. Remove the watermelon seeds; it's okay if the slices don't stay intact. Using a cake ring or glass slightly smaller than the mouth of a 14- to 16-ounce martini glass or champagne coupe, cut out 16 slices from watermelon and 16 slices from honeydew. Save the nicest 4 watermelon slices for the top.

continued

Melon Salad with Lemongrass Shrimp continued

Set out four 8- to 12-ounce martini glasses or champagne coupes. Layer 2 slices of watermelon and honeydew in each glass, lightly sprinkling each melon layer with lemongrass dressing, chopped basil, chopped cilantro, and salt and pepper. (You may need to trim melon slices so they fit neatly into the glasses, which should be half full at this point.) Divide shrimp among the glasses, arranging them in concentric circles. Season shrimp with dressing, basil, cilantro, and salt and pepper. Layer glasses with the melon in reverse order: the honeydew, then the watermelon, seasoning each layer as before. Top each salad with a reserved watermelon slice and sprinkle lightly with dressing, basil, cilantro, and salt and pepper. Garnish each salad with a basil and cilantro leaf. Refrigerate at least 1 hour before serving (the melon and shrimp taste best when well chilled).

Yield: 4 servings

Historical Society of Palm Beach County

Since its founding in 1937, the Historical Society of Palm Beach County has assembled an extraordinary collection of historically significant documents, photographs and artifacts that tell a fascinating story of the people who made Palm Beach County an exceptional area in which to live, work and learn. When the restoration of the 1916 Palm Beach Courthouse is complete in 2007, the Historical Society will open the first-ever, countywide history museum and educational resource center. Inside they will offer interactive exhibits, rotating exhibits, and their vast collection of historical photographs, documents, and artifacts detailing over 12,000 years of local history.

Mandarin Salad

This salad has a fresh, delightful, and surprising taste. Your taste buds will be intrigued as you try to figure out what's in it.

Dressing:

¼ teaspoon salt
1 tablespoon sugar
⅛ cup vegetable oil
¼ teaspoon Tabasco sauce

1 tablespoon tarragon
    vinegar
Freshly ground pepper

Salad:

1 head butter lettuce
1 cup celery, thinly sliced
    on the diagonal
2 spring onions, including
    tops, sliced on the
    diagonal

¾ cup Mandarin oranges
¼ cup slivered toasted
    almonds
2 tablespoons chopped
    parsley

Combine dressing ingredients. Tear lettuce into bite-sized pieces. Add celery, onions, oranges, almonds, and parsley. Toss salad with dressing just before serving.

Bibb or romaine lettuce may be substituted for the butter lettuce.

Soups & Sandwiches

Soups & Sandwiches

Red Lentil Soup with
  Garlic and Cumin
Moroccan Golden Split Pea
  and Butternut Squash Soup
Brandied Pumpkin Soup
Sweet Potato Soup
Dan's Tomato Basil Soup
Pasta Fagioli,
  Café Chardonnay
Cucumber & Avocado Soup
  with Tomato and Basil Salad
Cream of Poblano Chile Soup
  with Cheese
Conch Chowder
Lobster Chowder
Lobster Bisque
She Crab Soup
Spicy Salmon Chowder
Shrimp Chowder
Seafood Bar Gazpacho,
  The Breakers Palm Beach
Croissants filled with Ham
Grilled Turkey Burger,
  The Breakers Palm Beach
Lobster Roll
Ham, Brie, and Mango
  Chutney "Sidillas"
Hot and Creamy
  Turkey Sandwiches
Sazio Skirt Steak Sandwich,
  Sazio Restaurant

Red Lentil Soup
with Garlic and Cumin
(Shurit Ad – Egypt)

In the Bible, Jacob's red lentil soup was so delicious that his brother, Esau, sold his birthright for a bowlful.

2 cups dried, hulled, split
   red lentils
2 quarts chicken broth
1 medium-sized onion,
   peeled and quartered
1 medium-sized tomato,
   quartered
2 teaspoons minced garlic

1 tablespoon butter
1 tablespoon finely chopped
   onion
2 teaspoons ground cumin
1 teaspoon salt
Freshly ground pepper
3 tablespoons butter
Lemon wedges

Wash lentils in a large sieve or colander under cold running water until draining water runs clear. Remove any small stones.

In a heavy 4- to 5-quart saucepan, bring broth to a boil over high heat. Add lentils, quartered onion, tomato, and garlic. Reduce heat to low and simmer partially covered for 45 minutes or until lentils are tender.

Meanwhile, in a small skillet, melt 1 tablespoon butter over moderate heat. When foam begins to subside, add chopped onion and cook 10 minutes, stirring frequently, until onions are soft and deeply browned. Remove from heat and set aside.

Purée soup through a food mill, or pour entire contents of saucepan into a sieve set over a deep bowl and force ingredients through sieve with the back of a large spoon, pressing down hard on vegetables before discarding pulp. Return soup to saucepan and cook over low heat, stirring constantly, 3 or 4 minutes to heat through. Stir in cumin, salt, and pepper and taste for seasoning. Just before serving, stir in remaining 3 tablespoons butter.

To serve, ladle soup into a heated tureen, sprinkle lightly with the reserved browned onions. Serve with lemon wedges on the side.

Yield: 6 servings

Moroccan Golden Split Pea and Butternut Squash Soup

How about starting your dinner with a warm simmered bowl of exotic flavors? Excellent for lunch, too.

3 quarts chicken broth	1 tablespoon ground ginger
1 quart cold water	2 large pinches saffron
1 pound (2 cups) dried	threads, crumbled
yellow split peas	2 pounds butternut squash,
3 bay leaves	peeled and diced
½ cup olive oil	½ cup pearl barley
2 large onions, chopped	Salt and freshly ground
1 tablespoon ground	pepper, to taste
cinnamon	

In a large soup pot, combine broth, water, peas, and bay leaves and bring to a boil. Skim off and discard any white foam that forms on the surface. Reduce heat and simmer about 1 hour or until peas become tender.

In a separate pan, heat oil over medium heat. Add onions, cinnamon, ginger, and saffron. Cook until onions are translucent. Add mixture to soup along with squash and barley. Simmer 30 to 40 minutes or until squash is soft. Remove and discard bay leaves. Season to taste with salt and pepper and serve.

Yield: 8 servings

You can use diced red pumpkin or calabaza in place of the butternut squash.

Seagrape

The seagrape is a versatile, highly salt tolerant South Florida native tree. Its fruit, hanging in grape-like clusters, ripens in the fall and makes an excellent jelly. The round, firm, leathery leaves can be used as disposable, environmentally friendly "plates" for picnics at the beach.

Brandied Pumpkin Soup

Lovely color and texture to entice the appetite.

2 tablespoons unsalted
   butter
1 cup onion, finely chopped
3 cups pumpkin purée
4 cups chicken broth
2 cups whole milk, at room
   temperature
⅛ teaspoon ground cloves
¼ teaspoon ground
   cardamom
⅛ teaspoon ground cayenne
   pepper

½ cup sour cream, at room
   temperature
2 tablespoons brandy
1 teaspoon salt
¼ teaspoon freshly ground
   pepper, or to taste
Additional sour cream, for
   garnish (optional)
Finely chopped fresh chives
   (optional)

Melt butter in a large heavy saucepan over medium heat. When foam subsides, add onion. Reduce heat to medium-low and sauté onion, stirring occasionally, until softened but not browned, about 5 minutes. Stir in pumpkin purée until thoroughly blended; gradually stir in broth and milk. Add cloves, cardamom, and cayenne pepper; reduce heat to very low. Heat soup to very gentle simmer and cook, partially covered, about 25 minutes, adjusting heat if necessary to prevent soup from boiling.

Stir in sour cream and brandy, then season with salt and pepper. Heat through briefly; do not allow to boil. Ladle into warmed soup bowls and serve immediately, garnished with sour cream and chives, if desired.

Yield: 6 to 8 servings

Sweet Potato Soup

Sweet potatoes are loaded with complex carbohydrates, fiber, and important nutrients like beta carotene, an antioxidant that is believed to help prevent cancer. This soup can be paired with any pork, chicken, lamb, tuna, turkey, or ham entrée and is great with a nice salad. It can be made ahead of time and refrigerated; reheat slowly to serve.

1½ tablespoons olive oil
1⅔ cups coarsely chopped onion
1 large garlic clove, coarsely chopped
1 tablespoon coarsely chopped ginger
1 teaspoon ground cumin
½ teaspoon ground coriander
¼ teaspoon ground cardamom
¼ teaspoon turmeric
⅛ teaspoon hot pepper flakes (optional)
2½ pounds sweet potatoes, peeled and sliced ¼-inch thick
6 cups no-salt-added chicken broth
Salt and freshly ground pepper, to taste
8 teaspoons fresh goat cheese

Heat oil in a nonstick pot large enough to hold all of the ingredients. Sauté onions until they begin to brown, about 10 minutes. Add garlic and sauté, stirring for 30 seconds. Add ginger, cumin, coriander, cardamom, turmeric, and hot pepper flakes and stir well. Add sweet potatoes and broth and bring to a boil. Reduce heat and simmer about 20 minutes, until sweet potatoes are soft. Purée soup in batches in a blender or food processor. Season with salt and pepper. If soup is too thick, add a little more stock. Ladle into mugs or bowls, top each serving with a teaspoon of goat cheese, and stir to melt cheese a little.

Yield: 8 cups

Sea Oats

Sea Oats are grasses that grow in coastal areas and are valuable for stabilizing dunes and beaches. They prevent beach erosion through elaborate and extensive root systems. Once popular for dried flower arrangements, they are now protected by a Florida statute making it unlawful to pick them.

Dan's Tomato Basil Soup

Try making your own fresh tomato soup. What a delicious way to eat your vegetables!

4 tablespoons butter
1 cup finely diced Spanish
  onions
1 cup finely diced carrots
1 cup finely diced celery
½ cup finely diced fresh
  sweet red peppers

2 tablespoons tomato paste
4 cups diced tomatoes
4 cups heavy cream
2 bunches fresh basil,
  minced
1 teaspoon coarse salt
1 teaspoon pepper

Melt butter in a heavy pot. Add onions, carrots, celery, and sweet red peppers; sauté until translucent. Add tomato paste and let the color mix in thoroughly. Add tomatoes and simmer 15 minutes, then add cream, basil, salt, and pepper. Heat thoroughly. Process all ingredients with a hand-held food processing stick or place it in small batches in a standard food processor. After mixture is puréed, taste and adjust flavor as needed.

Yield: 2 quarts

Old School Square

Old School Square Cultural Arts Center, a National Historic Site housing restored school buildings, was the catalyst for the renaissance of downtown Delray Beach. Slated for demolition in the mid 1980s, the buildings are now the community's gathering place. Old School Square offers visual and performing arts opportunities through the Cornell Museum of Art & History in the old 1913 elementary building and Crest Theatre in the old 1925 high school building and hosts a variety of festivals. It is a classic example of how the arts and historic preservation make downtown revitalization come alive.

102

Pasta Fagioli

This Italian bean soup was contributed by Chef Frank Eucalitto, owner of Café Chardonnay *in Palm Beach Gardens.*

½ cup diced carrot
1½ cups diced onion
1½ cups diced celery
3 garlic cloves, chopped
1 small ham hock
6 ounces tomato paste
1 quart dried navy beans or
    other white beans, rinsed
    and picked through for
    small rocks, etc.

2 quarts chicken broth
1 quart water
2 teaspoons salt
1 teaspoon pepper
2 ounces olive oil
½ pound ditalini pasta,
    cooked al dente
4 ounces grated Parmesan
    cheese

Heat oil in a large heavy soup pot. Add carrots, onions, and celery and sauté 3 to 4 minutes. Add garlic and sauté 2 minutes longer. Add ham hock and tomato paste and cook 1 minute, stirring. Add beans, broth, and water, then add salt and pepper. Bring to a boil and lower to a simmer. Simmer 1½ to 2 hours until beans are tender. Add more water while cooking if soup becomes thick.

Remove ham hock, add pasta, and serve. Top each serving with Parmesan cheese.

Yield: 12 servings

Cucumber and Avocado Soup with Tomato and Basil Salad

Serve this chilled soup as a first course, or by itself for lunch.

Soup:

1 large English hothouse cucumber, peeled and diced (about 2½ cups)

2½ cups lowfat (1%) buttermilk

1 avocado, quartered, pitted, and peeled

4 tablespoons chopped red onion

2 tablespoons chopped fresh basil

Salt and pepper, to taste

Salad:

2 tablespoons chopped red onion

1 tablespoon chopped fresh basil

½ cup seeded chopped tomato

2 teaspoons fresh lime juice

Topping:

4 tablespoons plain nonfat yogurt

Combine cucumber and buttermilk in a blender. Chop ¼ of the avocado; set aside for the salad. Cut remaining avocado into chunks and add to blender, then add 2 tablespoons onion and 1 tablespoon basil. Blend until very smooth. Season with salt and pepper. Cover and refrigerate until chilled, about 1 hour.

Mix reserved avocado, 2 tablespoons onion, 1 tablespoon basil, tomato, and lime juice in a small bowl.

To serve, ladle soup into bowls. Top each with 1 tablespoon yogurt; then with tomato salad, and serve.

Yield: 4 servings

Soup and salad can be prepared 1 day ahead; cover separately and refrigerate.

Lake Worth

Lake Worth, the body of water, was the early nexus of the greater West Palm Beach area. It was named for William Jenkins Worth, colonel in the Seminole Indian War. (Colonel Worth is also the namesake of Ft. Worth, Texas.) The Seminole Indians called this lake 'Hypoluxo'. Roughly translated, it means "water all around – can't get out."

Cream of Poblano Chili Soup with Cheese

Rich and hot with fire, perfect to begin an exciting dinner.

8 poblano chili peppers
1 serrano chili pepper
1½ tablespoons clarified
   butter
1 medium yellow onion,
   diced
1 carrot, diced
2½ tablespoons flour
5 cups strong chicken
   broth

2 medium baking potatoes,
   peeled and diced
2 cups heavy cream
1 tablespoon fresh cilantro
Salt, to taste
2 blue corn tortillas, julienned
   and fried crisp
2 red chili corn tortillas,
   julienned and fried crisp
8 slices Monterey Jack cheese

Char one poblano chili over an open flame, then peel, seed, and dice. Remove seeds and stems from remaining poblano chilies and the serrano chili. Wear plastic gloves to avoid irritating your skin, and do not touch your eyes while working with the peppers.

Place butter, onion, and carrot in a soup pot and sauté slowly for 5 minutes. Add flour and continue to stir for another 4 to 5 minutes. Whisk in chicken broth, then add potatoes and raw poblano and Serrano chili peppers. Simmer 25 to 30 minutes.

Remove soup from heat and purée in blender, then strain mixture back into soup pot using a fine-meshed strainer (soup may be made ahead to this point).

Shortly before serving, preheat broiler. Add cream and cilantro to the purée. Season to taste with salt and reheat. Ladle into ovenproof bowls. Top each with some of the tortilla crisps, then add a slice of cheese. Finish with roasted, diced poblanos and place under broiler until cheese is melted.

Yield: 8 servings

Oleander

Oleanders have been cultivated in Florida since 1565 and are popular landscape plants. They flower freely and thrive under difficult conditions, growing well in sandy, coastal soil and in the polluted air along busy highways. Oleander derives its name from "oleandra" which means "olive-like" in Greek. But that's only in appearance; unlike the olive, the oleander is quite poisonous, all parts of it: the leaves, the flowers, and the branches are highly toxic. So do not be tempted to roast your hot dogs or marshmallows on an oleander stick-even the smoke from burning oleander branches will make you sick!

Conch Chowder

Take a quick trip to the Bahamas with a bowl of this traditional flavorful chowder.

Conchtown

What is now Riviera Beach was once known as Conchtown, a reference to the diet of the people inhabiting the area. By 1922, residents had incorporated the area in an attempt to avoid a takeover by its neighbor to the south, West Palm Beach. Then hard times hit, starting with the devastating hurricane of 1928, followed by the Great Depression.

¼ pound salt pork, diced
2 onions, chopped
4 or 5 cloves garlic, minced
1 green pepper, chopped
2 (1-pound) cans tomatoes
1 (6-ounce) can tomato
   paste
2 quarts hot water
2 tablespoons vinegar
10 bay leaves
1 tablespoon oregano
1 teaspoon basil
1 teaspoon poultry seasoning
1½ teaspoons salt
½ teaspoon pepper
Few drops Tabasco sauce
6 large conchs
3 or 4 medium potatoes,
   diced
1 (12-ounce) can whole
   kernel corn, drained
   (optional)

Fry salt pork slowly until crisp. Remove, set aside. In the remaining hot drippings, cook onion, garlic, and green pepper until tender.

Stir in all remaining ingredients except conch and potatoes. Simmer 15 minutes.

To tenderize conch, pound with a mallet or side of heavy saucepan until tissue is somewhat broken up; alternatively, conch may be put through a food grinder or chopped very fine.

Add conch to hot tomato mixture. Bring to a boil, then reduce heat and simmer 3 hours or until conch is tender. Add potatoes, and corn if desired; cook until potatoes are done, approximately 15 minutes. Taste; add more salt, pepper, and Tabasco sauce, if needed.

Yield: 8 servings

Lobster Chowder

The most discerning New Englander would be delighted with the aromatic steam of this Lobster Chowder.

2 (1½-pound) live Maine
   lobsters
3 gallons water
¾ cup salt
8 cups water
2 bay leaves
2 bacon slices, chopped
1 cup chopped green
   onions
1 teaspoon Hungarian
   sweet paprika

½ teaspoon cumin
2 cups diced peeled baking
   potato
1 cup half & half
2 teaspoons sugar
½ teaspoon salt
¼ teaspoon white pepper
2 cups fresh corn kernels
   (about 4 ears)
Chopped fresh chives

Boil lobsters, covered, in 3 gallons water and salt in a 5-gallon stockpot for 10 minutes or until shells are bright orange-red and tails are curled. Remove from pan and cool. Remove meat from shells (reserving shells), coarsely chop, and refrigerate.

Combine lobster shells, 8 cups water, and bay leaves in stockpot. Bring to a boil, reduce heat, and simmer 1 hour. Strain broth through a colander into a large bowl. Discard shells. Reserve 4 cups of broth.

Cook bacon in a large Dutch oven over medium-high heat until crisp. Add green onions and sauté 2 minutes. Stir in paprika and cumin. Add reserved broth and potato. Bring to a boil and cook until potato is tender; remove from heat. Stir in lobster meat, half & half, sugar, salt, and pepper. Cover and refrigerate 1 hour, if desired. Return pan to low heat. Add corn and cook 5 minutes. Garnish with chives.

Yield: 8 servings

Lobster Bisque

An elegant beginning for a gourmet meal or great by itself with a loaf of bread. The simmered lobster shells give the trademark flavors of a spectacular bisque.

2 (1½-pound) fresh lobsters, split and cleaned
1½ sticks unsalted butter, divided
1 cup carrots, diced
1 cup onions, chopped
¼ cup shallots, chopped
2 tablespoons fresh Italian (flat leaf) parsley
4 tablespoons brandy
1 cup chicken broth
⅔ cup dry white wine
3 tablespoons Madeira wine
½ cup all-purpose flour
1 cup milk
3 cups half & half
2 plum tomatoes, diced
1 pinch cayenne pepper
1½ cups chicken broth
Salt, to taste
2 tablespoons brandy
1 teaspoon dried tarragon (or 2 tablespoons fresh)

Cut lobster halves into four pieces; crack claws. Melt 6 tablespoons butter in large saucepan over medium-low heat. Add carrots, onions, and shallots and cook 5 to 7 minutes, until onions are translucent, not brown.

Add lobster and parsley to saucepan and toss. Cook over medium-low heat until lobster shells turn red, 5 to 7 minutes. Pour 4 tablespoons brandy over lobsters and carefully ignite. When flames diminish, add 1 cup broth and white wine. Simmer 15 minutes partially covered over low heat. Remove from heat.

Remove lobster from pan and allow to cool; reserve broth in saucepan. Remove meat from shells and coarsely chop. Place diced lobster in a small bowl and toss with Madeira wine; cover and reserve. Coarsely crush lobster tail shells and reserve.

In a separate saucepan, melt remaining 6 tablespoons butter. Add flour and blend with a wire whisk over low heat for 1 minute.

Bring milk and half & half to a boil in another saucepan. Add this all at once to the flour mixture

continued

The Old Inlet

Before settlers arrived in south Florida, Lake Worth was a true lake. In 1877 settlers dug a channel through what is now the northern portion of Singer Island, connecting the lake with the ocean. This old inlet was just south of the Black Rocks, across the lake from and a little north of the hamlet of Riviera. Twelve years later heavy storms blocked up the old inlet and cut away a new inlet about a mile to the south. The settlers re-cut the inlet at Black Rocks. But after 1923, when the present inlet between Palm Beach and Palm Beach Shores was deepened, the old inlet silted up and there is no trace of it today.

Lobster Bisque continued

and whisk constantly over low heat for 1½ minutes; add to reserved broth. Stir in tomatoes, cayenne, tarragon, and crushed lobster shells. Cover, and simmer over low heat for 15 minutes. Add 1½ cups broth, cover, and simmer another 45 minutes. Season with salt.

Pour soup through a very fine strainer, pressing down on the shells and vegetables with the back of a spoon. Return soup to saucepan and heat through. Stir in 2 tablespoons brandy and reserved lobster meat. Serve immediately.

Yield: 8 servings

Eat!

Have a banana, Hannah,

Try the salami, Tommy,

Give with the gravy, Davy,

Everybody eats when they come to my house!

~Cab Calloway

She-Crab Soup

An elegant soup from Chef Mark Ramsay.

1 medium onion, chopped	1 dash Worcestershire sauce
4 tablespoons butter	Salt, to taste
1 pound white crabmeat	1 teaspoon cornstarch
2 quarts milk	½ cup milk
8 tablespoons butter	½ cup sherry wine

Sauté onions over low heat in 4 tablespoons butter until soft; add crabmeat and heat through. Add 2 quarts milk and additional 4 tablespoons butter and bring to a simmer – don't boil. Season with Worcestershire sauce and salt to taste.

Stir cornstarch into ½ cup cold milk. Pour into soup to thicken. Add sherry and stir well; serve.

Yield: 8 servings

Spicy Salmon Chowder

Salmon's nutrition makes it one of the most valuable foods you can store in your pantry. It is rich in Omega 3 fatty acids and high in protein, vitamin A, and the complex of B vitamins. This creamy, chunky chowder is an incredibly easy, tasty, and inexpensive way to get more salmon into your diet.

Omega-3s

The American Heart Association's dietary guidelines recommends that healthy adults eat at least two servings of fish per week, particularly fish such as mackerel, lake trout, herring, sardines, albacore tuna and salmon. These fish contain two omega-3 fatty acids. A third kind, alpha-linolenic acid, is less potent. It comes from soybeans, canola, walnut and flaxseed and oils made from those beans, nuts and seeds.

4 medium-to-large turnips, peeled and cut into small cubes
2 medium onions, chopped
3 ribs celery, chopped
2 teaspoons dill seed
2 bay leaves
4 cups vegetable broth or water

2 (12-ounce) cans wild salmon
2 cups lowfat buttermilk
2 cups fat-free plain yogurt
2 tablespoons butter
3-4 teaspoons Tabasco sauce
½ teaspoon salt
1 teaspoon ground pepper
½ teaspoon dried tarragon
Fresh dill, to garnish

In a large saucepan, combine turnips, onions, celery, dill seed, bay leaves, and broth or water. Bring to a boil over high heat. Reduce heat to medium and simmer 12 minutes or until vegetables are tender.

Reduce heat to low. Stir in salmon, buttermilk, yogurt, butter, Tabasco sauce, salt, pepper, and tarragon. Cook 5 minutes or until just heated through. Remove and discard bay leaves before serving. Garnish each bowl with fresh dill.

Yield: 8 servings

Shrimp Chowder

¼ cup butter
4 large onion, peeled and
    sliced
1 cup hot water
6 medium potatoes, peeled
    and cubed
1 teaspoon salt
½ teaspoon pepper

6 cups whole milk
2 cups (8 ounces) shredded
    pasteurized process cheese
2 pounds shrimp, shelled and
    deveined
3 tablespoons minced fresh
    parsley

In a 5-quart Dutch oven over moderate heat, melt butter and cook onions until tender. Add water, potatoes, salt, and pepper. Reduce heat to low; cover and cook 15 minutes or until potatoes are tender. Do not drain.

In a 3-quart saucepan over low heat, cook milk and cheese until cheese has melted. Do not let mixture boil; stir often. Add shrimp to potato mixture and cook 2 to 3 minutes or until shrimp are pink and tender. Add hot cheese mixture to potato mixture; heat but do not boil. Place in tureen, garnish with parsley, and serve.

Yield: 8 servings

The Kravis Center

The highest point in Palm Beach County, the downtown site of the Raymond F. Kravis Center for the Performing Arts, has long been a spot where people have gathered for entertainment. For more than 60 years, the property was home to Connie Mack Field (formerly Wright Field), a baseball facility named after Mack, a Hall of Famer and baseball manager for over 50 years. As a spring training camp Connie Mack Field saw action from some of the greatest names in baseball: Babe Ruth, Lou Gehrig, Jackie Robinson, Joe DiMaggio, and Mickey Mantle among them. Today, a commemorative plaque on the grounds of the Kravis Center marks the spot of home plate.

Seafood Bar Gazpacho from The Breakers

From The Seafood Bar *restaurant, overlooking the Atlantic Ocean.*

The Breakers in the 1920's

The Breakers was an unrivaled masterpiece for the times whose guest register read like a "who's who," with many guests staying for the winter season. Featuring outdoor recreation, a Mediterranean-style beach casino, a saltwater swimming pool, dining in the Florentine Dining Room, and a selection of fine shops, The Breakers established itself as a destination resort early on while still upholding the somewhat formal nature of the times.

1 (20-ounce) can Roma tomatoes
1 cup cucumber, small dice
½ cup sweet red pepper, small dice
½ cup yellow pepper, small dice
½ cup onion, small dice
1 teaspoon minced garlic
¼ cup watermelon juice
¼ cup Pomace olive oil
½ cup vegetable broth

3 ounces white balsamic vinegar
1 lemon, juiced
1 lime, juiced
1 teaspoon Dijon mustard
1 teaspoon rice wine vinegar
1 tablespoon Italian flat leaf parsley, roughly chopped
1 teaspoon cilantro, minced
2 basil leaves, finely cut
1 dash Tabasco sauce
1 tablespoon sugar
Salt and pepper, to taste

Garnish:

Crusty French bread
Olive oil
Salt and pepper, to taste
½ seedless cucumber

12 ounces cooked lobster meat
12 ounces sour cream

To make the gazpacho, break up tomatoes into small pieces using your hands. Measure and combine all remaining ingredients (except garnish) in a mixing bowl. Remove 1 cup of mixture and purée using a hand mixer or blender; add back into the gazpacho mixture. Season with salt and pepper.

continued

Seafood Bar Gazpacho from The Breakers continued

Preheat oven to 400 degrees. Cut French bread into six ½- to 1-inch thick slices. Brush bread with oil and season with salt and pepper. Bake bread slices until they are crispy. Cut cucumber lengthwise in half and then cut each half lengthwise into three long pieces.

To serve, ladle gazpacho into a bowl or martini glass. Spoon sour cream on top in center of gazpacho. Place 2 ounces cooked lobster on top of the sour cream. Slide French bread and cucumber spear in the soup, resting on the side.

Yield: 6 8-ounce servings

Schinkengipfeli
(Croissants Filled with Ham)

½ pound ham
Thyme, to taste
2 bunches fresh green
    onions, chopped
2 teaspoons mustard

2 tablespoons white wine
4 tablespoons whipped
    cream
Puff pastry sheets
1 egg yolk, beaten

Preheat oven to 350 degrees. Cut ham very fine or chop; add thyme and green onions. Mix mustard with wine and combine with ham. Add as much cream as necessary to bind mixture.

Cut pastry into desired size triangles and put rounded tablespoon of mixture on each triangle. Brush water all around ends and roll from larger end up, pressing down edges to keep filling in. Beat egg yolk and brush over pastry. Bake approximately 15 minutes.

Yield: About 30 pieces, depending on size

Grilled Turkey Burger from The Breakers, Palm Beach

This is served in The Beach Club *at* The Breakers.

Turkey Patties:

2 pounds ground turkey breast, skinless
1 large Spanish onion, chopped
2 tablespoons chopped garlic
⅛ bunch parsley, chopped
¾ cup grated Parmesan cheese
½ cup Apple Chutney
2 tablespoons olive oil
Salt and pepper, to taste

Apple Chutney:

2 shallots, diced
1½ tablespoons minced ginger
1½ tablespoons butter
¼ cup sugar
¼ cup white wine
3 ounces apple juice
4 Granny Smith apples, peeled and wedged
3 star anise
1 tablespoon lemon juice
1 bunch green onions, thinly sliced

To Assemble:

6 turkey patties
6 Brioche buns, toasted
1½ cups apple chutney
12 leaves red oak lettuce

continued

The Breakers Fire of 1925

Shortly after a fire on March 18, 1925 destroyed the hotel, the Florida East Coast Hotel Company announced that it would not only build the world's finest resort on the site of The Breakers but also that it would do so in time for the opening of the 1926-27 winter season, little more than a year away. More than 1,200 construction workers labored around-the-clock along with 75 artisans from Italy to complete the magnificent paintings on the ceilings of the lobby and first-floor public rooms. The immense structure was completed in a scant 11½ months and opened on December 29, 1926.

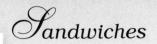

Grilled Turkery Burger from The Breakers continued

Combine turkey with onions, garlic, and parsley. Add Parmesan cheese, oil, and apple chutney. Season with salt and pepper. Mix well and form into 8-ounce patties.

To make the Apple Chutney, sauté shallots and ginger in butter until translucent in a non-reactive saucepan. Add sugar and stir until completely dissolved. Deglaze with white wine and apple juice; reduce by ⅓. Add apple wedges and star anise (in a cheesecloth) and simmer on low heat approximately 20 minutes. Add lemon juice. Stir and remove from heat; cool. Remove cheesecloth with star anise and fold in green onions.

Grill patties until golden-brown. Finish in a hot oven until cooked all the way through (165 degrees). Place a patty on each toasted brioche bun. Serve each sandwich with 2 ounces Apple Chutney on top of red oak leaves.

Yield: 6 servings

Grilling Tips

Oiling the grill rack is a vital step in preparing to barbecue meat unless there is oil in the marinade or the food you are cooking has built-in lubricants such as sausages or chicken with the skin on. Either spray the rack before it is put on the grill with a cooking spray or dip several folded paper towels in vegetable or olive oil and rub it over the grill rack.

Lobster Roll

New Englanders have loaned us this great recipe.

4 cups cooked lobster
    meat, cut into bite-sized
    pieces
½ cup mayonnaise
¼ cup chopped green
    onions
1 tablespoon chopped
    celery

1 tablespoon lemon juice
½ teaspoon salt
1 dash hot sauce
4 hot dog buns
Butter
Chopped lettuce and tomatoes

Combine lobster meat, mayonnaise, green onions, celery, lemon juice, salt, and hot sauce. Split, lightly butter, and toast buns. Spoon ¼ of the mixture into each bun. Garnish with lettuce and tomatoes as desired.

Yield: 4 servings

Ham, Brie, and Mango Chutney "Sidillas"

Serve this with a fresh baby green salad - delicious! Homemade mango chutney has the best flavor and will keep for 1 week, but store-bought is also good and saves time. The chutney is also good with cheeses (e.g., Brie), sandwiches, or fish.

Mango Chutney:

1 ripe mango, cut into small cubes

2 tablespoons white vinegar

2 tablespoons chopped green pepper or 1 tablespoon jalapeño pepper

½ cup sugar

½ teaspoon ginger powder

¼ cup onion, chopped

Ham and Brie "Sidillas":

1 flour tortilla

¼ tablespoon butter

2 or 3 thin ham slices

2 tablespoons mango chutney

3 or 4 slices Brie cheese

Combine all chutney ingredients in a saucepan. Bring mixture to a boil, stirring frequently. Reduce heat and simmer until mixture begins to thicken. Cover and refrigerate.

Melt butter over medium-high heat, being careful not to let it burn. Place a flour tortilla in bottom of pan and add ham slices on one-half of tortilla. Spread mango chutney over ham evenly and arrange Brie slices over chutney. Using a spatula, carefully fold over tortilla in half. When browned, flip tortilla and brown other side. Remove, place on plate, and slice into wedges.

Yield: 1 serving

Hot and Creamy Turkey Sandwiches

A wonderful recipe for Thanksgiving turkey leftovers, or you can make these sandwiches with deli turkey slices.

¼ pound white mushrooms, thinly sliced
4 tablespoons butter
3 tablespoons all-purpose flour
1 cup whole milk, heated
1 cup chicken broth, heated
¼ cup grated sharp Cheddar cheese
¼ cup grated Parmesan cheese
1 teaspoon minced fresh sage
1 teaspoon minced fresh thyme
Salt and pepper, to taste
8 slices country bread, toasted
8 ounces thinly sliced turkey
6 slices bacon, cooked and crumbled
Fresh green onions, chopped, for garnish

Cook mushrooms in butter in a large skillet over moderately low heat, stirring until most of the liquid given off by the mushrooms is evaporated. Add flour and cook, stirring, 3 minutes. Add milk and chicken broth in a stream while whisking; bring mixture to a boil. Simmer 3 minutes and stir in cheeses, sage, thyme, salt, and pepper.

Preheat broiler. Arrange bread slices in a single layer on a sheet pan. Divide turkey slices evenly on top of bread and spoon some of the sauce over each toast. Broil slices 2 to 3 minutes or until golden and top each toast with bacon and green onions.

Yield: 8 servings

Monstera deliciosa

Also known as windowpane philodendron and Swiss cheese plant, the monstera's big, tropical leaf is represented in the Mounts Botanical Garden logo. It is one of our most delicious and interesting edible treats. The fruit, which tastes like a cross between mango, banana, and papaya, must be absolutely ripe before it is eaten because of a high level of oxalic acid in unripe fruit. You might want to place nearly-ripe fruits in a paper bag and check daily for kernels that have ripened and fallen off-a process that can take place over a few days, since the fruit ripens unevenly.

Sazio Skirt Steak Sandwich

Chef Dave DeLisa of Sazio restaurant in Delray Beach contributed this fabulous recipe.

Marinade:
8 ounces soy sauce

1 teaspoon freshly chopped garlic

1 pinch parsley

1 pinch rosemary

Steak Sandwich:
2 ounces butter

8 ounces marinated skirt steak

2 ounces sliced white onions

1 (10-inch) baguette, split

3 ounces sliced Brie cheese

Pour soy sauce into a bowl. Add garlic, parsley, and rosemary. Place skirt steak into bowl, cover, and refrigerate overnight.

Preheat oven to 350 degrees. Melt butter in pan. Add steak and onions and sauté until steak is cooked. Place steak and onions in baguette and top with Brie. Place sandwich in oven until cheese is melted; serve.

The Everglades Club

Paris Singer had a love of architecture and invited his friend, Addison Mizner, to Palm Beach to recuperate from a leg injury. Together, they built a convalescent club for soldiers returning from World War I. This structure, known today as the Everglades Club on Worth Avenue on Palm Beach, was the trendsetting basis for our still popular Mediterranean style of architecture. Mizner went on to establish a wildly successful career building winter homes for Palm Beach society.

Vegetables

Vegetables

Sunset Asparagus
Green Beans &
  Mushrooms in
  Garlic Sauce
Jamaican Golden
  Bammy Slices
Mustard Greens
Bacon Braised Greens
Black-eyed Peas
  with Ham
Praline Sweet Potatoes
Palm Beach Coconut Yams
Apricot Sweet Potatoes
Creamy Parmesan
  Cauliflower
Carrot and Sweet
  Potato Puree
Spinach and Artichoke
  Casserole
Cauliflower and Potato Fry
Seasoned Cauliflower
Glazed Carrots
Cumin Roasted Potatoes
Broiled Tomatoes
Saffron Carrots & Turnips

Sunset Asparagus

Orange pieces give this dish a different slant.

3 tablespoons butter, melted
3 tablespoons all-purpose
  flour
2 cups milk
¾ teaspoon salt
¼ teaspoon ground white
  pepper

2 medium oranges, peeled
  and sectioned
2½ pounds fresh asparagus,
  steamed
Salt, to taste
½ cup cashews, roasted and
  chopped

Melt butter in a small saucepan. Stir in flour. When
bubbles form, slowly add milk, stirring constantly.
Cook over low heat until mixture thickens. Add salt
and pepper. Strain sauce through sieve. Cut orange
sections into medium pieces and gently add to sauce.

Arrange steamed asparagus on serving dish and
sprinkle with salt. Pour sauce over asparagus and
sprinkle with cashews.

Yield: 8 servings

The Florida State 'Tree'?

Also known as the Sabal palmetto, the native cabbage palm is Florida's official state tree. The palm, however, is not a tree; it is a relative of grasses. The "cabbage" is the edible, succulent base of the central leaf bundle. It was a staple food of Indians and pioneers and is still served as "swamp cabbage" in restaurants around Lake Okeechobee. It is more popularly know as 'hearts of palm'.

Green Beans and Mushrooms in Garlic Sauce

Vegetables with an Asian flair and flavor.

¼ cup soy sauce
1 tablespoon minced garlic
1 tablespoon honey
2 teaspoons minced fresh
  ginger

1 pound fresh green beans,
  trimmed
6 ounces mushrooms, sliced
2 tablespoons olive oil

Combine soy sauce, garlic, honey, and ginger. Sauté
green beans and mushrooms in oil about 3 minutes
or until beans are crisp and tender. Add sauce and
boil until sauce thickens, about 4 minutes.

Yield: 4 to 6 servings

Jamaican Golden Bammy Slices

Bammies are a flat cake made from yucca, a starchy root vegetable from South America. Serve instead of rice or potatoes, with any meat stew or curry. They can be purchased at Caribbean grocery stores or your local grocery.

2 (6-inch) bammies	½ teaspoon salt
3 cups cold water or milk	4 tablespoons butter

Preheat oven to 350 degrees. Slice each bammy into four pieces and soak in milk for 5 minutes (slices should be completely covered). Check bammies; they should not be too soft, as some bammies have very little starch to hold them together. If bammies are still hard, soak a bit longer. Pour off milk.

Melt butter in a skillet; place bammies in skillet and cover. Fry until sides are brown. Remove bammies from skillet and place on a cookie sheet. Bake for about 10 minutes. Bammies are done when crispy brown.

Yield: 8 slices

Mustard Greens

Mustard greens are an excellent source of vitamins A and C, thiamine, and riboflavin

2 pounds mustard greens	2 garlic cloves, minced
2 tablespoons olive oil	2 tablespoons chicken broth
1 medium onion, coarsely chopped	2 teaspoons lime juice
2 small shallots, minced	½ teaspoon salt
	¼ teaspoon pepper

Wash greens thoroughly to remove all sand. Strip stems out of leaves. In a large pot, heat oil over moderate heat. Sauté onion, shallots, and garlic until golden, about 8 minutes. Add broth. Place greens, torn into pieces, on top. Cover and cook until tender, turning greens after about 20 minutes. Toss in lime juice, salt, and pepper.

Yield: 6 servings

Bahamian Immigration

During the first two decades of the 20th century, close to 12,000 residents of the Bahamas made their way to Miami to take advantage of work opportunities made available by the development of South Florida. Boats making repeated trips from Nassau to Miami were reportedly crowded to the point of standing room only. Many of the men found construction work, while women and children collected wages by working in orange groves and truck farms.

Bacon Braised Greens

These greens will add a Southern touch to your Thanksgiving dinner.

3-4 pounds greens (mustard, turnip, collard, kale, etc.)	1 garlic clove, crushed
	1 teaspoon chili pepper flakes or powder
6 slices thick cut bacon, julienned	1 teaspoon salt
	1 teaspoon sugar
1 onion, sliced thin	Freshly ground pepper, to taste

Wash greens thoroughly to remove grit and sand; do not dry - leave wet. Trim and cut greens into wide ribbons. Set aside.

In a large pot over medium heat, cook bacon until just barely crisp. Remove and drain on paper towels. Set aside.

In remaining bacon grease in pot, add onion, garlic, and chili pepper flakes. Sauté until onion is translucent. Add wet greens. Cover pot and cook until greens have just withered down. Uncover and add salt, sugar, and pepper. Increase heat to medium-high and partially cover. Cook until greens are just tender, about 15 minutes.

Yield: 8 servings

Black-Eyed Peas with Ham

In the South, black-eyed peas are eaten traditionally on New Year's Eve for good luck and prosperity in the new year.

3 cups presoaked black-eyed peas	2 tablespoons red wine vinegar
3 cups chicken broth	1 tablespoon minced garlic
½ cup chopped ham	1 bay leaf
¼ cup chopped onion	½ teaspoon dried thyme
	¼ teaspoon cayenne pepper
	Salt and pepper, to taste

Bring all ingredients to a boil in a large saucepot. Reduce heat and simmer approximately 45 minutes, until peas are tender. Season with salt and pepper.

Yield: 6 servings

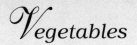

Praline Sweet Potatoes

Sweet and scrumptious. Don't wait for Thanksgiving to try these.

3 cups cooked mashed sweet potatoes	1 cup firmly packed brown sugar
½ cup sugar	1 cup chopped pecans or walnuts
2 large eggs, beaten	½ cup all-purpose flour
¼ cup milk	4 tablespoons butter
½ teaspoon salt	
¼ teaspoon vanilla extract	

Preheat oven to 350 degrees. Combine sweet potatoes, sugar, eggs, milk, salt, and vanilla in a blender or food processor. Cover and process until smooth. Spoon mixture into a greased, shallow 2-quart baking dish.

Combine brown sugar, nuts, flour, and butter; sprinkle over sweet potato mixture. Bake 25 to 30 minutes or until thoroughly heated.

Yield: 8 to 10 servings

Palm Beach Coconut Yams

1 tablespoon butter, melted	1 teaspoon salt
6-10 medium yams, half-cooked and peeled	2 cups firmly packed brown sugar
3 tablespoons butter	1 cup shredded coconut

Preheat oven to 350 degrees. Brush bottom of a shallow 2½-quart casserole with 1 tablespoon melted butter. Arrange peeled yams in casserole and dot with 3 tablespoons butter. Sprinkle salt and brown sugar evenly over top of yams. Bake 35 minutes.

Remove from oven and sprinkle top with shredded coconut. Continue to bake until yams are tender and coconut is lightly browned.

Yield: 12 servings

To half-cook yams, place peeled yams, arranged in a circle (like petals on a flower) on a paper towel. Microwave for 5 to 8 minutes.

How to Julienne

Also known as a matchstick, the ideal julienne is a long thin strip about two inches long. When done properly, a julienne enhances the presentation of many vegetables. First, peel the skin from the vegetable if necessary. Then trim away any root or stem parts. If the vegetable is round, cut it in half and lay it cut side down on the cutting board to keep it from rolling. Cut the edible part of the vegetable into slices about ¼-inch thick, cutting around the seeds if necessary. Cut these slices into even strips ¼-inch thick.

Apricot Sweet Potatoes

Almost a dessert, this recipe has helped a generation of children overcome their aversion to vegetables. This has been a family favorite for over 40 years.

1 (40-ounce) can sweet potatoes
1 (15.25-ounce) can apricot halves, cut into small pieces
¾ cup sugar
¾ teaspoon cinnamon
2 tablespoons cornstarch mixed in ½ cup water
¼ teaspoon salt
½ cup pecan halves

Preheat oven to 375 degrees. Drain and reserve juices from sweet potatoes and apricots. Heat juices in a saucepan. Gradually add sugar, salt, cinnamon, and water/cornstarch mixture. Boil down sauce until thickened.

Place potatoes in a greased casserole. Add apricot pieces to casserole and stir to mix. Pour thickened sauce over potato and apricot mixture. Bake 45 minutes. Sprinkle top with pecan halves and serve.

Yield: 6 servings

Creamy Parmesan Cauliflower

This makes for an impressive mashed potato rival.

1 head cauliflower, florets only
2 tablespoons butter
½ cup half & half
½ cup freshly grated Parmesan cheese
Salt and freshly ground pepper, to taste

Microwave cauliflower 10 minutes or until soft. Position knife blade in a food processor and add cauliflower, butter, half & half, Parmesan cheese, salt, and pepper; process until smooth. Add additional half & half if needed.

Yield: 4 servings

For a healthier version, use a butter substitute and fat-free half & half – still very tasty.

Soak 4 threads of saffron in 2 tablespoons of hot water and add to ingredients when processing.

Coontie

Coontie is a native, ancient plant dating back to the age of dinosaurs. It is salt tolerant and will thrive in any well drained soil. Indians and early settlers obtained edible starch from coontie's poisonous underground stems after a thorough and lengthy detoxification process.

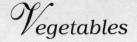
Carrot and Sweet Potato Purée

Great for Thanksgiving, this may be prepared in advance.

6 large sweet potatoes
   (about 5½ pounds)
1 ½ pounds carrots, peeled
   and cut into 1-inch
   pieces
1 tablespoon butter
1½ cups water
2 tablespoons sugar

½ teaspoon salt
½ teaspoon freshly ground
   black pepper
7 tablespoons butter
½ cup lemon lowfat yogurt
½ teaspoon ground nutmeg
¼ teaspoon cayenne pepper

Preheat oven to 350 degrees. Wash sweet potatoes and pat dry. Prick several times with a fork. Arrange potatoes in a circle on paper towels in microwave oven, spaced 1 inch apart. Microwave on high for 35 to 40 minutes or until tender, rotating sweet potatoes at 10-minutes intervals. Cool to touch, peel, and cut into chunks.

Position knife blade in a food processor. Add half the sweet potatoes. Process until smooth. Transfer to a large bowl. Repeat procedure. Set aside.

Combine carrots, 1 tablespoon butter, water, sugar, salt, and pepper in a medium saucepan. Bring to a boil and cook 10 to 15 minutes or until tender and liquid is evaporated. Position knife blade in food processor and add carrot mixture, 7 tablespoons butter, yogurt, nutmeg, and cayenne. Process until smooth. Stir into sweet potatoes. Bake uncovered for 30 to 45 minutes or until thoroughly heated.

Yield: 8 to 10 servings

After combining sweet potatoes and carrots, you can cover and refrigerate overnight, if desired. Remove and let stand at room temperature for 30 minutes before baking. Also may be frozen; thaw in refrigerator.

Marjorie Merriweather Post

Mar-a-Lago was the Palm Beach estate of Marjorie Merriweather Post, daughter of CW Post. (Think Grape Nuts.) Her love of the arts and fine craftsmanship inspired this opulently decorated home. The ballroom was a frequent venue for her favorite party – the square dance. Over the course of her life she developed a strong sense of charity in response to the Depression of the 1930's. She is reputed to have held Palm Beach's first charitable event, setting the stage for the busy social whirlwind which happens during the high season every year.

Spinach and Artichoke Casserole

This is an old Louisiana recipe that found its way to Florida. The water chestnuts give it a delicious crunch.

3 (10-ounce) packages frozen chopped spinach

1 (8-ounce) package cream cheese

1 stick butter

½ teaspoon salt

¼ teaspoon pepper

1 teaspoon Worcestershire sauce

1 can sliced water chestnuts, finely chopped

2 (8½-ounce) cans quartered artichoke hearts

Topping:

6 tablespoons butter

½ cup breadcrumbs

Preheat oven to 350 degrees. Prepare chopped spinach according to package directions; drain very well. While still hot, mix right away with softened cream cheese and 1 stick butter. Add salt, pepper, Worcestershire sauce, and water chestnuts. Place half the spinach mixture in a 2-quart casserole, cover evenly with artichokes, and layer rest of spinach mixture on top.

Melt 6 tablespoons butter on stovetop and add enough breadcrumbs to make a crumbly mixture. Top casserole with buttered breadcrumbs and bake 30 to 35 minutes.

Yield: 6 to 8 servings

This recipe can be made a day ahead and refrigerated or frozen; if frozen, thaw in refrigerator before heating.

Henry Morrison Flagler (1830-1913)

Henry Morrison Flagler was one of the leading figures of America's Gilded Age. Flagler was a founding partner of Standard Oil, the most profitable corporation in American history, and the earliest and most important developer of Florida. In fact, it would not be an exaggeration to say that Henry Flagler literally invented modern Florida. Flagler's Florida East Coast Railway linked the entire east coast of Florida from Jacksonville to Key West.

Cauliflower and Potato Fry

This is an Indian recipe. Garam masala powder is a prepared blend of spices including coriander, pepper, cumin, cardamom, and cinnamon. It is available at most large supermarkets.

3 tablespoons oil
2 onions, cut lengthwise
1 small piece fresh ginger,
    minced
4 garlic cloves, minced
1 teaspoon chili powder
1 teaspoon coriander powder
½ teaspoon turmeric powder

½ teaspoon pepper
½ teaspoon garam masala
    powder
1 head cauliflower, cut into
    florets
3 potatoes, cut into 1-inch
    cubes
Salt, to taste

Heat oil in a frying pan and sauté onions, ginger, and garlic until onions are transparent. Add chili powder, coriander powder, turmeric powder, pepper, and garam masala powder. Mix well and sauté for 1 minute.

Add cauliflower, potatoes, and salt. Sprinkle with a little water and cover. Cook on low heat until vegetables are done. Open lid, stir, and sauté until mixture turns light golden brown.

Yield: 6 to 8 servings

Henry Morrison Flagler continued

The series of luxury hotels Flagler built along Florida's east coast and the two million acres of land he developed established agriculture and tourism as the foundation of Florida's economy during the last 100 years. Flagler's completion of the Over-Sea Railroad was the most ambitious engineering project ever undertaken by an individual and was considered by some to be the "eighth wonder of the world".

Seasoned Cauliflower

Easy to make. Fresh herbs can be used if you grow your own.

1 head cauliflower, cut into
   florets
1 tablespoon olive oil
4 garlic cloves, minced
Breadcrumbs from 1 slice
   of bread

½ teaspoon thyme
1 teaspoon basil
½ teaspoon marjoram
½ teaspoon salt
¼ teaspoon pepper

Steam cauliflower until tender, about 15 to 20 minutes.

Meanwhile, heat oil and sauté garlic. Stir in breadcrumbs. Add spices and toss all ingredients into cauliflower.

Yield: 4 servings

Jewel Cut

Try this technique for cutting carrots; it makes interesting shapes when you don't want 'coins'. Lay the carrot on its side. Make a diagonal cut. Turn it ¼ turn and make another diagonal cut in the same direction. Keep turning and cutting just like that.

Glazed Carrots

Carrots have been renowned for over 2,000 years for their health-giving properties and high vitamin A content.

1 stick butter
3½ pounds peeled baby
   carrots
6 tablespoons sugar

½ cup balsamic vinegar
Salt and pepper, to taste
¼ cup chopped fresh chives

Melt butter in a pan over medium heat. Add carrots and sauté 5 minutes. Cover and cook until carrots are crisp-tender, stirring occasionally, about 7 minutes. Stir in sugar and vinegar.

Cook uncovered until carrots are tender and glazed, stirring frequently, about 12 minutes longer. Season with salt and pepper. Add chopped chives and toss to blend. Transfer to a bowl and serve.

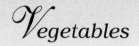

Cumin Roasted Potatoes

Roasting the cumin seeds releases a fragrant aroma and flavor.

1½ teaspoons whole cumin seeds	1¼ teaspoons salt
3 tablespoons olive oil	2 pounds russet potatoes (3 potatoes), peeled and cut into 1-inch pieces
¾ teaspoon paprika	

Preheat oven to 450 degrees. Heat cumin seeds in small pan over medium heat until just fragrant (45 seconds). Transfer seeds to a 13x 9-inch baking pan. Add olive oil, paprika, and salt and whisk together. Add potatoes; stir to thoroughly coat. Spread in single layer and bake 35 minutes, stirring every 12 minutes.

Yield: 4 servings

The Tomato

Botanically a fruit, specifically a berry, the tomato was officially proclaimed a vegetable in 1893 by the U.S. Supreme Court, a result of a tariff dispute. The tomato was brought to Europe by Spanish explorers in the sixteenth century. Europeans believed that the plant was poisonous and used it only as an ornamental houseplant. Not until the nineteenth century was the tomato widely accepted as a food. Now, tomatoes are the second most popular vegetable eaten by Americans (the potato is first). Florida produces about 45 percent of the total U.S. tomato supply.

Broiled Tomatoes

Like the potato and eggplant, the tomato is a member of the nightshade family. It's the fruit of a vine native to South America.

3 medium tomatoes	1 garlic clove, crushed
3 tablespoons mayonnaise	Salt and freshly ground pepper, to taste
1 teaspoon Dijon mustard	
1 tablespoon chives, finely chopped	1 tablespoon grated Parmesan cheese
2 tablespoons grated Parmesan cheese	

Preheat oven to 400 degrees. Cut tomatoes in half crosswise or into 1½-inch-thick slices. Place cut side up in a single layer in an ovenproof baking dish.

Mix together mayonnaise, mustard, chives, 2 tablespoons Parmesan cheese, garlic, salt, and pepper. Spoon and spread mayonnaise mixture on top of each tomato slice. Sprinkle with remaining Parmesan cheese. Bake until hot, 10 to 12 minutes. Turn oven to broil and broil tomatoes until glazed brown and bubbling. Serve hot.

Yield: 6 servings

Saffron Carrots and Turnips

Enticing color and flavors – beautiful presentation with little effort. Try pairing this with turkey or roast chicken.

½ pound carrots, peeled and cut into ¼-inch julienne strips

2 tablespoons unsalted butter

¼ teaspoon crushed saffron threads or ¹⁄₁₆ teaspoon powdered saffron

1 cup chicken broth

Salt and freshly ground pepper, to taste

¾ pound turnips, peeled and cut into ¼-inch julienne strips

In a large saucepan, combine carrots, butter, saffron, broth, salt, and pepper. Heat to boiling. Reduce heat, cover, and simmer 5 minutes. Add turnips and continue to simmer uncovered until vegetables are tender and liquid is reduced.

Yield: 6 servings

Burt Reynolds and Friends Museum

The Burt Reynolds and Friends Museum, one of the largest celebrity museums in the country, is filled with memorabilia from some of Hollywood's greatest actors. The collection also includes a large sports and western area, two of Mr. Reynolds favorite areas of interest. Glistening trophies, radiant chandeliers, and prestigious awards are displayed in mirrored cases in an atmosphere of varnished mahogany columns, granite and coquina counters, creating a beautiful tribute to Hollywood.

Entrées
Poultry, Meat & Seafood

Entrées

Poultry, Meat & Seafood

Sesame Chicken
Lemon-Honey Chicken
Chicken with Wine Sauce
Key Lime Broiled Chicken
Chicken Marbella
Indian Chicken Cutlets
Chicken Kurma
Morikami Chicken Curry
Chicken a la Vineyard
Chicken with Sun-Dried
  Tomatoes
Easy Paella
Chicken with Cold
  Sesame Noodles
Moo Goo Gai Pan
Yakitori Chicken
Tia Mirta's Arroz con Pollo
Peruvian Chicken Stew
Pan Roasted Duck Breast
  with Mission Figs,
  Café Chardonnay
Veal Oscar,
  The Breakers, Palm Beach
Ropa Vieja
Filet of Beef "Chateaubriand"
Grilled Steaks with Martini Twist
Beef in Spicy Tomato Sauce
  with Black Beans
Stuffed Leg of Lamb
Lamb Curry
Leila's Classic Lamb Kebab,
  Leila Restaurant
Pan Roasted Pork Chop,
  The Ritz Carlton, Palm Beach
Macadamia Crusted
  Rack of Lamb,
  PGA National Resort and Spa

Grilled Mongolian Pork Chops
Easy Grilled Fish with
  Fresh Dill Sauce
Spice Rubbed Atlantic Salmon,
  City Cellar
Baked Pompano
Fish Pepper Delight
Fish Picatta Shack Style,
  The Food Shack
Gingered Chilean Sea Bass,
  Nirvana Restaurant
Pecan Encrusted Sea Bass with
  Red Pepper Sauce
Grilled Dolphin with
  Mango Corn Salsa
Mango Nut Grouper, Tabica Grill
Pan Seared Mahi Mahi with
  Shrimp Creole Sauce,
  Café Chardonnay
Snapper Caprice with
  Island-Style Chutney
Almond Crusted Grouper,
  The Morikami
Macadamia-Crusted Yellowtail
Snapper with Tropical Fruit Salsa,
  Café Chardonnay
Snapper with Shrimp Sauce
John's Trinidad Yellowtail
  Snapper, Palm Beach Yacht Club
Island-Style Baked Snapper,
  The River House Restaurant
Seafood Casserole Supreme
Swordfish with Tomato Vinaigrette
Cornmeal Crusted Soft Shell
  Crabs, Café Chardonnay
Conch Salad
New Orleans Shrimp Remoulade
Barbecued Garlic Shrimp
Shrimp Dijonaise,
  Café Chardonnay
Polynesian Prawns with
  Tropical Fruit Sauce
Scalloped Florida Lobster
Spoto's Bouillabaisse
Zuppa de Pesce,
  Café Chardonnay

Sesame Chicken

This dish goes well with Cold Sesame Noodles (see Index for recipe).

¾ cup all-purpose flour
3 tablespoons sesame seeds
1 teaspoon spicy Montreal
   steak seasoning

4 chicken breasts, boneless
   and skinless
3 tablespoons soy sauce
⅓ cup butter, melted

Preheat oven to 400 degrees. Combine flour, sesame seeds, and steak seasoning. Slice chicken breasts in half horizontally so they are thin. Dip chicken pieces into soy sauce and dredge in sesame seed mixture. Place chicken in a 9x13-inch baking dish, drizzle with butter, and bake 25 to 30 minutes.

Yield: 4 servings

Lemon-Honey Chicken

A great grilled barbecue dish.

¼ cup lemon juice
2 tablespoon cooking oil
2 small garlic cloves, minced
½ teaspoon salt

½ teaspoon paprika
½ teaspoon pepper
½ teaspoon honey
2 pounds chicken pieces

In a saucepan, mix together all ingredients except chicken. Simmer, let cool, and pour over chicken. Marinate in refrigerator for several hours. Stir frequently to keep marinade evenly distributed.

Grill on high heat, bone-side down, then reduce heat to low. Grill 30 minutes, turn over, and grill 20 minutes more.

Yield: 6 servings

Chicken with Wine Sauce

1½ tablespoons flour	½ pound mushrooms, thinly
½ teaspoon salt	sliced
⅛ teaspoon pepper	¼ cup chopped onion
2 large boneless, skinless	¼ cup chopped parsley
chicken breasts, split	1 cup white wine or chicken
4 tablespoons butter	broth
	2 cups hot cooked rice pilaf

Combine flour, salt, and pepper; coat chicken with mixture. Shake off and reserve excess flour. Melt 2 tablespoons butter in a large skillet over medium heat. Brown chicken; remove from skillet. Add remaining butter and mushrooms, onion, and 2 tablespoons chopped parsley; sauté until onion is transparent. Remove from heat. Stir in reserved flour and blend in wine. Bring to a boil, stirring frequently. Add chicken. Cover, reduce heat, and simmer 25 minutes or until chicken is tender. Serve with rice and garnish with remaining parsley.

Yield: 4 servings

If desired, you can cut chicken in chunks before coating. Double the amount of flour/salt/pepper and add an extra tablespoon butter or oil for browning.

You can substitute 2 tablespoons butter and 2 tablespoons canola oil for the 4 tablespoons butter.

Lake Worth Playhouse

The Lake Worth Playhouse occupies the former Oakley Theatre, the oldest building on the Register of the Art Deco Society. It was constructed during the wave of movie mania sweeping the country in the early 1920's. Early productions were performed in the un-air-conditioned third floor auditorium of the old Lake Worth City Hall. In 1975 the Lake Worth Playhouse purchased and renovated the Oakley Theatre. Currently, the organization offers a season of traditional musicals and plays on the main stage; contemporary productions in the Stonzek Theatre; vibrant educational programs; and much more.

Key Lime Broiled Chicken

Key limes impart a unique taste to this dish – they have a stronger and more complex acidic flavor than Persian limes.

2½ pounds chicken pieces
½ teaspoon Key lime zest
¼ cup Key lime juice
1 tablespoon vegetable oil
3 garlic cloves, minced

1 tablespoon finely minced
   fresh basil
¼ teaspoon salt
1 teaspoon pepper

Rinse chicken and pat dry. Place skin-side down on a greased broiler pan. Broil 5 to 6 inches from heat for 20 minutes.

Mix remaining ingredients in a small bowl. Turn chicken over in broiler pan and brush with mixture. Return to oven. Baste with mixture every 5 minutes for an additional 5 to 10 minutes or until done.

Yield: 6 servings

Chicken Marbella

½ head garlic, peeled and
   chopped
2 tablespoons dried oregano
¼ cup olive oil
½ cup pitted prunes
¼ cup green olives, pitted
¼ cup capers with a little
   juice

3 bay leaves
¼ teaspoon salt, or to taste
¼ teaspoon pepper, or to
   taste
5 pounds chicken
½ cup brown sugar
½ cup white wine
6 sprigs fresh cilantro leaves

Combine garlic, oregano, oil, prunes, olives, capers, bay leaves, salt, and pepper. Marinate chicken in mixture overnight.

Preheat oven to 350 degrees. Arrange chicken in a baking pan in a single layer and cover with marinade. Sprinkle chicken with brown sugar and add wine. Bake 50 minutes, basting frequently. Arrange on a platter and garnish with cilantro.

Yield: 10 servings

Indian Chicken Cutlets

Try this served with fresh tomato slices, lemon rings,
or your choice of chutney.

½ pound boneless, skinless
   chicken
1 small piece ginger, sliced
   thinly with skin
3 small garlic cloves,
   minced
1 teaspoon chili powder
1 teaspoon salt
½ cup cilantro, chopped
2 medium russet potatoes,
   peeled, boiled, and
   mashed

1 cup finely chopped onions
6 green chilies, finely chopped
2 slices bread, torn into small
   pieces
1 teaspoon pepper
1 teaspoon garam masala
   powder
1 egg, beaten with a pinch of
   salt
½ cup oil

Wash chicken and boil with ginger, garlic, chili
powder, and salt. Remove from heat when tender.
Remove chicken, set aside to cool, then dry and shred.

In a mixing bowl, add remaining ingredients except egg
and oil to shredded chicken and mix well.

Divide mixture into small lemon-sized balls and flatten
between palms to make oval-shaped cutlets. Dip
cutlets into egg and fry in oil until golden brown.

Yield: 4 to 6 servings

Bird of Paradise

Its official name
is "Strelitzia reginae",
but South Floridians
know it as the Bird
of Paradise. This
beautiful tropical
plant has no trunk
and can grow as high
as five feet tall. The
flower itself is nothing
short of spectacular
and got its name
because its shape
resembles an exotic
bird's beak and head
plumage.

Chicken Kurma

This is wonderful served with rice or chapati, a flat, round Indian bread made without yeast.

1 cup fresh coconut, shredded (¼-½ of a whole coconut)
5 green chili peppers
1 teaspoon poppy seeds
6 cashew nuts
½ cup fresh cilantro leaves
¼ cup fresh mint leaves
2 cups chopped onions
¼ cup olive oil
2 additional cups chopped onions
10 garlic cloves, finely chopped
1 small piece ginger, finely chopped
5 cloves
1 cinnamon stick, broken into 3 pieces
5 whole cardamoms
2 bay leaves
1 teaspoon turmeric powder
1 cup plain yogurt
2 cups warm water
Salt, to taste
2½ pounds chicken, cut into small pieces
Juice from 1 lemon

Combine coconut, chili peppers, poppy seeds, cashew nuts, cilantro, mint, and onions in a food processor and grind into a smooth paste. Set aside.

Heat oil in a large pan. Add remaining 2 cups of onions and sauté 2 minutes. Add garlic and cook until lightly browned. Add ginger, cloves, cinnamon, cardamoms, turmeric, and bay leaves and sauté 1 minute.

Add smooth paste and mix. Reduce heat and slowly fold in yogurt. Add warm water while stirring slowly; mix completely and salt to taste. Add chicken and increase heat to medium. Cover and simmer on low 15 to 20 minutes or until done.

Mix in lemon juice before serving.

Yield: 8 servings

Cardamom

Cardamom is a member of the ginger family. If a recipe calls for ground cardamom, the seeds can be removed from the pods and ground or the entire pod may be ground. When the whole cardamom is called for, as in this recipe, lightly crush the shell of the pod and add to recipe. The shell will disintegrate while the dish cooks.

Morikami Chicken Curry

A hearty, homestyle stew that is a meal unto itself from Chef Fu Chen of the Cornell Café, *located overlooking the gardens of the Morikami Museum and Japanese Gardens in Delray Beach.*

1 pound chicken meat, cut in large chunks (dark meat, such as chicken thighs, is preferred, with or without the bone)

1 large potato, cut into medium chunks

1 large carrot, cut into medium chunks

1 small onion, cut into small chunks

2 pieces curry paste (this is sold in packages of small concentrated blocks like bouillon cubes, e.g., S & B Golden Curry Sauce Mix, Medium Hot)

2 cups steamed white rice

Place meat in a large pot and add enough water to just cover the meat. Bring to a boil. Change the water. Add potatoes and carrots and continue cooking with enough water to just cover the ingredients. Add onion and bring to a second boil. Add curry paste cubes and mix thoroughly until cubes are completely dissolved. Continue cooking on low heat until mixture reaches a third boil. Stew sauce should be thick and creamy, chicken cooked through, and vegetables tender. Serve hot over steamed white rice.

Yield: 4 servings

Other vegetables such as green pepper or celery can be included for variety.

Morikami Gardens

Hidden in the natural recesses of southern Florida is a destination of eastern elegance, natural serenity, and cultural beauty. For more than 25 years, The Morikami Museum and Japanese Gardens has served as a gateway to the world of Japan. Roji-en, also known as the George D. and Harriet W. Cornell Japanese Gardens, features six Japanese garden styles. Situated on 16 acres, the gardens surround Morikami Pond, and lead walkers approximately a mile through meandering greenery, past towering bamboo and rushing waterfalls and beside beds of carefully raked pebbles.

137

Chicken à la Vineyard

Red Chilean grapes are a different twist on chicken for dinner.

2 tablespoons all-purpose
   flour
½ teaspoon salt
½ teaspoon dried basil
   leaves, crushed
¼ teaspoon dried tarragon
   leaves, crushed
¼ teaspoon paprika
⅛ teaspoon white pepper
4 skinless, boneless
   chicken breasts, halved
   lengthwise

1 tablespoon olive oil
2 garlic cloves, minced
¾ cup chicken broth
1 tablespoon white wine
   vinegar
1 teaspoon lemon juice
2 cups red Chilean grapes,
   halved and seeds
   removed
1 tablespoon fresh parsley,
   finely chopped

In a shallow bowl, combine flour, salt, basil, tarragon, paprika, and pepper. Add chicken pieces and toss to coat; reserve excess flour mixture.

Heat oil in skillet over medium-high heat until hot. Add chicken and brown on both sides.

Add garlic and sprinkle with reserved flour mixture. Add broth, vinegar, and lemon juice; cover and cook 5 minutes.

Add grapes and cook uncovered 5 minutes more or just until chicken is fork tender.

Remove chicken and grapes to heated serving platter. Boil pan liquid 1 minute and pour over chicken. Sprinkle with parsley.

Yield: 4 servings

Chicken with Sun-Dried Tomatoes

Sun-dried tomatoes give a gourmet touch and a burst of flavor to this dish.

3 tablespoons olive oil
1 onion, chopped
8 white mushrooms, sliced
1 garlic clove, minced
½ cup sun-dried tomatoes, sliced with scissors
4 boneless, skinless chicken breasts

1 cup all-purpose flour
Salt and pepper, to taste
1 cup chicken broth
½ cup black olives
½ cup milk or cream
½ cup marinara sauce
2 tablespoons chopped parsley

Heat oil in a large skillet over medium heat. Sauté onion until soft and translucent. Stir in mushrooms, garlic, and sun-dried tomatoes. Dredge chicken in flour and place in pan. Season with salt and pepper. Cook chicken 5 minutes on each side. Stir in chicken broth, olives, milk or cream, and marinara sauce. Simmer until sauce is reduced to desired consistency. Sprinkle with parsley before serving.

Yield: 4 servings

The South Florida Science Museum

The South Florida Science Museum has provided hands-on science fun for over 44 years in Dreher Park in West Palm Beach. The Buzz Aldrin Planetarium features daily star shows and a weekend laser concert. The famous astronaut dedicated the planetarium two years before walking on the moon. The Museum also features ocean life from around the world, an Egypt gallery with authentic mummy and artifacts, and a science themed mini-golf course. Rotating exhibitions complete your experience in this interactive center.

139

Easy Paella

Paella is one of the most famous Spanish dishes. There is no single way of making it - every chef has his or her own technique, and the list of ingredients can differ as well. Here's a wonderful example.

1 (7-ounce) can chopped clams; reserve liquid
2 tablespoons vegetable oil
8 chicken thighs
1 large onion, chopped
1½ cups parboiled long-grained white rice
2 garlic cloves, minced
6 cups chicken broth
½ teaspoon ground turmeric or ground saffron
½ teaspoon pepper
1 (10-ounce) package frozen peas
½ pound medium shrimp, peeled and deveined
½ lemon, sliced into rounds
¼ cup parsley sprigs (optional)

Drain clams, reserving liquid. Add enough water to clam liquid to make 1¼ cups; set aside.

Heat oil in a 6-quart Dutch oven and brown chicken on all sides on medium-high heat. Remove chicken and set aside.

Reduce heat, add onion, rice, and garlic; cook, stirring often, until rice is lightly browned. Add reserved clam liquid, broth, turmeric or saffron, pepper, and chicken. Heat to boiling. Reduce heat to low, cover, and cook 30 minutes or until chicken is no longer pink and juices run clear.

Stir in clams, peas, and shrimp. Cover and cook 5 minutes or until shrimp turn pink and opaque. Serve with lemon and garnish with parsley, if desired.

Yield: 8 servings

Jasmine

Confederate jasmine, a tropical vine, produces an abundance of lovely small white flowers with a delightful fragrance. Although the blooming period lasts only about two months, the vine's attractive dark-green leaves look good throughout the year. It is among the few plants that are well adapted to extremes of temperature, thriving in the warmth and humidity of south Florida as well as the freezes of north Florida. The name "Confederate" does not refer to the American Confederacy; instead, it derives from the confederacy of the Malay Sultanates formed by the British in the early 1800's.

Chicken with Cold Sesame Noodles

As an alternative, you can use Sesame Chicken (see Index for recipe) in place of the marinated chicken. This dish also works well with grilled teriyaki chicken breasts.

1 (8-ounce) chicken breast

Marinade:

¼ cup soy sauce

¼ cup rice wine (mirin)

2 tablespoons brown sugar

1 teaspoon grated ginger root

Cold Sesame Noodles:

4 tablespoons peanut
    butter

3 garlic cloves, crushed

6 tablespoons soy sauce

6 tablespoons sesame oil

3 tablespoons rice vinegar

1 teaspoon grated
    gingerroot

½ cup chicken broth

3 red hot peppers, crushed

¼ cup minced green onions

3 tablespoons sesame seeds

1 pound thin egg noodles or
    angel hair pasta

Thinly sliced cucumber for
    garnish (optional)

Combine marinade ingredients; marinate chicken in mixture 20 minutes. Sauté chicken in marinade. Cool and slice against the grain.

In a blender, mix all Cold Sesame Noodle ingredients except noodles. Cook noodles and rinse with cold water. Combine all ingredients and garnish with cucumber.

Bromeliads

Bromeliads, native to the American tropics and sub-tropics, are members of the pineapple family. The two best-known members of this family are the pineapple and Spanish moss. Most bromeliads are epiphytes ("epi" means "upon" and "phyte" means "plant"). Epiphytes grow on trees but not as parasites; their roots function primarily as a support and anchoring system; they absorb water and minerals through their leaves. Other bromeliads are terrestrial, they grow on the ground. Whether epiphytic or terrestrial, bromeliads can thrive equally well if forced to switch places and lifestyles.

Moo Goo Gai Pan

Why get take-out when you can make this at home?

1 pound boneless, skinless
  chicken breasts
1 teaspoon salt
¼ teaspoon white pepper
1 teaspoon cornstarch
1 teaspoon dry sherry or
  Chinese cooking wine
1 teaspoon cornstarch

4 tablespoons cooking oil
8 ounces fresh mushrooms,
  thinly sliced
1 green pepper, sliced into
  1-inch strips or 1 cup pea
  pods
½ teaspoon salt
¼ cup water (optional)

Cut chicken diagonally into slices, 1x1x¼-inches. Mix 1 teaspoon salt, pepper, and 1 teaspoon cornstarch with sherry; add chicken. In a small bowl, mix remaining 1 teaspoon cornstarch with water; set aside and stir occasionally.

Heat oil in frying pan over high flame. Add seasoned chicken and stir constantly approximately 2 minutes until chicken turns white. Drain chicken in a small colander or strainer over a bowl.

Return oil from bowl to same skillet. Over medium heat; add mushrooms, pepper or pea pods, and remaining ½ teaspoon salt. Mix thoroughly. If mixture is too dry, add 1 tablespoon water. Mix in well-stirred cornstarch mixture and cooked chicken meat. When liquid thickens, serve immediately.

Yield: 4 servings

Civil War and the Lighthouse

The lighthouse was completed and lit in 1860 just in time for the Civil War. It was a boon to the Union Navy. In 1861 the assistant keeper of the Jupiter Lighthouse took matters into his own hands. He seized and hid the Fresnel Lens for the duration of the war. This eliminated the aid to navigation for the Northern troops.

Yakatori Chicken

Easy and colorful chicken on skewers.

Marinade:

¾ cup light teriyaki sauce
½ cup green onions, chopped
2 garlic cloves, minced

2 teaspoons dark sesame oil
2 pounds boneless, skinless chicken breast, cut into 1-inch pieces

Skewers:

8 large green onions, cut into ½-inch pieces
2 medium zucchini, cut into 1-inch chunks

2 sweet red peppers, cut into 1-inch pieces
24 small button mushrooms

Marinate chicken at least 30 minutes, reserving ¼ of the marinade for basting.

Arrange chicken and vegetables on skewers and baste with reserved marinade. Broil 7 to 10 minutes; turn and broil until cooked through.

Yield: 6 to 8 servings

The Jupiter Inlet Lighthouse

The lighthouse has been an active aid to navigation since 1860. It stands at the Jupiter Inlet, where the Loxahatchee River flows into the Atlantic Ocean. It was constructed in 1850 to warn boats of the dangerous offshore shoal near the inlet. Its First Order Fresnel Lens had an important role during the Civil War, as its powerful light shone 22 to 28 miles out to sea.

Today's red painted exterior reminds us of the tower's original brick construction.

Tia Mirta's Arroz con Pollo
(Aunt Mirta's Chicken with Rice)

A classic Spanish dish, and so easy.

1 tablespoon olive oil
1 large onion, chopped
2 bay leaves
6 cups chicken broth
1 teaspoon Bijol
1 teaspoon garlic powder
1 teaspoon salt
⅓ teaspoon pepper
1 whole chicken, cut into
    8 pieces
1 teaspoon ground cumin

1 teaspoon oregano
½ cup white wine
12 ounces beer
1 (8-ounce) can tomato sauce
1 (15-ounce) can peas,
    reserve liquid
1 (8-ounce) jar pimientos,
    reserve liquid
1 cup long-grained white
    rice, presoaked in water
    for 30 minutes

In a large pot, heat oil on medium heat. Add all ingredients except peas, pimentos, and rice; add liquid only from peas and pimientos. Cook 25 minutes.

Preheat oven to 325 degrees. Remove chicken from broth and place in a baking pan. Bake 20 to 30 minutes

Add rice to pot of liquid broth; cover and cook on low for 25 minutes, stirring occasionally. When rice is ready, warm peas 5 minutes and fold peas into each serving of rice. Serve with chicken and garnish with pimentos.

Yield: 6 to 8 servings

For family-style dinning, place half the rice in the center of a large platter. Spoon on warm peas, add remaining rice, and place chicken on top. Garnish with pimientos.

Bijol powder is used in many Latin American dishes. If you can't find it at your local grocery store, you can substitute equal parts turmeric and paprika.

Peruvian Chicken Stew

2 pounds chicken thighs,
   legs, and breasts
1 package chicken giblets
1 large onion, coarsely
   chopped
7 garlic cloves, minced or
   finely sliced
3 tablespoons tomato paste
4 plum tomatoes, quartered
   and seeded

½ cup raisins
4 carrots, pared and quartered
6 small red potatoes,
   quartered
⅛ teaspoon allspice
2 bay leaves
2 cups chicken broth
⅔ cup red wine
1 pound sliced mushrooms
1 cup frozen peas

Brown chicken and giblets in a large pot; remove and
set aside. On medium heat, sauté onions, then garlic.
Add tomato paste, tomatoes, raisins, carrots, potatoes,
allspice, bay leaves, chicken broth, wine, and browned
chicken and giblets. Simmer for 40 minutes or until
potatoes are soft. Add mushrooms and peas. Stir and
cook 10 minutes longer.

Yield: 8 servings

Spady Cultural Heritage Museum

The Spady Cultural Heritage Museum is a tribute to Delray Beach's African American roots by showcasing photographs and artifacts of pioneering black families. The only African American museum in Palm Beach, it is housed in the former mission revival style home of Solomon D. Spady, the third educator for black children in Delray Beach from the early 1920s to the 1950s. Exhibits include kerosene appliances, wooden furniture hand made by school students, photographs, and oral histories. Traveling exhibits, programs for children, trolley tours, and old-fashioned events round out the African American cultural heritage experience.

Pan-Roasted Duck Breast
with Mission Figs and
Honey Balsamic Glaze over Polenta

*This recipe comes from Chef Frank Eucalitto of
Café Chardonnay in Palm Beach Gardens.*

4 (8-ounce) boneless duck breasts, trimmed of all excess fat

Marinade:

2 ounces olive oil

1 teaspoon each fresh
chopped thyme, sage,
rosemary, and marjoram

2 sliced shallots

2 garlic cloves, sliced

¼ teaspoon coarse salt

½ teaspoon freshly ground
pepper

2 tablespoons honey

2 tablespoons balsamic
vinegar

Entrée:

1 tablespoon vegetable oil

Marinated duck breasts

12 cipollini or pearl onions

4 ounces diced fresh fennel

2 shallots, sliced

2 garlic cloves, finely
chopped

2 ounces balsamic vinegar

1 ounce honey

½ teaspoon each fresh
chopped thyme,
rosemary, sage, and
marjoram

8 ounces veal or chicken
broth

4 ounces dried mission figs,
sliced in half

4 ounces veal or chicken
broth

Salt and freshly ground
pepper, to taste

Polenta or mashed potatoes

Mix marinade ingredients together and marinate
duck breasts for 1 hour.

Preheat oven to 350 degrees. Heat oil in ovenproof
sauté pan. Place duck breasts skin-side-down in a
pan and sauté until browned over medium heat; this
will reduce the amount of fat under the skin. Drain
fat from pan and turn breasts. Add onions and
continue to sauté 3 minutes. Add fennel, shallots,
and garlic. Sauté 1 minute, stirring continually. Add
balsamic vinegar, honey, and herbs and simmer 30
seconds. Add 8 ounces broth and figs. Bring to boil,
then place in oven for 10 minutes.

continued

Pan Roasted Duck Breast continued

Remove duck from pan. Add remaining 4 ounces broth. Bring liquid to a simmer and reduce until slightly thickened. Season with salt and pepper and remove from heat.

To serve, place a slice of polenta (or mashed potatoes) on each plate. Slice breasts on a bias and arrange. Spoon sauce and figs over breasts and serve.

Yield: 4 servings

Garnish with steamed asparagus and sautéed cherry tomatoes, if desired.

The Maltz Jupiter Theatre

Originally built by Burt Reynolds in 1978 as a dinner theatre, and occupied during the 80's and early 90's by Burt Reynolds and his successors, the landmark building was acquired in October 2001 by the not-for-profit Palm Beach Playhouse, Inc. Following a successful capital campaign that raised in excess of $6.5 million, the 28,000 square foot theatre was renovated and re-named the Maltz Jupiter Theatre in recognition of major benefactors, Milton and Tamar Maltz. The Maltz Jupiter Theatre is a 550-seat, nonprofit community-based regional theatre. The theatre presents a wide variety of top quality theatrical productions, concerts and other special events.

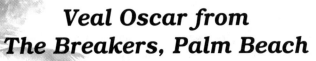

Veal Oscar from The Breakers, Palm Beach

This is served in the Flagler Steakhouse, *overlooking the golf course at The Breakers.*

Béarnaise Sauce:

2 egg yolks
4 tablespoons white wine
1 cup clarified butter
½ tablespoon lemon juice

Tabasco sauce, to taste
Salt and pepper, to taste
1 tablespoon white wine
½ teaspoon dried tarragon

Black Bean Sauce:

1 tablespoon chopped bacon
½ cup onion, chopped
¼ teaspoon cumin
1 cup black beans, soaked in water
4 cups chicken broth
1 tablespoon lime juice

4 tablespoons chopped cilantro
1 tablespoon chopped garlic
4 tablespoons rice wine vinegar
4 tablespoons butter
Salt and pepper, to taste

Veal:

12 (4-ounce) veal tenderloin fillets
Salt and freshly cracked pepper, to taste
12 ounces jumbo lump crabmeat

30 asparagus spears, blanched
Olive oil, as needed
1 ounce Béarnaise sauce
2 ounces black bean sauce

For Béarnaise Sauce, combine egg yolk and wine. Whisk over a double-boiler until mixture is thick (approximately 8 minutes) Remove from double-boiler. Slowly add butter to egg mixture while whisking until all butter is incorporated. Add lemon juice and Tabasco sauce. Season with salt and pepper. In a small sauté pan, add white wine and tarragon and reduce over low heat until all liquid is evaporated. Add tarragon to egg mixture.

To make the Black Bean Sauce, cook bacon until crisp in a medium pot. Add onion and cook until translucent. Add cumin, beans, broth, lime juice, and cilantro. Cook for 2 hours or until beans are tender. Blend and strain mixture. Add rice wine vinegar and butter to finish. Season with salt and pepper.

continued

Veal Oscar from the Breakers continued

Season veal with salt and pepper and cook until desired doneness. Sauté crabmeat and asparagus; season with salt and pepper. Place 5 asparagus spears on top of the veal, then place 2 ounces crabmeat on top of the asparagus. Place 1 ounce Béarnaise sauce over crabmeat and asparagus. Place 2 ounces black bean sauce in front of the veal. Serve with your choice of vegetables and/or starch.

Yield: 6 servings

The Breakers

From its opening in 1894, the Royal Poinciana Hotel, located on the Intracoastal Waterway, proved so popular that Henry Flagler built a second hotel – the Palm Beach Inn – on the beachfront portion of the Royal Poinciana's property overlooking the Atlantic Ocean. It was fully booked for most of its opening season in 1896. Instead of asking for rooms at the Royal Poinciana, many regular guests asked for rooms "over by the breakers." The name stuck, and when Flagler doubled the size of the Palm Beach Inn for the 1901 season, he renamed it The Breakers.

Ropa Vieja

A slowly simmered Spanish stew.

2 pounds beef stew meat,
cut in 1-inch cubes
2 tablespoons olive oil
8 ounces (total combined
weight) onions, bell
peppers, and sweet red
peppers
2 garlic cloves, minced
1 tablespoon salt
1 tablespoon Mrs. Dash
garlic and herb seasoning

4 ounces ham, diced
1¼ ounces chorizo sausage,
skinned and diced ⅛-inch
thick
1 (12-ounce) bottle dark beer
1 package Sazon seasoning
2 heaping tablespoons salad
olives
1 tablespoon capers

In a large heavy pot, brown meat in oil over high heat
for about 15 to 20 minutes. Add onions and peppers,
garlic, salt, Mrs. Dash, ham, half a link of diced
sausage, and beer. Entire mixture should be covered
in about ½ inch of liquid. Simmer covered for 3
hours or until meat becomes tender. Stir frequently.

Add remaining sausages and Sazon; simmer
1½ hours longer. Meat should be falling apart. About
30 minutes before serving, add olives and capers.

Filet of Beef (Chateaubriand)

Beef tenderloin (allow
8 ounces per serving)
Butter, melted, or olive oil

Salt, pepper, granulated
garlic, and thyme leaves,
to taste

Remove meat from refrigerator about 1 hour before
cooking. Preheat oven to 500 degrees. Remove
surplus fat and skin from a 5- or more pound
tenderloin. Fold over thin end of filet and secure with
butchers' twine. Spread meat with melted butter or
olive oil, season with salt, pepper, granulated garlic,
and thyme leaves.

Place meat on a roasting rack pan. Place pan in oven
and reduce heat to 400 degrees. Bake 30 minutes.
Tenderloin is usually cooked rare when internal
temperature reaches 120 degrees. Remove from oven
and let rest 5 minutes before slicing.

An Early Restaurateur

Bessie DuBois was known for her cooking expertise and operated a restaurant called the DuBois Fishing Camp from 1929 until the start of World War II. Her oysters were cooked in a crisp cocoon of browned egg and cracker meal. Some were over 6" long! Turtle eggs were sometimes used when the mosquitoes plagued the chickens into a state of not laying. Turtle eggs were strong, and for omelets, cheese was used to mask the flavor.

Grilled Steaks with Martini Twist

A great recipe from Chef Mark Ramsay. Fire up your grills!

4 green onions, finely chopped	1 teaspoon crushed black peppercorns or very coarsely ground black pepper
¼ cup gin	
1 tablespoon olive oil	
1 teaspoon finely shredded lemon peel	Salt, to taste
4 boneless beef top loin steaks, cut 1-inch thick (approximately 2 pounds)	2 tablespoons sliced stuffed green olives
	Lemon twists

Make marinade by combining green onions, gin, oil, and lemon peel. Place steaks in a ziplock bag; add marinade, seal bag, and turn to coat steaks. Refrigerate 30 minutes while grill is heating.

Remove steaks from marinade. Press peppercorns onto both sides of steak. Grill steaks to desired doneness, turning once; allow 8 to 12 minutes for medium-rare and 12 to 15 minutes for medium. Season to taste with salt.

To serve, garnish with sliced olives and lemon twists.

Yield: 4 servings

Grill Marks

Any backyard chef can make the attractive grill marks found on food prepared by the world's greatest chefs. It's simple. Just rotate the food you are grilling by 45 degrees about halfway through the cooking process. The crosshatch marks lend a professional look to your home grilled food.

Beef in Spicy Tomato Sauce with Black Beans

Serve this over yellow rice.

1 large onion, sliced
1 garlic clove
1 sweet red pepper, cut in
   strips
1 tablespoon olive oil
6 ounces tomato paste
½ tablespoon ground cumin
1 tablespoon chopped
   cilantro

1 teaspoon Tabasco sauce
2 cups water
1 tablespoon olive oil
1 (6-ounce) can black beans,
   drained
2 pounds sirloin steak, thinly
   sliced

Heat 1 tablespoon oil and sauté onions, garlic, and pepper until soft. Stir in tomato paste, cumin, cilantro, and Tabasco sauce. Cook, stirring, 1 to 2 minutes. Stir in water and simmer, uncovered, about 45 minutes.

In a separate pan, heat 1 tablespoon oil and gently sauté beans. Sauté beef until cooked rare. Drain beef juices into the sauce and reduce sauce over medium-high heat, stirring constantly. Add beef to sauce and toss in beans.

Paris Singer

Paris Singer was one of 19 children of Isaac M. Singer, of Singer Sewing Machine fame. He inherited a love of architecture and invited Addison Mizner to Palm Beach to recuperate. Paris Singer provided the 'deep pockets' that got Addison Mizner started. Paris's mother, Isabella, is rumored to be the model for the Statue of Liberty.

Stuffed Leg of Lamb

This makes a beautiful Easter dish. You'll need some butcher's twine to prepare this recipe.

2 Granny Smith apples, peeled and chopped
2 tablespoons minced shallots
1 tablespoon butter
1½ cups crumbled goat cheese

1 cup pine nuts, toasted
½ cup chopped mint
Salt and pepper, to taste
1 (5-pound) leg of lamb, butterflied
1 tablespoon olive oil

Preheat oven to 375 degrees. Cut six 2-foot lengths of butcher's twine. In a small skillet, sauté apples and shallots in butter for 1 minute or until lightly browned. Transfer to a small bowl and mix well with goat cheese, pine nuts, and mint; season with salt and pepper. Arrange lamb on work surface, inside facing up. Place a sheet of plastic wrap over lamb and pound with a meat mallet to flatten meat slightly, if needed, until leg is a fairly even thickness. Remove plastic wrap and generously season inside and outside of lamb. Mound stuffing mixture lengthwise along one side of lamb; roll up lamb over stuffing, tucking in ends. Space five pieces of twine under lamb roll and tie them firmly, starting at outside and working in. Tie roll lengthwise with remaining piece of twine.

In a large skillet, heat oil over high heat. Add lamb roll and sear all over, about 6 minutes. Transfer lamb to a rack set in a roasting pan and roast until browned and tender, 25 minutes for rare or 30 minutes for medium-rare, basting occasionally. Remove from oven and let stand for 10 minutes, covered loosely with foil.

To serve, discard strings, slice in 12 pieces, and serve 2 slices per serving

Yield: 6 servings

This is good with roasted rosemary potatoes.

Lamb Curry

This is wonderful served with Basmati rice.

2 pounds lean boneless
   lamb, cut in 1- to
   2-inch cubes
½ teaspoon salt
1 cup chopped onion
1 (1-inch) piece fresh
   ginger, minced
2 garlic cloves, minced
2 teaspoons ground
   coriander

1 teaspoon cumin
⅛ teaspoon ground cloves
½ teaspoon cinnamon
2 bay leaves
2 cups chicken broth
1 (14.5-ounce) can diced
   tomatoes
½ cup plain yogurt
1 tablespoon garam masala
8 fresh mint leaves, chopped

Sprinkle lamb with salt. Cook lamb in a Dutch oven over medium-high heat, stirring often, 5 minutes or until lamb is lightly browned. Remove meat and set aside.

Sauté onion and ginger in Dutch oven 1 to 2 minutes over medium-high heat. Add garlic and cook 1 minute. Stir in coriander, cumin, cloves, cinnamon, and bay leaves. Add lamb, broth, and tomatoes; bring to a boil. Cover, reduce heat, and simmer 1 hour or until lamb is tender.

Remove from heat; add yogurt and garam masala, stirring until blended. Sprinkle with mint.

Yield: 6 servings

Boca Raton Museum of Art

The Boca Raton Museum of Art hosts an annual Outdoor Juried Art Festival each February that attracts more than 50,000 people from all over the state and beyond. Only one of three museum-sponsored art festivals in the state, the Boca Raton Museum Art Festival has been ranked one of the Top 100 Art Festivals in the country, featuring 250 of the finest artists from around the world.

154

Leila's *Classic Lamb Kebab*

This signature Middle Eastern recipe comes from Leila in West Palm Beach.

Marinade:

¾ teaspoon sea salt, or to taste
¾ teaspoon freshly ground allspice
⅛ teaspoon freshly cracked black pepper

¼ teaspoon ground cinnamon
⅛ teaspoon freshly grated nutmeg
¼ large onion, finely minced in the food processor
2 cups olive oil

Kebabs:

2 pounds lamb strip loin, cut into 1½-inch cubes
20 shallots, halved

1 large red bell pepper, cut into 1½-inch pieces

Combine dry ingredients and dry rub the lamb until well coated. Combine onion and olive oil and pour over the spice-rubbed lamb, mix well to combine. Let marinate for up to 10 hours in the refrigerator.

Remove lamb from marinade. Alternating lamb cube, half shallot, and red bell pepper, thread four pieces of each onto a skewer (wooden skewers are fine); make 10 skewers. Cook over a hot grill to desired temperature.

Yield: 5 servings (10 skewers)

DuBois Pioneer Home

Harry DuBois met his wife Susan Sanders in February 1898 on a blind date at the top of the Jupiter Lighthouse. They built their home in the same year. Harry raised vegetables and fruits, fished, and hauled freight. But he was most successful at keeping bees and selling honey. The Loxahatchee River Historical Society operates the DuBois Pioneer Home.

Pan Roasted Pork Chop
with Garlic Smashed Potatoes, Zucchini, and Bacon and Irish Cheddar Emulsion

This recipe comes to us from Chef Kai Lermen at the Ritz-Carlton, *Palm Beach. Mâche is baby lettuce that is found in specialty stores.*

Pork Chop:

1 (12-ounce) pork chop
1 garlic clove, cut into
  slivers
Olive oil
1 teaspoon fresh rosemary,
  minced

1 zucchini boat (½ zucchini
  sliced lengthwise, seeds
  scooped out and
  blanched)
3 tomato skirts
Mâche, for garnish

Make small cuts in pork chop with a sharp knife and insert garlic into cuts. Sear pork chop on both sides in pan with oil and rosemary. Finish to desired doneness in a 400-degree oven.

Garlic Smashed Potatoes:

3 to 4 Red Bliss potatoes,
  whole
1 ounce butter
1 garlic clove, minced
2 ounces milk

Salt and pepper, to taste
½ teaspoon parsley,
  chiffonade (thin strips or
  shreds)
Sour cream, to taste

Wash potatoes and simmer until completely cooked through. Leave whole, do not cut. Melt butter; add garlic and sweat down, then add milk. Season with salt and pepper. Drain water from pot until water evaporates. Using a stiff whisk, smash potatoes lightly and add butter/milk mixture. Do not over mash, potatoes should be quite chunky. Adjust seasoning and add parsley. Fold in sour cream.

Bacon and Irish Cheddar Emulsion:

1 slice smoked bacon,
  minced
2 shallots, sliced
2 sprigs thyme
1 pinch chicken base

2 ounces Irish Cheddar
  cheese, shredded
6 ounces heavy cream
Salt and pepper, to taste

continued

Pan Roasted Pork Chop continued

Render bacon in a pot. Add shallots, thyme, and chicken base. Allow to foam; scrape well. Cook until shallots are translucent. Add cream and bring to a boil. Remove from heat, whisk in cheese, and season with salt and pepper. Using a small hand blender mix and strain through a chinois.

Assembly:

Rest pork chop for a few minutes, then slice bottom of chop on an angle so the chop will stand up and tip forward. Spoon garlic mashed potato on side of plate, place chop onto mash, standing up. Place small amount of potatoes on other side of plate, place zucchini boat on top. Spoon sauce onto boat and place 3 tomato skirts on top. Spoon a small amount of sauce onto pork and drape mâche over.

Yield: 1 serving (multiply as needed)

Lynn University

Forty-three years ago, few could have envisioned the phenomenal progress of Boca Raton and a small two-year women's college that had just opened off a dirt road called Military Trail. Then known as Marymount College, the fledging institution fell upon hard times and nearly closed. Fortunately, its young, visionary college president, Donald E. Ross transformed the institution into today's thriving Lynn University. Like the community it grew up with, Lynn is recognized worldwide,enrolling more than 2,300 students from 46 states and 90 nations, and offering bachelor's, master's, and doctoral programs of study.

Macadamia Crusted Rack of Lamb

with Papaya and Vidalia Onion Applesauce and Roasted Sweet Potatoes

Contributed by Roger Dikon, Executive Chef at PGA National Resort & Spa in Palm Beach Gardens.

Papaya

Native to the Americas, papaya is a horticultural wonder, growing from seed to a 20-foot fruit-bearing tree in less than 18 months. Once reaching that size, it bears fruit all year long. Green papaya and the leaves of the papaya tree contain papain, a digestive enzyme that breaks down proteins. Caribbean cooks wrap meats in papaya leaves before baking or grilling; they also marinate meats and poultry with chunks of unripe papaya. Though the glossy black seeds are generally discarded, they are edible and have a spicy, pepper-like flavor. The seeds can be rinsed and used as garnish, like capers, or dried and ground to the consistency of ground pepper for use as seasoning.

Papaya and Vidalia Onion Applesauce:

1 tablespoon olive oil

½ cup Vidalia onions, julienned

1 cup apples, peeled and chopped into ½-inch cubes

½ cup papaya, peeled and chopped into ½-inch cubes

1 teaspoon garlic, chopped

⅓ teaspoon fresh ginger, chopped

½ teaspoon salt and pepper, mixed

2 cups chicken broth

Roasted Sweet Potatoes:

4 sweet potatoes

Vegetable oil, enough to rub on potatoes

Macadamia Crusted Rack of Lamb:

4 (16- to 18-ounces each) racks of lamb, defatted and frenched

3 tablespoons Dijon mustard

2 tablespoons English Mustard (mixed with water to paste consistency)

⅓ cup Macadamia nuts, ground to a granular consistency

⅔ cup Panko breadcrumbs or fresh breadcrumbs

1 tablespoon fresh parsley, chopped

½ teaspoon fresh garlic, chopped

½ teaspoon salt and pepper, mixed

To make the applesauce, sauté onions in oil until transparent. Add apples, garlic, and ginger and sauté for 2 minutes. Add salt, pepper, papaya, and chicken broth and bring to a boil. Reduce heat and simmer 20 minutes. Adjust seasoning if necessary.

continued

Macadamia Crusted Rack of Lamb *continued*

For the roasted sweet potatoes, preheat oven to 400 degrees. Wash sweet potatoes and rub with a little vegetable oil. Roast on a sheet pan or cookie sheet until fork-tender (approximately 45 minutes). Cut into quarters and serve warm.

Broil or sear lamb racks for 2 minutes under a preheated broiler or on a hot sauté pan; remove any excess fat. Season with salt and pepper.

Combine mustards and set aside. Mix ground macadamia nuts with Panko breadcrumbs, parsley, garlic, salt, and pepper. Lightly brush lamb racks with mustard to cover top of rack, bottom, and the two end chops. Cover with and pat on the breadcrumb mixture and set aside.

Bake in a preheated 375-degree oven for about 17 minutes to a medium-rare doneness. Slice into individual chops and place on top of the Papaya and Vidalia Onion Applesauce. Serve with Roasted Sweet Potatoes.

Yield: 4 servings

Loggerhead Marinelife Center

Visit the sea turtle hospital in Juno Beach ... and you'll feel better! Sea turtles are prehistoric creatures. In much of the world they're a "protected" species, though some cultures still rely on them for food. Southeast Florida's coast is the number one Loggerhead sea turtle nesting habitat in the U.S. Over 1,500 sea turtles, hatchling through adult, will be brought to the Loggerhead Marinelife Center in Juno Beach each year for diagnosis, treatment, and release back into the sea.

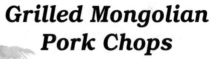

Grilled Mongolian Pork Chops

Marinated meat may turn bitter if it chars, so be sure to cook it longer and slower on the grill rather than shorter and hotter.

6 (10-ounce) center-cut double pork chops
1 cup hoisin sauce
1 tablespoon sugar
1½ tablespoons tamari soy sauce
1½ tablespoons sherry vinegar
1½ tablespoons rice vinegar
1 scallion, white and two-thirds of the green part, minced
1 teaspoon Tabasco sauce
1½ teaspoons Lee Kum Kee black bean chili sauce
1½ teaspoons peeled and grated fresh ginger
1½ tablespoons minced garlic
¾ teaspoon freshly ground white pepper
¼ cup fresh cilantro leaves and stems, minced
1 tablespoon sesame oil

Trim excess meat and fat away from ends of chop bones, leaving bones exposed. Put chops in a clean plastic bag and lightly sprinkle with water to prevent meat from tearing when pounded. Using the smooth side of a meat mallet, pound meat down to an even 1-inch thickness, being careful not to hit bones. Alternatively, have your butcher cut thinner chops and serve 2 per serving.

To make marinade, combine all remaining ingredients in a bowl and mix well. Coat pork chops liberally with marinade and marinate in refrigerator at least 3 hours or up to overnight.

Place chops on grill and grill 5 minutes on each side, rotating a quarter turn after 2 to 3 minutes on each side to produce nice crosshatch marks. Baste with marinade as meat cooks.

Yield: 6 servings

Easy Grilled Fish with Fresh Dill Sauce

Choose your favorite fish fillet and serve with the remaining chilled wine.

4 fresh fish fillets, boned, skinned, and bloodline removed

Milk, enough to cover fish
4 tablespoons olive oil
Salt and pepper, to taste

Fresh Dill Sauce:

1 cup cream
½ cup white Bordeaux
1 dash sugar
¼ cup chilled butter, cut into 6 pieces

4-6 tablespoons finely chopped fresh dill
Salt and white pepper, to taste

Rinse fillets in water, then pat dry. Place in a flat container and cover with milk. Let stand at least 15 minutes in refrigerator. Rinse and pat dry again. Brush olive oil on both sides of fillets and sprinkle with salt and pepper. Place on an oiled grill. Grill until done, 4 to 7 minutes on each side, depending on thickness of fish.

To make the fresh dill sauce, combine cream, wine, and sugar in a medium saucepan. Simmer mixture gently until reduced to ½ cup. Remove from heat and whisk in butter, one piece at a time, adding the next just before the last piece melts. Stir in dill, salt, and pepper. Place sauce on individual platters, top with fish, and garnish with fresh dill sprig, if desired.

Yield: 4 servings

Don't Forget The Fish

Many cooks shy away from grilling fish because of its tendency to get overcooked quickly over a fire and its tendency to stick to the grill. But many types of fish are ideal for outdoor cooking and can be just as satisfying as a rib-eye steak. Chose fish that has been cut to an even thickness such as halibut, tuna, shark, and salmon steaks. Fish steaks are much easier to turn on the grill than fillets. Put the fish on a very hot grill and leave it alone for at least two minutes, long enough for a crust to form. And finally, buy the freshest fish you can find.

Spice-Rubbed Atlantic Salmon
with Tomato Couscous, Cucumber Salad, and Orange Dill Vinaigrette

This is a very delicious and healthy dish that is popular at City Cellar in West Palm Beach. The vinaigrette sauce is healthy and the sweet tangy flavor goes well with the spice rub on the fish. Since the couscous salad is served chilled and the salmon is served at room temperature, it is a great party dish – no last minute cooking. All can be done in advance.

4 (7-ounce) salmon fillets

Tomato Couscous:

1 cup water	2 cups couscous
1 cup tomato juice	4 leaves chopped basil
3 tablespoons extra virgin olive oil	1 teaspoon chopped fresh garlic
1 tablespoon lemon juice	1 cucumber, thinly sliced

Orange Dill Vinaigrette:

2 ounces sherry vinaigrette	Zest of 1 orange
6 ounces extra virgin olive oil	1½ teaspoons dry dill weed
1 teaspoon salt	1 tablespoon orange juice
1 teaspoon pepper	1 tablespoon fresh lemon juice
2 teaspoons orange juice concentrate	

Spice Rub:

¼ teaspoon paprika	¼ teaspoon thyme
¼ teaspoon cumin	¼ teaspoon ginger
¼ teaspoon black pepper	¼ teaspoon allspice
¼ teaspoon turmeric	3 teaspoons kosher salt

To make the couscous, bring water, tomato juice, oil, and lemon juice to a boil. In a bowl, add boiling liquid to dry couscous. Cover with plastic wrap and let steep 15 minutes. Fluff with a fork and add basil and garlic. Chill in refrigerator.

Whisk together vinaigrette ingredients and reserve.

continued

Zesting Citrus

Many Florida home cooks have discovered the beauty of zesting our state's delicious citrus fruits. Simply put, the zest of the fruit is the skin. It is flavorful and can serve as a beautiful garnish. The easiest way to zest fruit is with a tool called a citrus zester, which has small holes at the top that allows you to cut shallow thin ribbons of the skin. One word of caution: the flavorful zest is the colored part of the rind. If you zest too enthusiastically you may scrape off some of the white bitter pith underneath the skin.

Spice-Rubbed Atlantic Salmon *continued*

Combine spice rub ingredients and mix well. Lightly dust salmon fillets with spice rub and grill until desired doneness - about 4 minutes on each side will leave the fish pink or medium-rare in center.

Serve salmon topped with vinaigrette. Garnish chilled couscous with thinly sliced cucumbers.

Yield: 4 servings

Fresh dill may be substituted for dried dill weed, and any type of citrus can be substituted in the vinaigrette.

The Gulf Stream

Look out to the ocean's horizon on a windy winter day and you'll see that it might be anything but smooth. A northerly wind will whip up some pretty tall waves. The Gulf Stream passes very close to our shores on its way up north. For centuries, ships have caught a ride on the strong flowing currents of the Gulf Stream. Early treasure ships also caught this current, hence the name 'the Treasure Coast."

Baked Pompano

Pompano is considered by many to be America's finest fish found in the waters off south Atlantic and Gulf states.

2 whole shallots, minced
½ pound butter
2 pounds pompano fillets
   (4 nice fillets)

1 cup almonds, sliced
½ cup white wine

Preheat oven to 450 degrees. Sauté shallots in butter. Place fillets in shallow baking pan and top with sautéed shallots and almonds. Bake 20 minutes, basting every 5 minutes to prevent fish from becoming dry. Remove pan from oven, add wine, and broil 2 to 3 minutes.

Yield: 4 servings

Fish Pepper Delight

A small mortar and pestle comes in handy here to crush the fennel seeds.

1 pound fish pieces
½ teaspoon turmeric
Salt, to taste
Oil, for frying
3 onions, chopped
1 garlic clove, chopped
6 cashew nuts
½ cup coconut, grated
1 teaspoon fennel seeds
3 tablespoons oil

5 green chilies, cut lengthwise
4-5 whole garlic cloves
2 teaspoons pepper
2 teaspoons breadcrumbs
2 cups warm water, salted to taste
2 teaspoons fresh lemon juice
2 tablespoons cilantro leaves, chopped

Wash fish well. Mix turmeric powder and salt. Marinate fish in the mixture for 20 minutes, then deep fry in hot oil on both sides to a very light brown. (Fish should be half-fried.) Set fish aside.

Grind onions, chopped garlic clove, nuts, coconut, and fennel seeds to a fine paste in a mixer. Heat 3 tablespoons oil and fry chilies and whole garlic cloves for 1 minute. Add pepper and ground mixture; stir and fry for 2 minutes. Add breadcrumbs and stir well. Gradually add warm water. Stir and let simmer 5 to 10 minutes, then add fried fish and lemon juice. Let simmer until gravy thickens. Remove from heat and garnish with cilantro.

Yield: 2 servings

The Celestial Railroad

The Celestial Railroad was the first railroad to service our area. Its name was coined because of the towns that it served: Jupiter, Mars, Venus, and Juno. Mars and Venus no longer exist, but Jupiter and Juno Beach continue to thrive today. When Henry Flagler's Florida East Coast Railroad came to the area, the Celestial Railroad was retired.

Fish Picatta Shack Style

This recipe from Mike Moir of The Food Shack *in Jupiter is very simple and can be varied with different herbs and cheeses.*

2-3 ounces vegetable oil	1 pound of thin white fish
4 eggs	(snapper is a great choice)
2 ounces Parmesan cheese, shredded	All-purpose flour for dredging
	2 ounces capers
1 small handful fresh basil, chopped	½ lemon, sliced
	1 ounce Parmesan cheese,
Salt and freshly ground pepper, to taste	shredded

Heat oil in a large skillet over medium heat. Beat eggs in a bowl; add 2 ounces Parmesan cheese and basil, then season with salt and pepper. Dredge fish in flour and dip in egg mixture (kind of like French toast). Cook fish until lightly browned, then turn over and repeat until done (5 to 7 minutes). Garnish with capers, lemon, and cheese.

Yield: 2 servings

This dish is great served over some fresh spinach or arugula while it is still warm so the greens will just start to wilt. Caesar, blue cheese, lemon, roasted pepper, sun-dried tomato, and balsamic vinegar are all great dressings that also go well with this fish dish.

East Coast Railway

Flagler's Florida East Coast Railway linked the entire east coast of Florida from Jacksonville to Key West. The series of luxury hotels Flagler built along Florida's east coast and the two million acres of land he developed, established agriculture and tourism as the foundation of Florida's economy during the last 100 years.

Flagler's completion of the Over-Sea Railroad was the most ambitious engineering project ever undertaken by an individual and was considered by some to be the "eighth wonder of the world".

Gingered Chilean Sea Bass

This comes from Chef Ricky Gopeesingh of Nirvana restaurant in Boynton Beach.

Ginger Glaze:

6 ounces pickled ginger in heavy syrup

¼ cup red wine vinegar

1 teaspoon chopped garlic

1 teaspoon chopped shallots

½ cup cilantro

¼ cup soy bean and olive oil blend

Haden Mango Molasses Rum Sauce:

1 ripe Haden mango

1 teaspoon garlic

1 teaspoon shallots, chopped

¼ cup red rum

¼ cup water

1 tablespoon molasses

¼ cup rice wine vinegar

1 tablespoon olive oil

Salt and pepper, to taste

Sea Bass:

2 (7-ounce) Chilean sea bass fillets

Salt and pepper, to taste

2 tablespoons olive oil

In a food processor, purée ginger into a paste. Add vinegar, garlic, and shallots and purée 1 minute. Add cilantro and purée until blended into the other ingredients. Slowly add oil to finish the emulsification process. Remove from processor and reserve.

For the mango sauce, peel mango and remove pulp from pit. Dice into ½-inch cubes. In a sauté pan, sweat the garlic and shallots in 1 tablespoon olive oil, deglaze with rum, and allow alcohol to cook off, about 2 minutes. Add water, mango, molasses, and rice wine vinegar and cook 5 minutes. Season with salt and pepper. Do not cook more than 5 minutes or the sauce will lose its bright yellow color. Allow to cool, and purée in a food processor until smooth, and reserve.

Preheat oven to 300 degrees. Season fillets with salt and pepper. Heat 2 tablespoons oil in a sauté pan and sear fillets on one side to a golden-brown color. Turn fillets over and place in preheated oven; bake 5 minutes. Remove from oven and ladle 3 ounces ginger glaze over each fillet; bake 10 minutes longer. Remove from oven and place over your favorite vegetable and starch, using 3 ounces mango sauce for each serving.

Yield: 2 servings

Pecan-Encrusted Sea Bass with Red Pepper Sauce

Chilean sea bass is an excellent moist fish, medium-textured with a mild nutty flavor.

6 Chilean sea bass fillets, soaked in milk for 15 minutes, rinsed, dried

1½ cups pecans, crushed

Roasted Red Pepper Sauce:

2 red peppers
1 pint heavy cream

1 garlic clove
1 dash salt

Sugar Paste:

4 tablespoons dark brown sugar

2 tablespoons Dijon mustard

To make sauce, broil peppers until black. Let cool in a closed plastic bag; remove skin and seeds. Cut into thin strips. Mix sauce ingredients in a food processor until puréed. Pour into small pot and warm on medium low heat. Set aside and keep warm.

For sugar paste, cook brown sugar and Dijon mustard in a small pot over medium heat until sugar is dissolved. Set aside and keep warm.

Dip both sides of fillets in sugar paste and place in large glass baking dish. Sprinkle crushed pecans on top. Bake at 350 degrees for 20 minutes or until done.

To serve, ladle equal portions of sauce on each plate, then add a fish fillet.

Yield: 6 servings

Jarred roasted red peppers can be substituted for fresh roasted red peppers.

Florida Atlantic University's School of the Arts

Florida Atlantic University's School of the Arts provides a wealth of cultural offerings in music, theatre, dance, and visual arts. With the School's 488-seat University Theatre and 175-seat Studio One Theatre, top graduate students and visiting equity actors present a variety of plays each year. The University Theatre also holds dance performances and world-renowned music faculty and visiting musicians give over 50 concerts each year. FAU's Schmidt Center Gallery and Ritter Art Gallery feature several art exhibitions each year from visiting visual artists, along with public programs including lectures by visiting scholars and artists.

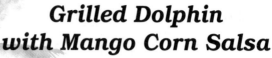

Grilled Dolphin with Mango Corn Salsa

A popular fish also known as mahi-mahi, dolphin is delicious grilled and served with this colorful salsa that combines the fresh flavors of summer.

Mango Corn Salsa:

4 ears fresh corn, cooked 4-5 minutes, kernels cut from cob

2 fresh mangoes, diced

2 roasted red peppers, fresh or jar

½ cup diced red or Vidalia onion

½ cup fresh cilantro or parsley, chopped

3-4 tablespoons balsamic vinegar

5-6 tablespoons olive oil

Salt and pepper, to taste

1 garlic clove, minced

1 (15-ounce) can black beans, drained and rinsed (optional)

Grilled Dolphin Fillets:

4 (6-7 ounce) skinless dolphin fillets

¼ cup olive oil

Salt and freshly ground pepper, to taste

To prepare the salsa, use equal parts corn, mangoes, and red peppers. Mix all ingredients together and refrigerate at least 3 hours before serving.

Heat grill. Remove any dark, reddish meat from dolphin fillets. Brush fillets with oil and sprinkle with salt and pepper. Place fillets on hot grill. Grill 4 to 6 minutes per side or longer, depending on thickness of fish. Serve with chilled Mango Corn Salsa.

Yield: 4 servings

To roast fresh peppers, place whole pepper on grill and char until black; can also be done under broiler of oven. Let pepper cool, enclosed in a bag, then peel and seed.

Grilling Temperature Control

Try grilling with a two-tiered charcoal fire. Place one-third of the coals on one side (the cooler side) and the remaining ones on the other side (the hot side). This allows you to sear the food on the hot side then move it to the cooler side to finish. Or you can move the food back and forth during the cooking process. This trick gives a charcoal grill some of the temperature variety of a gas unit.

Mango Nut Grouper

This delicious recipe comes from Tabica Grill *in Jupiter.*

2 pounds grouper fillets,
    cut into 8-ounce
    portions
6 ounces hazelnuts
6 ounces Panko
    breadcrumbs
6 ounces heavy cream
1 tablespoon vegetable oil

2 large fresh local mangoes,
    peeled and diced
6 ounces good quality white
    wine
4 ounces cold butter, cut into
    small pieces
Salt and white pepper, to taste
1 tablespoon vegetable oil

Combine hazelnuts and breadcrumbs in a food processor and pulse until nuts have been broken down into a medium-fine texture. Put cream and nut-crumb mixture in separate shallow bowls. Gently dip one side of the fish fillets into the cream, followed immediately by the nut-crumb mixture, pressing firmly to ensure maximum adhesion of the nut-crumb mixture to the fillets. Set fillets aside, nut-crumb-side up. Refrigerate fillets to help adhere crust.

To prepare sauce, heat 1 tablespoon oil in a small saucepot to medium and add mango pieces. Simmer until mangoes are softened and begin to break down (about 5 minutes). Add wine and simmer 3 minutes. Add butter all at once and remove sauce from heat. Whisk in butter until it is completely incorporated; season with salt and pepper. The sauce should be thick enough to coat a spoon; add more butter if necessary to reach desired consistency. Set sauce aside at room temperature.

Preheat oven to 350 degrees. Heat a sauté pan over medium-high heat. Add 1 tablespoon oil to sauté pan and place one fillet nut-crumb-side down in the pan. Allow nut-crumb mixture to brown slightly on the fish, then turn fish onto a baking sheet or ovenproof dish using a spatula. Repeat with remaining three pieces of fish. Bake fish in oven for 12 to 15 minutes, depending on thickness of fillets. Remove fish, place on serving plate, and top with sauce.

Yield: 4 servings

The Young Singers of the Palm Beaches

The Young Singers of the Palm Beaches provides a truly unique musical experience for students in Palm Beach County. They are the only stand-alone children's community choir in Palm Beach County and represent students from Boca Raton to Jupiter. Their members are from public and private schools, and represent a variety of cultural, ethnic, and socio-economic backgrounds. The group's mission is to increase opportunities for Palm Beach County children to participate in high quality music programs, to enhance and expand children's music programs, and to provide the community with professional concerts.

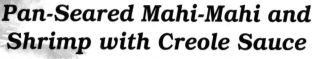

Pan-Seared Mahi-Mahi and Shrimp with Creole Sauce

This recipe was contributed by Chef Frank Eucalitto from Café Chardonnay in Palm Beach Gardens. Sofrito is a seasoning sauce of Spanish origin made with garlic, salt pork and/or ham, peppers, onion, garlic, tomato, and spices; it can be purchased at most grocery stores.

Frank Eucalitto

Our Suncoast parent and celebrity chef, Frank Eucalitto, holds a degree in Business Management and Culinary Arts from Johnson and Wales. He moved to Jupiter in 1981 to become the Day Chef at Café l'Europe on Palm Beach. Between 1982 and 2001, he opened and operated Cobblestone Café, Café Chardonnay, three locations of No Anchovies!, Frank's Sandbar & Grill, and Off the Vine Market & Bistro. He continues with Café Chardonnay, Chardonnay Catering, Eucavani's Creative Sauces, and the Wine Seller, his retail wine company. Café Chardonnay is a DRONA Award and Wine Spectator Award recipient.

Creole Sauce:

⅓ cup olive oil
1 medium Spanish onion, diced
1 red bell pepper, seeded and diced
1 green bell pepper, seeded and diced
1 tablespoon chopped garlic

1 pinch crushed red pepper flakes
1 pinch dried thyme
½ cup Sofrito
Salt and pepper, to taste
1 (28-ounce) can Italian plum tomatoes, puréed or finely chopped
Tabasco sauce, to taste

Mahi-Mahi:

¼ cup flour
¼ teaspoon each salt, pepper, garlic powder, and dried thyme
1 pinch cayenne pepper
4 ounces vegetable oil
2 (8-ounce) mahi-mahi fillets

8 shrimp (21 to 25 size), peeled, deveined, and cut into 2 pieces each
4 ounces white wine
2 cups Creole sauce
2 cups steamed rice

To make the Creole sauce, heat oil in a sauté pan over medium heat. Sauté onion, peppers, and garlic until softened. Add red pepper flakes, thyme, Sofrito, salt, pepper, and tomatoes with their juice. Bring to a boil; reduce heat to a simmer. Cook uncovered stirring occasionally for 30 to 40 minutes until excess liquid has evaporated. Season to taste; add Tabasco sauce if desired.

Heat oven to 350 degrees. Combine flour, salt, pepper, garlic powder, thyme, and cayenne pepper. Heat oil in an ovenproof sauté pan. Dredge fillets in seasoned flour and place flesh-side down in heated oil. Sauté 2 to 3 minutes until lightly browned; turn

continued

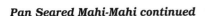

Pan Seared Mahi-Mahi continued

fish and cook 2 minutes. Add shrimp to pan and sauté 1 minute, stirring occasionally. Add white wine and reduce by half. Add hot Creole sauce and place in oven for 5 to 7 minutes until fish is cooked; it should be firm to the touch. Remove fish from oven.

Place 1 cup steamed rice on each plate. Put a piece of fish on the rice and top with shrimp Creole sauce. Garnish with cilantro leaves or fried sweet plantains.

Yield: 2 servings

This sauce can be made adding any diced tropical vegetables (yucca, boniato, plantain, chayote, etc.) at the same time as the onions and peppers.

Sauce can be made up to 3 days in advance and refrigerated; reheat before using.

Snapper Caprice with Island-Style Chutney

Island Style Chutney:

1 cup onion, diced
1 cup mango, diced
1 cup apple, diced
1 cup banana, diced
½ cup raisins

¼ cup white wine, drinking quality
¼ cup oil
¼ cup red wine vinegar

Snapper:

4 fresh snapper fillets, soaked in milk 15 minutes, rinsed, patted dry

1 cup flour
½ teaspoon salt
½ teaspoon pepper
1 tablespoon olive oil

Mix chutney ingredients together and sauté on low heat for 25 to 30 minutes. Set aside and keep warm.

Combine flour with salt and pepper. Dredge fish in flour. Sauté in oil 3 to 4 minutes each side. Arrange fish on platter and top with warm chutney.

Yield: 4 servings

Almond-Crusted Grouper

This recipe is a creation of Chef Fu Chen of the Cornell Café at the Morikami Museum and Japanese Gardens in Delray Beach. A citrus-coconut sauce makes this lightly battered fish heavenly.

Sauce:

2 tablespoons honey

4 tablespoons cream of coconut

6 tablespoons orange juice (no pulp)

1 teaspoon salt

1 pinch white pepper

2 tablespoons white vinegar

4 tablespoons white cooking wine

Fish:

2 cups tempura flour

1 cup water

4 grouper fillets or other sweet white fish

Vegetable oil, for frying

Sliced or slivered almonds

Prepare sauce first. Mix all sauce ingredients except wine in a saucepan over low heat. Add wine while sauce is cooking; cook until thick. Put sauce aside but keep hot.

Mix tempura flour and water to make a light and loose batter; add water or flour to adjust until proper consistency. (When tested with a chopstick, batter should easily slide off but should not be watery.)

Heat vegetable oil in a deep fryer to 300 degrees. Dip fillets into batter to be completely covered and quickly transfer to fryer. Cook 4 minutes until light golden in color. Remove with slotted spatula and let drain on paper towels to catch excess oil. Place on serving platter or individual plates and pour sauce over batter-fried fillets. Sprinkle almonds generously to cover each fillet.

Yield: 4 servings

Serve with steamed white rice garnished with sesame seeds or chopped parsley, and a side vegetable such as sautéed string beans.

The Morikami Museum

Inside the main gallery of The Morikami, a schedule of rotating exhibitions, along with a 5,000-piece Permanent Collections Gallery, bring alive the artistry, history, and complexity of Japanese culture. Curator Tom Gregerson selects from a wide range of creative perspectives to introduce west to east.

Macadamia-Crusted Yellowtail Snapper
with Tropical Fruit Salsa

From Café Chardonnay in Palm Beach Gardens; this is one of their signature dishes.

Tropical Fruit Salsa:

2 cups mixed diced fruit
Juice of 1 lime
¼ cup freshly squeezed orange juice
2 tablespoons chopped fresh cilantro
1 teaspoon sugar

½ chili pepper (Serrano or Scotch bonnet), finely diced
½ small red bell pepper, finely diced
1 scallion, sliced into thin rounds
Salt and white pepper, to taste

Snapper:

½ cup crushed macadamia nuts
¼ cup flour
Salt and white pepper, to taste
4 (8-ounce) yellowtail snapper fillets, skin and bones removed
½ cup milk

½ cup vegetable oil or clarified butter
¼ cup white wine
¼ cup freshly squeezed orange juice
1 teaspoon chopped fresh chives
1½ cups Tropical Fruit Salsa

To make the salsa, place fruit in a glass mixing bowl and add lime juice, orange juice, cilantro, sugar, peppers, and scallion; mix well. Season with salt and pepper. Let sit for 30 minutes before serving.

For the snapper, mix nuts with flour, salt, and pepper. Dip fillets in milk, then dredge in nut mixture. Heat oil in a sauté pan over medium heat. Place fish in pan flesh-side down and sauté until lightly browned. Turn fish and sauté for 2 more minutes. Remove oil from pan, reserving 2 tablespoons; add wine and orange juice. Reduce by one-half and add chives. Remove fillets to a plate. Spoon 1 tablespoon sauce over fish and top with 2 tablespoons Tropical Fruit Salsa.

Yield: 4 servings

For the mixed fruit, choose from mango, papaya, kiwi, carambola, pineapple, blackberry, orange, watermelon, or any sweet tropical fruit.

Sport Fishing

As West Palm Beach is the closest place on the U.S. mainland to the Gulf Stream, fishing is one of our favorite sports. Sailfish, Kingfish, snapper, and a wealth of other species make for great sport and great eating. Whether you fish on a charter boat, in a tournament, on your own pleasure craft, from the pier or from the bridge, we are a prime spot for this year round activity.

Snapper with Shrimp Sauce

If you are an avid fisherman or just a seafood lover, you'll enjoy the smooth flavors and textures of this entrée.

4 fresh snapper fillets, skinned	Juice of 1 lemon
2 tablespoons olive oil	2 tablespoons heavy cream
Salt and pepper, to taste	2 tablespoons butter
10 small shrimp, peeled and deveined	1 avocado
2 tablespoons drinking quality white wine	1 tomato, seeds removed, diced
	¼ cup fresh basil leaves, cut into thin strips

Soak snapper fillets in milk for about 15 minutes. Rinse and dry fillets. In a large sauté pan, heat oil over medium heat. Season fillets with salt and pepper, then add to pan. Sauté 3 to 4 minutes on each side; remove from pan. Sauté shrimp in pan for 3 minutes; add wine, lemon juice, and heavy cream. Remove pan from heat and whisk in butter.

Cut avocado in half and remove seed. Slice lengthwise in skin and scoop out with a large spoon to create slices. Arrange fillets on platter, place avocado and tomato over fish, and pour shrimp sauce over everything. Garnish with basil.

Yield: 4 servings

Tastes wonderful with any type of snapper: red, yellowtail, etc. Also delicious with hogfish (also known as hog snapper).

Boynton Beach Arts District

Twenty years ago, artist Rick Beau Lieu founded his sculpture studio in the industrial area of Boynton Beach. The area was rough – a high crime neighborhood that was often used as a dump site. In 1999, Rick assembled a team of people who cleaned up the street, leading Mayor Jerry Broening to name the area the Boynton Arts District. Now thriving, The Neighborhood Art Gallery hosts monthly open houses where artists, patrons, and visitors can mix and mingle. Many artists have studios in the area as well. It's the place to be for the Arts in Boynton Beach.

John's Trinidad Yellowtail

Compliments of Chef John Jones of The Palm Beach Yacht Club. A west Indian flair to a classic beurre blanc sauce, to complement the delicate yellowtail snapper.

Pineapple Mango Salsa:

1 sweet red pepper, diced
½ cup fresh pineapple, diced
½ cup fresh mango, diced
½ cup fresh papaya, diced
½ cup red onion, diced
Fresh cilantro, chopped

Passion Fruit Beurre Blanc Sauce:

½ cup white wine
2 teaspoons white vinegar
1 tablespoon diced shallot
2 tablespoons heavy cream
Salt and pepper, to taste
½ cup unsalted butter, chopped
½ cup fresh passion fruit juice

Macadamia Crusted Yellowtail Snapper:

4 fresh yellowtail snapper fillets
1 cup flour
2 beaten eggs
1 cup crushed macadamia nuts
2 tablespoons olive oil

Combine all salsa ingredients; set aside in refrigerator.

Combine all sauce ingredients in a saucepan, except butter and passion fruit juice. Reduce mixture by half over medium heat. Whisk in butter until mixture is smooth; remove from heat and whisk in passion fruit juice. Set aside.

Rinse and pat dry fillets. Dredge fillets in flour, dip in egg, then coat with nuts. On medium heat, sauté fillets in olive oil on both sides until brown. Remove from heat.

To serve, place fish gently on plate and drizzle with Passion Fruit Beurre Blanc Sauce; place approximately ½ cup Pineapple Mango Salsa on plate. Garnish with additional cilantro, if desired.

Yield: 4 servings

Island-Style Baked Snapper

This delicious recipe comes from the River House *restaurant at Soverel Harbour in Palm Beach Gardens.*

4 (8-ounce) snapper fillets, cleaned

Salt and white pepper, to taste

1 peach, sliced, skin on

1 mango, sliced

2 ounces butter, melted

3 ounces bottled mango juice

4 ounces macadamia nuts, crushed

3 ounces crème fraîche

Preheat oven to 375 degrees. Place snapper on buttered or oiled baking dish and season with salt and pepper. Wash fruit and slice. Place thin slices of fruit on fish, alternating peaches and mangoes. Drizzle butter on fruit, then sprinkle nuts on the butter, pressing lightly. Bake 12 to 15 minutes; reserve juices.

Mix "oven juices" with mango juice, then mix in crème fraîche. Cover plate with sauce and place fish on sauce, then drizzle a little sauce on top of fish.

Mango juice can be found in the juice aisle of most grocery stores.

Yield: 4 servings

Mar-A-Lago Today

Owned by billionaire Donald Trump, better known as "The Donald", Mar-A-Lago has been the site of many large celebrity-filled parties. Mar-A-Lago, which was formerly owned by cereal heiress Marjorie Merriweather Post, has more than 100 rooms. Trump meticulously restored the building and grounds and established it as a private club. He paid a mere $10 million for the estate in 1985. Today the home, whose name is Spanish for "from lake to sea", is priceless.

Seafood Casserole Supreme

This might become a family favorite.

½ pound shrimp
1 (6-ounce) can crabmeat
½ pound scallops
½ pound cod, cut into bite-
    sized pieces (any firm
    white fish will work)
½ stick sweet butter
1 teaspoon minced garlic
Freshly ground black
    pepper, to taste

1¼ pints light whipping cream
Freshly grated Romano cheese
Freshly grated Parmesan
    cheese
¾ cup Italian seasoned
    breadcrumbs
1 (16-ounce) package spinach
    fettuccine noodles
Parsley

Preheat oven to 350 degrees. Place cleaned seafood in a large casserole. Add breadcrumbs and combine.

Bring some water to a boil in the bottom of a double-boiler. Melt butter in the top of the double-boiler. Add garlic and pepper and blend. Add whipping cream, stirring constantly. Add equal amounts of Romano and Parmesan cheeses, stirring constantly until melted together (the amount of cheese used will vary depending on the flavor you prefer); continue stirring. Pour sauce over seafood in casserole and mix together. Sprinkle breadcrumbs on top. Cover casserole and bake 45 minutes.

Prepare fettuccine noodles al dente. When casserole is done, remove from oven, uncover, and allow to sit for 5 minutes. On a platter, place seafood casserole over the noodles. Serve with crusty Italian bread for dipping.

Yield: 4 to 6 servings

The Jeaga

The Jeaga Indians occupied an area stretching from today's Jupiter to southern Palm Beach County. As hunter-gatherers they ate deer, fish, turtles and other sea life. They also ate sea grapes and palm berries. They lived on top of a large shell mound overlooking the Jupiter Inlet in wigwam style homes.

Swordfish with Tomato Vinaigrette

Try this Italian flavor combination – it complements the swordfish beautifully.

¼ cup red onion, chopped
1 tablespoon chopped garlic
2 tablespoons olive oil
1 (28-ounce) can diced tomatoes with juice
¼ cup fresh basil, chopped
1 tablespoon balsamic vinegar
1 tablespoon red wine vinegar
1 tablespoon Worcestershire sauce
1 teaspoon Tabasco sauce
½ cup olive oil
2 tablespoons Dijon mustard
Salt and pepper, to taste
8 (8-ounce) swordfish steaks

Sauté onions and garlic in 2 tablespoons oil. Add tomatoes with juice and simmer until thick. Add basil, vinegars, Worcestershire sauce, and Tabasco sauce. Stir and remove from heat. Gradually whisk in ½ cup oil, mustard, salt, and pepper. Cover and let stand. This mixture can be made 4 hours ahead of time.

Heat grill. Broil fish 6 inches from flame, about 5 minutes per side. Simmer vinaigrette while whisking constantly. Serve over fish.

Yield: 8 servings

The 1928 Hurricane

It was September 1928 and South Florida was about to experience one of the nation's worst natural disasters. These were the days before named storms. The hurricane that crashed ashore near West Palm Beach and continued westward toward Lake Okeechobee was a solid Category 4 storm, packing winds of 150 miles per hour. Once the damage was assessed, including the wiping out of entire communities around Lake Okeechobee, the death count was reported to be as high as 3,500. Many still consider it the state's worst recorded tragedy.

Cornmeal-Crusted Soft Shell Crabs

As a rule, soft shell crabs are in season from mid-May to mid-October. Yes, you should eat the whole crab. Yet another fantastic recipe from Chef Frank Eucalitto of Café Chardonnay in Palm Beach Gardens.

½ cup milk
1 egg
Salt and pepper, to taste
4 ounces clarified butter
2 soft shell crabs, cleaned
½ cup each yellow and blue cornmeal
2 ounces whole butter
1 garlic clove, thinly sliced
2 tablespoons pecans, chopped

2 ounces diced mango
¼ serrano chili pepper, seeded and deveined, finely diced
¼ chipotle pepper, diced fine
2 ounces white wine
Juice of 1 lemon
½ teaspoon Italian parsley, chopped
½ teaspoon cilantro, chopped

Whisk together milk, egg, salt, and pepper. Heat clarified butter in a heavy sauté pan over medium heat. Dip crabs in milk mixture. Place in cornmeal and press mixture onto legs and body. Place bottom-side down in clarified butter and sauté for 2 minutes, until browned. Turn and sauté 3 to 4 minutes until body is firm. Keep warm on plates.

Drain clarified butter from pan. Add whole butter and stir; add garlic, pecans, and mango and sauté for 30 seconds. Add peppers, wine, and lemon juice; bring to a boil. Add parsley and cilantro. Season with salt and pepper, pour over crabs, and serve.

Yield: 2 appetizers or 1 entrée portion

Frances and Jeanne

Floridians know the drill: gather flashlights, clear the patio, gas up the car, buy bottled water, and watch the weather reports. The 2004 hurricane season intensified our storm angst. A ferocious Hurricane Frances scored an indirect hit on Palm Beach County then tore through Martin, St. Lucie and Indian River Counties over the Labor Day weekend. With barely a breather, less than three weeks later, Hurricane Jeanne hit Frances' target nearly perfectly on the Treasure Coast with her crushing 120 mile-per-hour winds. Even a year later, many homes were protected only by "blue tarp roofs." Sure, we hunker down for 'canes but we luxuriate in our "Winter (and non-hurricane) Season" of Thanksgiving through Easter.

Conch Salad

1 cup raw conch meat, diced small
¼ cup celery
¼ cup onion, diced fine
½ cucumber, diced
⅔ cup fresh tomatoes, seeded and diced
⅓ cup Key lime juice
Hot pepper sauce and salt, to taste

In a glass bowl, combine all ingredients and mix thoroughly. Cover and refrigerate for 30 minutes. Mix before serving. Serve in small bowls with a bottle of your favorite hot sauce.

Yield: 2 servings

New Orleans Shrimp Rémoulade

The rémoulade sauce can be prepared and refrigerated for up to 1 week before completing the recipe.

2 hard cooked eggs, cooled
2 garlic cloves, crushed
1½ tablespoons Creole mustard
1½ cups mayonnaise
1 tablespoon Worcestershire sauce
2 tablespoons fresh lemon juice
2 tablespoons paprika, preferably Hungarian
1½ tablespoons horseradish sauce
1 dash Tabasco sauce
½ cup fresh parsley, minced, divided in half
2 pounds shrimp, peeled, deveined, cooked, and cooled
½ head lettuce or mesclun, shredded

In a food processor, make rémoulade sauce by processing all ingredients except shrimp, reserving ¼ cup parsley for garnish. Place lettuce on the center of each salad plate. Toss shrimp with enough rémoulade sauce to coat lightly, reserving some sauce for topping. Divide shrimp equally among the plates. Top each plate with a dollop of remaining sauce. Sprinkle with remaining parsley and serve.

Yield: 8 small dinner salad portions or 4 luncheon-sized portions

Being a Conch

Whether or not you liked being called a Conch seemed to depend on where you lived. In Key West, it was an honor. In fact, prominent outsiders were given the designation of 'Conch' in lieu of being handed the symbolic keys to the city. In Riviera Beach, however, being a Conch implied having mixed blood, and many Bahamian immigrants there were uncomfortable with the term.

Barbecued Garlic Shrimp

Serve with crusty bread to soak up the delicious marinade.

1¼ cups unsalted butter
12 green onions, chopped
15 garlic cloves, minced
2 cups dry white wine
6 tablespoons lemon juice
Freshly ground pepper, to taste

2 pounds large shrimp, unpeeled
¾ cup minced fresh parsley
Salt, to taste
Hot pepper sauce (such as Crystal)

Garnish:
¼ cup minced fresh parsley
3 tablespoons minced green onions

Lemon wedges

After Chopping Garlic

It is easy to get the garlic smell off your hands after handling fresh garlic. Just rub your fingers on something metal – a spoon or a stainless steel sink. Try it – it really works!

Melt butter in a heavy large skillet over medium-low heat. Add chopped green onions and garlic; sauté 3 minutes. Add wine and simmer 15 minutes. Mix in lemon juice and pepper. Transfer to a large bowl.

Cut shrimp down back and through shell; do not peel. Remove veins. Add shrimp and ¾ cup parsley to garlic butter mixture and mix well. Cover and chill 6 hours.

Heat grill to medium heat. Remove shrimp from marinade. To make a dipping sauce transfer marinade to a heavy medium-sized saucepan; simmer over medium heat until thick, stirring occasionally, about 12 minutes. Strain marinade and season with salt and hot pepper sauce. Spoon into 8 small ramekins. Sprinkle with ¼ cup parsley and minced green onions. Place one ramekin on each plate.

Place shrimp on grill and cook until just pink and cooked through; turning once after about 3 minutes. Divide shrimp among plates and garnish with lemon wedges.

Yield: 8 servings

Shrimp Dijonaise

A delicious seafood dish from Chef Frank Eucalitto of Café Chardonnay *in Palm Beach Gardens.*

Dijon Mustard

Dijon mustard is made from brown or black ground mustard seeds. Frenchman Jean Naigeon substituted a sour juice from unripe grapes (verjuice) for the mustard ingredient vinegar. The result was a smooth-tasting mustard.

2 tablespoons olive oil with garlic
1 pound shrimp (21 to 25 count size), peeled and deveined
Salt and pepper, to taste
1 teaspoon chopped fresh garlic
2 scallions, sliced
½ cup diced plum tomatoes

½ cup sliced roasted red pepper
6 artichoke hearts, halved
½ cup dry white wine
1 teaspoon lemon juice
1 cup chicken broth
1 teaspoon each Italian parsley and basil
2 teaspoons Dijon mustard
1 (10-ounce) bag fresh spinach, stems removed

In a large sauté pan, heat oil over medium heat. Dry shrimp and season with salt and pepper. Sauté until lightly browned; turn shrimp, add garlic, and toss well. Cook 10 seconds and add scallions, tomatoes, peppers, and artichokes; toss well. Add wine and allow to reduce by half. Add lemon juice, broth, and fresh herbs and let come to a boil. Stir in mustard. Season to taste with pepper (and salt, if needed).

Yield: 2 to 4 servings

Serve over wilted spinach.

Polynesian Prawns with Tropical Fruit Sauce

To save time, you can buy shrimp that are already peeled and deveined.

24 large prawns or shrimp (about 1½ pounds)

Tropical Fruit Sauce:

6 tablespoons rice vinegar

2 tablespoons dark sesame oil

4 teaspoons low-sodium soy sauce

1 cup thawed pineapple juice concentrate

½ teaspoon ground ginger

1 teaspoon minced garlic

2½ cups cooked brown rice

Peel and devein prawns, leaving tails attached. Combine Tropical Fruit Sauce ingredients in a blender and process until well mixed. Bring sauce to a boil in a large sauté pan. Add prawns and cook, turning frequently, until they turn from translucent to opaque (about 2 minutes). For each serving, top ⅓ cup hot cooked rice with 3 prawns and 1 tablespoon sauce.

Yield: 8 servings

Sue Archer

Our artist, Sue Archer, became involved with watercolors in 1980 after a 15-year career in physical education and coaching. What was a hobby when she moved to Florida in 1979, has now become a new, full time career. The artist enjoys meeting the people buying her work, so instead of showing through galleries, she sells her original watercolors at outdoor juried shows in Florida, doing approximately 15 shows a year. She also teaches 4-6 workshops a year. Since Sue began exhibiting her work in 1985, she has won over 100 state and national awards.

Scalloped Florida Lobster

On the first day of lobster season, you'll be hard pressed to find a few of your friends, as they'll be diving.

4 small Florida lobsters, boiled gently (reserve tail shells for serving)
2 tablespoons butter
2 tablespoons flour
1 cup chicken broth

Salt, red pepper, and paprika, to taste
½ cup heavy cream
2 egg yolks, beaten
½ cup sherry
Breadcrumbs, for topping
Butter, for topping

Florida Stage

Hidden within the island beauty of Manalapan is a cultural gem – Florida Stage. This year Florida Stage offers its 18th season of uncompromising theatre, in an intimate and warm setting. In the tradition of the finest small theatres from New York to San Francisco, a Florida Stage performance is a must visit for any tourist or resident.

Preheat oven to 400 degrees. Remove meat from lobsters and cut into small medallions. In a small saucepan, mix 2 tablespoons butter, flour, broth, and seasonings. Simmer a few minutes, then add cream and egg yolks. Stir mixture constantly until thick and smooth.

While lobster meat is still hot, add to sauce mixture, then stir in sherry. Fill reserved tail shells with mixture, sprinkle with breadcrumbs, and top each with a pat of butter. Bake until brown.

Yield: 4 servings

Instead of cooking sauce until thickened, add lobster and sherry and serve in puff pastry cups or over rice instead of in the tail shells.

Spoto's Bouillabaisse

*This creation from Chef Kevin Sawyer and Bill
Flatley at* Spoto's Oyster Bar *in West Palm Beach is
a delicious work of art.*

Bouillabaisse Base:

½ cup olive oil
¼ pound Spanish onions,
   julienned 2-inches long
2 tablespoons garlic,
   minced
¼ teaspoon saffron,
   pressed into spoon
1½ teaspoons fennel seed

½ pound leeks, julienned
   2-inches long
3 cups whole peeled tomatoes,
   canned
⅛ teaspoon cayenne pepper
2¼ cups dry cooking sherry
3 cups tomato juice
1 cup clam juice

Heat oil in a medium braiser pan until hot and just
smoking. Add onions and sauté until golden and
tender. Add garlic and cook 1 minute. Add saffron and
fennel seed and mix well. Add leeks and mix well;
cook 1 minute. Add tomatoes and cayenne pepper and
bring to a boil. Add sherry, tomato juice, and clam
juice and bring to a second boil. Reduce heat to
medium-low and simmer 15 minutes. Remove from
braiser and cool in an ice bath to 70 degrees for
2 hours, then cover and refrigerate for at least an
additional 4 hours.

Shellfish:

For each serving, use the following ingredients:

½ (1-pound) fresh lobster,
   split and cleaned
3 littleneck clams

6 mussels
4 ounces fresh fish pieces
8 ounces Bouillabaisse Base

Place shellfish and fish pieces into a hot kettle with
the bouillabaisse base and cook, covered, until all
shellfish are open and just cooked through,
approximately 8 to 10 minutes.

Arrange shellfish nicely in a pasta bowl, shells up.
Pour remaining broth over and around shellfish, and
place lobster on top in center of dish. Serve with
toasted garlic bread.

Yield: ½ gallon (6 to 8 servings)

Set your table with cocktail forks and a butter warmer.

Florida Lobster

*Often called Florida
lobster, the Caribbean
spiny lobster
(Panulirus argus) lives
in the tropical waters
of the Atlantic Ocean,
the Caribbean, and
the Gulf of Mexico. In
Florida, our regular
lobster season runs
from approximately
the first week in
August through the
end of March. The
primary difference
between Florida
lobster and American
lobster (or Maine
lobster, as it is known
to consumers) is the
claw meat: Maine
lobster has large
claws full of meat,
while Florida lobster
does not; you'll find
the meat solely in the
tail of the Florida
lobster.*

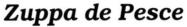

Zuppa de Pesce

The sauce for this fish is a culinary specialty that originated in Tuscany, Italy. Another wonderful recipe from Chef Frank Eucalitto of Café Chardonnay in Palm Beach Gardens.

Zuppa de Pesce Sauce:

2 cups extra virgin oil
12 ounces garlic, thinly sliced
2 cups white wine
½ teaspoon crushed red pepper
1 (4-ounce) package chopped Italian parsley leaves
1 (4-ounce) package chopped basil
1 teaspoon dry oregano
1 tablespoon salt
½ teaspoon pepper
2 cans tomato fillets

Seafood:

1 ounce olive oil
1 teaspoon chopped garlic
1 anchovy
4 clams
4 mussels
1 lobster tail
1 ounce white wine
1 teaspoon Italian parsley
1 teaspoon basil
Salt and pepper, to taste
8-10 ounces Zuppa de Pesce Sauce
2 ounces calamari
4 shrimp
3 ounces fish, cut into 2-inch pieces
2 ounces clam broth (optional)

To make the sauce, heat oil in a pot over medium heat. Cook garlic until lightly browned. Add wine and reduce by half. Add remaining ingredients and simmer over low heat for 30 minutes. Purée with wand.

To cook the seafood, heat oil in sauté pan. Add garlic and anchovy and sauté until slightly browned. Add clams, mussels, and lobster; sauté 1 minute. Add white wine, parsley, basil, salt, and pepper. Add Zuppa de Pesce Sauce and bring to a boil. Add all other seafood, cover, and simmer until clams are open and fish is cooked. Serve over spaghetti with garlic toast.

Pasta
Rice & Grains

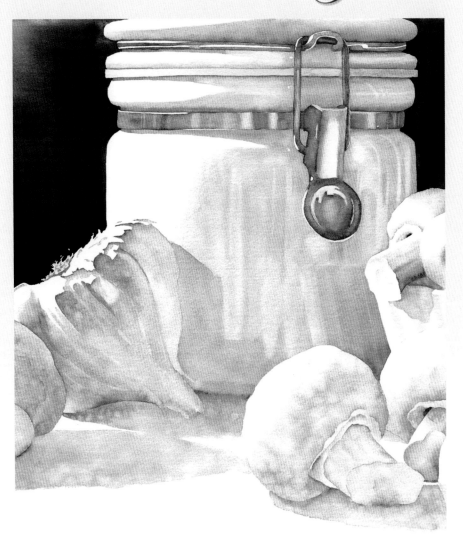

Pasta Rice & Grains

Angel Hair Pasta with
  Sun-Dried Tomato Sauce
Gnocchi
Spinach Gnocchi
Bice Pesto
Lobster Penne
Mediterranean Pasta
  with Shrimp
Linguine with
  Italian Sausage
Rigatoni with
  Grilled Vegetables
Spaghetti Primavera with
  Shrimp & Crabmeat,
  Café Chardonnay
Orecchiette Pasta with
  Broccoli & Chick Peas
Rigatoni with Broccoli
  Rabe and Sausage
Brown Rice Vegetable
  Casserole
Squash & Rice Casserole
Artichoke Hazelnut Risotto
Baked Gruyere Polenta
Fried Rice with Cashews,
  Chanterelles, &
  Pinenut Couscous

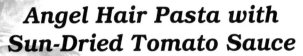

Angel Hair Pasta with Sun-Dried Tomato Sauce

Sun-dried tomatoes are no longer a difficult-to-find gourmet item. In most supermarkets they have moved from the specialty food aisle to the popular produce section, next to the fresh tomatoes.

6 to 10 sun-dried tomatoes
½ cup (or more) virgin olive oil
¼ cup capers
1 teaspoon anchovy paste or 2 anchovies, mashed into paste
1 teaspoon dried or 1 tablespoon fresh minced oregano
1 teaspoon dried or 1 tablespoon fresh minced basil
1-2 tablespoons pesto sauce (fresh pasta section of grocery store)
½-1 cup grated Parmesan cheese, preferably freshly grated
1 (8-ounce) package pasta of your choice

If tomatoes are packed in oil, drain them well. If not, boil 2 cups water and soak tomatoes to cover for 10 to 15 minutes, until soft. Drain well. Grind in food processor with olive oil. Add capers, anchovy paste or anchovies, oregano, basil, and pesto sauce and blend until well mixed. Cook pasta as directed on package. Drain and add sauce to coat. Add cheese and serve immediately.

Yield: 2 servings

Gnocchi

For a taste of Italy – this is delicious with either a red sauce or pesto sauce.

3 cups (about 5 medium) hot mashed potatoes
1½ cups flour
3 tablespoons grated Parmesan cheese
2 egg yolks
Prepared spaghetti sauce or pesto

Combine potatoes, flour, cheese, and egg yolks in a bowl and knead until smooth. Roll out on a floured board until ½-inch thick. Cut into 2-inch pieces. Cook in 6 quarts boiling water for 10 minutes. Drain and serve with sauce.

Spinach Gnocchi (Gnocchi Verde)

This is an amazingly delicious vegetarian dish.

2 (10-ounce) packages
   frozen chopped spinach,
   thawed and drained well
1 cup whole milk ricotta
   cheese
2 large eggs
⅔ cup freshly grated
   Parmesan cheese
3 tablespoons all-purpose
   flour

½ teaspoon salt
⅛ teaspoon ground pepper
⅛ teaspoon freshly grated
   nutmeg
1 cup all-purpose flour
Boiling salted water
3 tablespoons butter, melted
⅓ cup freshly grated
   Parmesan cheese

Early Loxahatchee River History

The site of the Jupiter Inlet Lighthouse is the likely location of the Indian village of Jobe, home of the Jeaga Indians who held Englishman Jonathan Dickinson and his party captive in 1696. Archeologists and students showed that the prehistoric village at the site extended over much of present day DuBois Park.

Squeeze spinach very dry and chop very fine; place in a medium bowl. Stir in ricotta cheese. Add eggs and mix well. Add ⅓ cup Parmesan cheese, 3 tablespoons flour, salt, pepper, and nutmeg; stir to mix very well. Refrigerate, covered, 1 hour.

Spread 1 cup flour in a shallow baking plan. Place a heaping tablespoon of spinach mixture between spoon and hand to form oval gnocchi; place on flour in pan. Repeat until all spinach mixture is used. Roll gnocchi in flour to coat evenly. Discard excess flour.

Slip 8 to 12 gnocchi into large pot of boiling, salted water. Reduce heat to medium. Cook uncovered until gnocchi are slightly puffed, rise to the surface, and are medium-firm to the touch (about 5 minutes). Remove gnocchi with a slotted spoon to a paper towel-lined plate, then transfer immediately to a buttered, broiler-proof shallow baking dish. Reheat water to boiling. Continue cooking and draining gnocchi in batches until all have been cooked. Arrange gnocchi in single layer in baking dish.

Heat broiler. Melt butter in small saucepan and spoon over gnocchi. Sprinkle with remaining ⅓ cup Parmesan cheese. Broil gnocchi 5 inches from heat source until cheese topping is light brown, 2 to 3 minutes. Serve immediately.

Yield: 24 gnocchi (4 to 6 servings)

Bice Pesto

This classic Italian sauce from Bice restaurant in Palm Beach is wonderful with pasta, on toasted French bread, or with chicken or fish. Be sure to use the freshest basil for rich green color.

1 pound fresh basil
3 cups olive oil
10 ounces Pecorino cheese, grated
20 ounces Parmesan cheese, grated
20 ounces pine nuts
Salt and pepper, to taste

Combine all ingredients in a food processor until well blended.

Garlic

Italian tradition says that one should plant garlic in October under the first full moon. If you do grow your own garlic, don't miss the opportunity to pick the 'scapes' that grow from the bulb. Similar to scallions, but infused with the flavor of garlic, they can be used in cooking as a substitute for scallions. They may also be used to make a variation in pesto.

Lobster Penne

Rich and savory, this turns penne into an elegant dish.

Sun-Dried Tomato Pesto:
2 garlic cloves
1 ounce fresh basil
1 cup sun-dried tomatoes
3 ounces olive oil

Lobster:
2 tablespoons olive oil
2 tablespoons chopped garlic
2 ounces dry sherry
8 ounces cooked lobster meat
⅔ cup heavy cream
⅔ cup chicken stock
2 tablespoons chopped fresh basil
4 ounces sun-dried tomato pesto
½ pound penne pasta, cooked to taste
Salt and pepper, to taste
1 tablespoon chopped fresh parsley

Combine all pesto ingredients in a food processor until well blended, set aside.

Heat oil in a sauté pan. Add garlic and sauté until golden brown. Deglaze pan with dry sherry. Add lobster meat, heavy cream, chicken stock, basil, and sun-dried tomato pesto. Stir well and cook approximately 1 minute. Toss in pasta and add salt and pepper to taste. Garnish with fresh chopped parsley and serve immediately.

Mediterranean Pasta with Shrimp

1 (8-ounce) package
   spinach or regular
   fettucine or linguine
1 tablespoon olive oil
4 garlic cloves, crushed
½ pound uncooked fresh
   medium shrimp, peeled
   and deveined

1 (28-ounce) can diced
   tomatoes
¾ cup pitted Kalamata olives,
   halved
1 tablespoon dry white wine
1 tablespoon capers
½ teaspoon pepper
½ cup shredded Parmesan
   cheese

Cook and drain pasta as directed. Heat oil in 10-inch skillet over high heat. Cook garlic and shrimp in oil 3 to 5 minutes, stirring occasionally, until shrimp are pink. Stir in tomatoes, olives, wine, capers, and pepper until hot. Stir in cheese and pasta and serve immediately.

Yield: 2 to 4 servings

The Jeannette Hare Art Gallery

The Jeannette Hare Art Gallery opened on Northwood University's campus in 1986 and was dedicated in the name of the Belgian-born sculptress after her death in 1995. Their exhibits rotate on a monthly basis to showcase young, rising artists as well as professional, established artist groups. The gallery is located in the Johann M. and Arthur E. Turner Education Center of the West Palm Beach campus of Northwood University. Features include a skylight and rounded wall with windows that overlook the Julia M. Edwards Bell Tower, and the Julia M. and William J. Edwards Bell Plaza and lake.

191

Linguine with Italian Sausage,
Baby Clams, Zucchini, and Grape Tomatoes

This delicious dish is served at No Anchovies! *in Palm Beach Gardens.*

2 (4-ounce) sweet Italian sausage links
¼ cup extra virgin olive oil
3 garlic cloves
2 anchovies
16 baby clams, well-scrubbed
1 small zucchini, sliced in ½-inch rounds
12 grape tomatoes
¼ bulb sliced fresh fennel

1 pinch crushed red pepper flakes (or to taste, if you like it spicy)
2 tablespoons chopped fresh basil
2 tablespoons chopped fresh parsley
¼ teaspoon chopped fresh rosemary
12 ounces clam broth
½ pound linguine cooked al dente

Preheat oven to 350 degrees. Roast sausage for 20 minutes. Let sausage cool until it can be handled, then slice into ½-inch rounds (this can be done in advance). Warm oil in large sauté pan. Sauté garlic over low heat for 1 minute. Add sausage slices and anchovies, and sauté 1 minute longer; do not brown garlic. Add clams, zucchini, tomatoes, and fennel and season with crushed red pepper, basil, parsley, and rosemary. Add clam broth and bring to a boil; reduce heat, cover, and simmer until clams open. Serve over hot linguine.

Yield: 2 servings

Lake Park

Few people may know that the town of Lake Park was the brainchild of Harry Kelsey, who at one time owned much of what is now North Palm Beach, Palm Beach Gardens, and Lake Park. He hired the Olmsted Brothers, the famous architects who designed New York's Central Park, to help him design the first zoned municipality in Florida, known as Kelsey City. The stock market crash dealt Kelsey City a severe financial blow, as did the hurricane of 1928. Flourishing Kelsey City crumbled and its city charter was nullified in 1930.

Rigatoni with
Grilled Vegetables, Extra Virgin Olive Oil, and Grated Parmesan

A delicious way to enjoy your vegetables from Café Chardonnay *in Palm Beach Gardens.*

1 small zucchini
1 small yellow squash
1 small red onion
1 large tomato, chopped
1 Portobello mushroom, stem and underside ribs removed
3 ounces extra virgin olive oil
Salt and pepper, to taste

8 medium fresh basil leaves
1 tablespoon Italian parsley, chopped
2 cloves garlic, crushed
1 pinch crushed red pepper
4 ounces chicken broth
½ pound rigatoni pasta, cooked al dente
2 ounces Parmesan cheese, grated

Grilling Tools

Choose grilling utensils with long handles that keep your fingers away from the fire. A complete grilling utensil set should include tongs, an offset spatula, a carving fork and a basting brush with natural, not nylon, bristles. It doesn't hurt to have a set of oven mitts and a good kitchen timer, as well.

Slice zucchini, squash, and onions into ½-inch thick rounds. Place vegetables along with Portobello top-side down on a sheet pan and brush with some of the oil. Add salt, pepper, basil, and parsley. Brown both sides of vegetables on hot grill and set aside until cool enough to handle.

Slice the Portobello into 8 slices and the rest of the grilled vegetables in half.

Warm remaining oil in pan; add garlic and sauté until lightly browned. Remove garlic from pan. Sauté grilled vegetables, then add tomatoes and sauté until warmed through, about 3 minutes. Season with salt, pepper, and red pepper. Add chicken broth and bring to boil. Simmer for 2 minutes. Toss with pasta and once more with grated Parmesan cheese. Serve immediately.

Yield: 2 to 4 servings

Spaghetti Primavera with Shrimp and Crabmeat

Served at Café Chardonnay in Palm Beach Gardens. Chef Frank Eucalitto demonstrated this recipe on television. This dish is best sautéed quickly, tossed with hot pasta, and served immediately.

6 garlic cloves, chopped fine
2 ounces good quality extra virgin olive oil
1 medium zucchini
1 medium yellow squash
6 thin asparagus spears
Coarse salt, to taste
1 pound Italian spaghetti, cooked al dente
2 ounces good quality extra virgin olive oil
1 pound shrimp, 21-25 count size, peeled and deveined
Coarse salt and freshly ground black pepper, to taste
½ cup white wine
1 pound jumbo lump crabmeat
2 ounces good quality extra virgin olive oil
½ cup sliced mushrooms
4 ripe roma tomatoes, peeled and finely chopped
16 basil leaves, cut into very thin strips
3 tablespoons coarsely chopped Italian (flat) parsley
1 pinch crushed red pepper flakes
16 ounces chicken or vegetable broth
4 ounces toasted pine nuts
Parmesan cheese (optional)

Chop garlic and place in a small container with 2 ounces olive oil. Wash and cut ends from zucchini and yellow squash; cut both in half, and stand each piece on end. Slice each into matchstick-sized pieces and reserve. Bring a large pot of water to a boil. Trim ends from asparagus. When water for pasta is boiling, add 2 tablespoons salt and blanch asparagus for 30 seconds, remove from water and reserve. When you are ready to begin cooking the shrimp, add spaghetti to water and cook for about 8 minutes. Drain and keep hot.

In large sauté pan, heat 2 ounces olive oil over medium heat. Season shrimp with salt and pepper and sauté shrimp, stirring frequently for 2 minutes. Add wine and simmer for 2 minutes. Add crabmeat and remove from heat. Pour onto a platter.

continued

Gumbo Limbo

The Gumbo Limbo is one of south Florida's best native trees. It is wind-tolerant and thus hurricane-resistant. It has two unusual characteristics: no two Gumbo Limbos have quite the same shape; and the thin, reddish bark peels off like sunburned skin – thus its nickname: the Tourist Tree. Pioneers used the leaves to treat snake bites and rashes and to brew a medicinal tea. Its branches root easily and are sometimes used to plant natural, living fences. The tree was given its name by the Somali Bantu tribe, which smeared its gummy resin on tree branches to trap birds.

Spaghetti Primavera continued

Rinse sauté pan and reheat with 2 ounces olive oil. When hot, add squashes, asparagus, and mushrooms and quickly sauté for 2 minutes. Season liberally with salt and pepper. Add tomatoes, basil, parsley, pine nuts, and crushed red pepper. Continue to sauté for 1 minute, then add broth. Add shrimp and crabmeat to vegetables and bring to a boil. Toss with hot spaghetti and serve with freshly grated Parmesan cheese.

Yield: 6 to 8 servings

Orecchiette Pasta with Broccoli and Chick Peas

Orecchiette means "little ears," which you will understand when you see their shape. Other shapes of pasta may be substituted, but the chick peas have a way of settling into the little nooks of the orecchiette.

1 head broccoli, florets only	1 medium zucchini, chopped
8 ounces orecchiette	in large pieces
(or rigatoni, bow ties,	1 can chick peas, drained and
or your favorite shape	rinsed
pasta)	2 garlic cloves, minced
1 tablespoon olive oil	1 large can diced plum tomatoes
1 small red onion, diced	Fresh basil, finely cut
1 (8-ounce) package sliced	Freshly grated Parmesan
mushrooms	cheese (optional)

Blanch broccoli florets until crisp tender. Cook pasta until al dente. Drain pasta and place in a large pasta bowl.

Heat oil in a large skillet over medium heat. Add onion, mushrooms, and zucchini and cook until tender. Add chick peas and garlic; warm mixture but do not let garlic brown. Add tomatoes and broccoli and cook just enough to warm. Add vegetable mixture to pasta and toss. Sprinkle basil and Parmesan cheese, if desired, and serve immediately.

Yield: 2 to 4 servings

It's easy to cut basil into thin strips by using scissors.

Ballot Bedlam

The whole nation voted on November 2, 2000, but for weeks after the election it seemed that Palm Beach County's voters were the only ones that really mattered. Florida was too close to call, and without Florida neither Bush nor Gore had enough electoral votes to claim the presidency. Democrats argued that Palm Beach's "butterfly ballot" had made thousands of confused Gore supporters pick Pat Buchanan. The whole world watched partisan squabbles over our "hanging chads". Finally, the Supreme Court ordered the end of all recounts and legal action. Gore conceded, the circus left town, and Bush became our President.

Rigatoni with Broccoli Rabe and Sausage

Broccoli rabe (pronounced rob) is also referred to as rabe or rapini. It has a slightly bitter taste and frequently is steamed or lightly sautéed in olive oil. Despite its name, it is not a type of broccoli, but the flower looks similar to broccoli florets.

3 teaspoons salt, divided in half

2 pounds broccoli rabe

1½ pounds sweet or hot sausage

1 pound rigatoni pasta

2 tablespoons extra virgin olive oil

1½ cups chopped yellow onion

1 tablespoon chopped garlic

1½ teaspoons salt

½ teaspoon pepper

5 tablespoons butter

⅓ cup extra virgin olive oil

2 cups grated Parmesan cheese; reserve ½ cup for topping

Fill a 5-quart pot ¾ full with water. Add 1½ teaspoons salt and place over high heat; cover.

In another pot, boil 3 inches of water and 1½ teaspoons salt. Remove bottom inch of broccoli rabe and discard. Chop remaining broccoli rabe into 1½-inch pieces and add to pot with 3 inches boiling water. Stir and cook, covered, 4 minutes. Strain broccoli and quickly place in ice bath to stop cooking and retain colors.

Remove sausage casing and add sausage to large sauté pan. Cook over medium heat for 10 to 12 minutes, chopping meat with wooden spatula, until meat is thoroughly browned and crumbly. Place sausage and liquid into separate pan; do not rinse sauté pan.

Add pasta to 5-quart pot of boiling water.

Place 2 tablespoons oil and onions in sauté pan and cook 7 to 8 minutes, until onions are translucent. Add garlic and cook 2 minutes. Remove from heat.

When pasta has cooked 10 minutes, combine sausage and its liquid and onions in sauté pan. Add 1½ teaspoons salt and pepper and bring to a simmer. Remove from heat and melt in butter.

continued

Rigatoni with Broccoli Rabe and Sausage continued

Place strained, cooled broccoli rabe in bottom of a colander and add cooked pasta to drain on top. Return pasta, broccoli rabe, and sausage to pasta pot and stir in ⅓ cup olive oil and 1½ cups grated Parmesan cheese. Top each serving with Parmesan cheese. Serve and enjoy.

Yield: 6 to 8 servings

Palm Beach Pops

Under the direction of Bob Lappin, The Palm Beach Pops is Florida's Premier Symphonic Pops Orchestra. Preserving the American Songbook for 13 years, 30 concerts are presented at The Kravis Center in West Palm Beach and Florida Atlantic University in Boca Raton November through April.

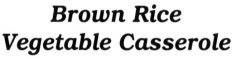

Brown Rice Vegetable Casserole

Brown rice is the entire grain with only the inedible outer husk removed. It is nutritious and high in fiber.

3 cups chicken broth
1½ cups uncooked brown rice
2 cups chopped onions, divided into 1-cup portions
3 tablespoons soy sauce
2 tablespoons butter
½ teaspoon dried thyme

4 cups cauliflower florets
4 cups broccoli florets
2 medium sweet red peppers, julienned
2 garlic cloves, minced
3 tablespoons olive oil
1 cup salted cashew halves
2 cups (8-ounces) shredded Cheddar cheese

Preheat oven to 350 degrees. In a greased 3-quart baking dish, combine broth, rice, 1 cup onion, soy sauce, butter, and thyme. Cover and bake 65 to 70 minutes or until rice is tender.

Meanwhile, in a large skillet, sauté cauliflower, broccoli, peppers, garlic, and remaining 1 cup onion in oil until crisp-tender: spoon over rice mixture. Cover and bake 10 minutes. Uncover and sprinkle with cashews and cheese. Bake 5 to 7 minutes longer or until cheese is melted.

Yield: 8 to 10 servings

Squash and Rice Casserole

A delicious side dish, also great for vegetarians.

1 medium onion, chopped
8 cups (about 2½ pounds) sliced zucchini squash
2 cups cooked rice
1 cup fat-free sour cream
1 cup shredded, sharp Cheddar cheese
2 tablespoons Parmesan cheese
¼ cup Italian seasoned breadcrumbs
1 teaspoon salt
½ teaspoon pepper
2 eggs, lightly beaten
¼ cup freshly grated Parmesan cheese

Microwave onion on high for 3 minutes. Add squash and microwave 10 to 12 minutes or until softened. Drain; partly mash with potato masher. Combine with rice, sour cream, Cheddar cheese, 2 tablespoons Parmesan cheese, breadcrumbs, salt, pepper, and eggs. Mix well and spoon into a 9x13-inch casserole dish. Microwave on high for 10 to 12 minutes or until bubbly.

Heat broiler. Sprinkle casserole with ¼ cup Parmesan cheese. Broil until lightly browned.

Yield: 10 servings

Sunfest

Florida's largest music, art and waterfront festival has grown significantly since the first-ever Sunfest was held along Flagler Drive in West Palm Beach in 1983. Performers at the first event included the Boca Raton Pops Orchestra and the event was marked by an art show, fireworks, and a regatta. Through the years, hundreds of thousands of locals and visitors have attended Sunfest and grooved to the tunes of a diverse group of entertainers, including Steve Winwood, the late Ray Charles, Bonnie Raitt, Jackson Browne, SouthsideJohnny, Billy Idol and The Johnny Clegg Band, to name just a few.

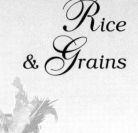

Artichoke Hazelnut Risotto

"Al dente" is an Italian phrase meaning "to the tooth." It is used to describe pasta, rice, or other food that is still slightly firm and offers some resistance when bitten into.

4 large artichokes
2 tablespoons fresh lemon juice
1 tablespoon extra virgin olive oil
1 small onion, chopped
2 garlic cloves, minced
1 pinch salt and pepper
3 cup chicken broth
2½ cups water

1 tablespoon extra virgin olive oil
1½ cups Arborio rice
1 cup fresh peas
½ cup grated Parmesan cheese
¼ cup hazelnuts, toasted
2 tablespoons freshly chopped parsley
1 tablespoon fresh lemon juice

Remove all tough outer leaves from the artichokes, leaving some of the tender inner leaves. Cut artichokes in half lengthwise and thinly slice; place in a large bowl of water with 2 tablespoons lemon juice. In a frying pan, warm 1 tablespoon oil and sauté onion until soft. Add garlic and sauté 1 minute. Drain artichokes and add to pan along with ½ cup lemon water and salt and pepper. Cover; cook until liquid evaporates and artichokes are tender, about 15 minutes.

Meanwhile, bring broth and water to a simmer. To the cooked artichokes, add 1 tablespoon olive oil and the rice, stirring constantly until edges are translucent, about 2 minutes. Add a ladleful of broth/water mixture. Continue to add broth a ladleful at a time, until rice is al dente. With 2 to 3 minutes left in the cooking process, add peas. When rice is firm but tender, remove from heat, add a ladleful of broth, Parmesan cheese, hazelnuts, parsley, and 1 tablespoon lemon juice.

Yield: 6 servings

Baked Gruyère Polenta

A time-tested dish that has circulated in the West Palm Beach area for many decades. Excellent served with fish as a side dish or at a breakfast or brunch.

4 cups milk	⅓ cup butter
1 cup butter, cut up	1 cup grated Gruyère cheese
1 cup quick grits	¼ cup grated fresh
1 teaspoon salt	Parmesan cheese
Pepper, to taste	

Bring milk almost to boiling. Add 1 cup cut up butter. Stir in grits slowly. Continue stirring until grits look like cream sauce. Add salt and pepper.

Pour mixture into a large bowl and beat with a mixer 5 minutes on medium speed. Pour into an 11x7-inch baking dish. Refrigerate until firm, usually overnight.

Using a knife, cut polenta into 1x2-inch rectangles. Place rectangles into a butter-greased 8x8-inch serving dish, standing on edge and stacked like fallen dominoes.

Preheat oven to 350 degrees. Melt ⅓ cup butter. Layer Gruyère cheese on top of polenta, then melted butter, then Parmesan cheese. Bake 15 minutes. Remove from oven. Turn on broiler. Return to oven and broil until cheese is lightly brown and bubbly, about 3 to 5 minutes.

Yield: 6 to 8 servings

Alligator

No visit to South Florida is complete without an alligator viewing, something that's easier to accomplish than you may think. Our gators are American alligators and are found not only in Florida but all over the southeastern United States. The males can grow to 15 feet and weigh as much as 400 pounds. They love fresh water and can tolerate the brackish waters of the Everglades National Park, where they hang out in droves. Limited gator hunting is allowed and, yes, they are edible, but here's a word of warning: Don't get too close to these temperamental carnivores or they may eat you first!

Fried Rice with Cashews

Your technique will improve the more you prepare this recipe – you can add your favorite meat, shrimp, or scallions.

3 tablespoons vegetable oil
5 garlic cloves, crushed
2 tablespoons small pieces
    of carrot
2 dried mushrooms,
    soaked in water and cut
    into small pieces

1 cup cooked rice
1 teaspoon sugar
1 tablespoon light soy sauce
2 tablespoons fish sauce
2 tablespoons roasted
    cashew nuts

Heat oil in a wok. When oil is hot, fry garlic until fragrant, then add carrots and mushrooms. Fry about 3 minutes. Add rice and stir-fry. Season with sugar, soy sauce, and fish sauce and continue to stir-fry, about 5 minutes. To serve, spoon onto a plate and sprinkle with cashews.

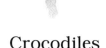

Crocodiles

What's the difference between an alligator and a crocodile? You might want to know because South Florida is the only place in the world inhabited by both species. But how can you tell them apart? Alligators have a larger, "U" shaped jaw while crocodiles have narrower jaws that leave their teeth exposed even when their jaws are shut. Crocs are often regarded as more aggressive than the commonly found alligator. In either case getting close for examination isn't generally recommended!

Chanterelles and Pine Nut Couscous

Chanterelles are a trumpet-shaped wild mushroom with a color that ranges from bright yellow to orange. They can be found dried or canned at many large supermarkets.

1 (5.6-ounce) box pine nut couscous
5 ounces fresh Chanterelle mushrooms, rinsed, trimmed, and sliced
1 tablespoon olive oil
2 tablespoons butter
2 tablespoons minced shallots
¼ cup freshly grated Parmesan cheese

Prepare couscous according to package directions; set aside.

In a skillet, sauté Chanterelles in oil and butter over moderate heat 3 minutes or until they give off liquid. Stir in shallots and sauté mixture 2 to 3 minutes or until Chanterelles are golden and tender. Stir Chanterelle mixture and Parmesan cheese into couscous.

Yield: 4 servings

Ballet Florida

Experience the dazzling artistry of Palm Beach County's only resident professional dance company. Feel the passion, the sweat, and the pure determination of this strong, charismatic and cutting edge dance troupe. Always protecting the integrity of the art but never afraid to redefine it, Ballet Florida is where the future of dance begins.

Desserts
Cakes, Cookies & Pies

Desserts
Cakes
Cookies & Pies

Tiramisu, Café Chardonnay
Peach & Pineapple Crisp
Almond Cake
Buttermilk Cake
Upside-Down Apple Cake
Tropical Key Lime Cheesecake
Osterkuchen - Easter Cake
Jane's Pound Cake with
  Lemon Jelly Icing
Chocolate Roll Cake
Chocolate Cheesecake
Tres Leches Cake
Pumpkin Roll
Holiday Cranberry Orange
  Pound Cake
Uncle Dennis' U.S.S. Coral Sea
  Chocolate Chip Cookies
Chunky Chocolate Drops
White Chocolate -
  Hazelnut Cookies
Frosted Lemon Cookies

Abuela's Puddin'
Chocolate Chambord
  Truffle Torte
Quebec Grand-peres
  au Sirop D'erable
Chocolate Raspberry
  Pavlovas
Mango Ice Cream
Easy Flan
Frozen Palm Beach
  Tropical Terrine
  with Mango Sauce
Icebox Potica
Passover Pralines

Lemon Cheesecake Bars
Coconut Macaroons
Grandma Rose's Mandel Brot
Mexican Churros
Rum Balls
Irish Coffee Ice Cream Pie
Mara Vaca Key Lime Pie
Margarita Key Lime Pie
Mango Pie
Classic Key Lime Pie
Old-Fashioned Raspberry Pie
Pear Pie with Walnut Topping
Mom's Pumpkin Chiffon Pie
Black Bottom Pie

Abuela's Puddin'

Grandma's bread pudding.

Caramel Topping:

1 cup sugar

1 tablespoon water

Bread Pudding:

6 eggs
½ cup sugar
1 (15-ounce) can
  evaporated milk
1 (14-ounce) can sweetened
  condensed milk

1 measured can (use
  evaporated milk can)
  regular milk
1 teaspoon vanilla extract
1 pinch salt
1 large loaf white bread, all
  crust removed

In a small pot, prepare caramel topping. Heat 1 cup sugar with 1 tablespoon water; stir constantly until sugar turns into a caramel liquid. Pour caramel immediately into a round Bundt cake pan, spreading to cover most of the sides and bottom of the pan. Set aside.

Preheat oven to 375 degrees. In a large mixing bowl, combine eggs, ½ cup sugar, milks, vanilla extract, and salt. Crumble bread and add to liquid mixture. Mix well; mixture will be slightly lumpy. Pour mixture on top of hardened caramel in Bundt cake pan. Bake 45 minutes or until inserted knife comes out clean; remove from oven.

Run a small knife around edges of pan to loosen; turn over onto a plate. Shake gently to release, allowing caramel syrup to run over bread pudding. Be very careful, caramel will be extremely hot. Refrigerate 45 minutes to 1 hour. Cut in wedge slices and serve.

Women in the Visual Arts

Women in the Visual Arts (WITVA) is a non-profit organization, founded in 1989, to promote public interest in the visual arts and support the artistic goals of its growing membership through activities and programs. WITVA sponsors a variety of juried events for artists to exhibit their work. Annual scholarships and prizes are awarded to Palm Beach County high school and college graduate level art students. WITVA's HOSPITALART program provides original multi-canvas painted murals to non-profit institutions, free of charge, to cheer and benefit patients, care givers, and visitors.

Chocolate Chambord Truffle Torte

The raspberries in this recipe contain a fair amount of iron, potassium, and vitamins A and C, in case you need an excuse to indulge.

1½ pounds bittersweet chocolate, melted
1¼ cups heavy cream
3 ounces Chambord liqueur

7 tablespoons unsalted butter
1 prepared chocolate cookie crust
Whipped cream
Fresh raspberries

Melt chocolate in large bowl over pot of simmering water. Heat cream but do not boil. Add chocolate and Chambord. Stir in butter until completely melted. Pour into prepared crust and refrigerate overnight. Slice into wedges and serve with whipped cream and fresh raspberries.

Quebec Grand-Peres au Sirop D'erable

(Dumplings in Maple Syrup)

A delicious dessert from our French Canadian neighbors.

1 cup water
1¼ cups maple syrup
1¼ cups cake flour
1 tablespoon sugar

3 teaspoons baking powder
½ teaspoon salt
¼ cup shortening
½ cup milk

In a large pot, bring water and maple syrup to boil. Meanwhile, combine flour, sugar, baking powder, and salt. With two knives or a pastry cutter, combine shortening with flour mixture. Add milk to flour mixture with a fork, mixing until just combined. Do not overhandle. Drop dough by tablespoonfuls in boiling syrup. Cover and let simmer 10 to 15 minutes without lifting the cover.

Serve hot with vanilla ice cream, adding additional syrup to the top if you wish.

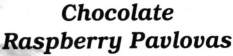

Chocolate
Raspberry Pavlovas

A New Zealand specialty, this truly spectacular dessert is best prepared in advance but assembled on each plate 20 minutes before being served. You can make the pavlovas ahead of time and store them in an airtight container.

Pavlovas:
1 cup ground almonds

⅓ cup cocoa powder, sifted

2 tablespoons cornstarch, sifted

6 egg whites

1 pinch salt

½ teaspoon cream of tartar

1½ cups superfine sugar

First Topping - Mascarpone Cream:
10½ ounces mascarpone cheese

⅓ cup whipping cream, lightly whipped

2 tablespoons superfine sugar

Second Topping - Chocolate Sauce:
3½ ounces semi-sweet chocolate

½ cup cream

Third Topping - Raspberry Sauce:
½ cup raspberries

3 tablespoons superfine sugar

2 teaspoons water

Final Decoration:
1 cup whipped cream

2 cups raspberries

2 tablespoons chopped almonds, toasted golden

Preheat oven to 225 degrees. Line two baking trays with nonstick parchment paper. In a bowl, combine ground almonds, cocoa powder, and cornstarch. In another bowl, beat egg whites, salt and cream of tartar together until soft peaks form. Gradually add superfine sugar while beating egg whites until they are thick, shiny, and stiff. Add a third of the almond mixture to the egg whites and fold in; fold in remaining two-thirds of the almond mixture.

continued

Chocolate Raspberry Pavlovas continued

Take approximately ½ cup of mixture and place it on a lined baking tray. Shape mixture into a small square shape with a flat top. Repeat process with remaining mixture, spacing squares well. Bake 45 minutes. Turn off oven and leave pavlovas to cook in oven as it completely cools (this helps prevent cracking).

To make Mascarpone Cream, combine mascarpone with whipped cream and superfine sugar. To make Chocolate Sauce, melt chocolate and cream together. To make Raspberry Sauce, gently simmer raspberries with superfine sugar and water until sugar dissolves and fruit softens, then mash with a fork.

To assemble, place each pavlova on a serving plate and drizzle with Chocolate Sauce. Top with a dollop of Mascarpone Cream, some whipped cream, and a little Raspberry Sauce; finish with fresh raspberries and a sprinkle of toasted almonds.

Yield: 10 to 12 individual desserts

Mango Ice Cream

Mango pulp can be purchased at Latin or Indian grocery stores.

2 eggs, separated	¼ teaspoon orange food
1 cup sugar	coloring (optional)
6 teaspoons flour	1 cup mango pulp, chilled
3 cups milk, boiled	1½ cups heavy cream

Mix egg yolks, sugar, and flour into milk and stir over heat until slightly thickened. Cool mixture and place in freezer until it begins to set.

Line an ice cream mold with waxed paper. Beat egg whites and mix into ice cream mixture. In a separate bowl, lightly mix orange food coloring (if using) and mango pulp together. In another bowl, beat chilled cream until it thickens. Combine mixtures, pour into mold, and cover with a lid. Freeze until firm.

Yield: 10 servings

Mango, The Apple of the Tropics

The mango originated in India, where it has been in cultivation for over 4,000 years. A highly esteemed tropical fruit; it is widely consumed in the tropics as the apple is in North America. Mangoes can be used at any stage of maturity. Green mango can be made into a sauce or, just like green papaya, used to tenderize meat. Green mango also can be substituted in recipes calling for tart apples; and medium ripe mangoes can be used in recipes calling for peaches. Mangoes were introduced into Florida in 1863, and more mangoes are commercially grown in Florida than in any other state.

Easy Flan

This is a very popular dessert in most Latin American countries. Bake the flan in an angel food cake pan to create a beautiful presentation.

Sugar, for caramelizing
2 cans condensed milk
2 cups cream

6-8 eggs
1 teaspoon vanilla

Cover the bottom of a baking pan with about ¼-inch of sugar. To caramelize sugar, heat it either in a 500-degree oven or on top of the stove. Heat sugar until it becomes amber in color, using a wooden spoon to smooth it. Remove from oven. Reduce heat to 325 degrees.

While sugar is caramelizing, mix condensed milk, cream, eggs, and vanilla together by hand, adding one egg at a time, making sure each egg is completely combined before adding the next. After ingredients are combined, pour mixture into the caramelized baking pan. Set the caramelized baking pan into a larger baking pan and fill larger pan with enough hot water to come halfway up the sides of the inside pan. Bake approximately 20 to 30 minutes. Check doneness as with a cake; when an inserted toothpick comes out dry, the flan is ready.

Allow flan to cool. To remove from pan, invert on a dish with some depth so syrup does not spill out.

Boynton Woman's Club

The Boynton Woman's Club has played a significant role in the community since 1908. The first Woman's Club building was built with lumber salvaged from the shipwreck of The Coquimbo which had floundered off Boynton in 1909. The ladies kept a lending library, held dances, bake sales, fish fries, community dinners, and beauty contests. In 1924, the women wanted a larger building. Major Boynton's heirs contributed $35,000 toward a new clubhouse and world famous architect Addison Mizner designed and supervised its construction. The building is one of two Boynton Beach area buildings on the National Register of Historic Sites.

Frozen Palm Beach Terrine with Mango-Blackberry Sauce

Purchased pineapple-coconut ice cream and mango and raspberry sorbets make this dessert easy. The terrine needs to freeze overnight before serving.

Terrine:

1 (7-ounce) package sweetened flaked coconut, toasted, divided

2 pints pineapple-coconut ice cream, divided
1 pint mango sorbet
1 pint raspberry sorbet

Sauce:

1 large mango, peeled, pitted, sliced
2½ pints blackberries

¼ cup sugar
1 vanilla bean, split lengthwise

Line a 9x5-inch metal loaf pan with two layers of plastic wrap in each direction, leaving overhang. Sprinkle 1¼ cups toasted coconut over bottom of pan. Microwave 1 pint pineapple-coconut ice cream on low in two or three 10-second intervals until slightly softened. Drop ice cream by large spoonfuls over coconut in pan, then spread in an even layer; freeze 15 minutes. Microwave mango sorbet on low in two or three 10-second intervals until slightly softened. Drop sorbet by large spoonfuls atop ice cream, then spread in an even layer; freeze 15 minutes. Repeat with raspberry sorbet, then with remaining 1 pint ice cream. Sprinkle remaining coconut over top; press to adhere (filling will extend slightly above pan). Cover with plastic wrap overhang; freeze overnight.

To make the sauce, combine mango, blackberries, and sugar in a medium bowl. Scrape in seeds from vanilla bean; add bean and toss. Let stand at room temperature until juices form, tossing occasionally, about 2 hours. Remove vanilla bean. Using plastic wrap as an aid, lift terrine out of pan; remove plastic wrap. Cut terrine into ¾-inch thick slices. Place on plates; spoon sauce on top and serve.

The terrine can be made 3 days ahead and kept frozen before preparing fruit sauce. Fruit sauce can be made up to 4 hours ahead; cover and chill.

Yield: 8 servings

Icebox Potica

Takes time, but worthwhile.

Dough:

2 cakes yeast
5½ cups flour
½ cup sugar
½ cup warm water
½ teaspoon salt

3 eggs, beaten
1 teaspoon vanilla
½ pint cream, sour or sweet
½ pound butter, melted

Filling:

⅓ cup milk
3 pounds ground walnuts
2 cups sugar
2 tablespoons cinnamon

2 eggs, beaten
¼ pound butter, melted
1 cup dates, ground
1 cup raisins, ground

To make the dough, crumble yeast cakes and add
1 tablespoon flour and 1 tablespoon sugar. Dissolve
in warm water and set aside. In a large bowl, sift
together flour and salt. In a medium bowl, beat
together eggs, sugar, vanilla, cream, and butter.
Combine with yeast mixture and add to flour. The
mixture will be sticky; do not be tempted to add
additional flour. Refrigerate dough 4 hours or
overnight.

Preheat oven to 325 degrees. Scald milk. Mix
remaining filling ingredients and add just enough
scalded milk to make filling mixture easy to spread.
Remove dough from refrigerator and divide into 4
equal parts. Roll out each part to about ¼-inch thick
in an oblong shape (about 9x18 inches). Spread
filling evenly over each portion. Roll up from the
short side. Score tops slightly, about ⅛-inch deep.
Place on baking sheets. Bake 50 to 60 minutes.

Passover Pralines

This is a recipe served at the Jewish Passover seder, a traditional meal commemorating Moses leading the Jews out of Egyptian bondage. Matzo, an unleavened bread, is eaten in place of regular bread during Passover as a reminder that there was no time for bread to rise before they began their journey. You don't have to be Jewish to love this recipe.

3-4 whole matzos
3 sticks unsalted butter
1½ cups dark brown sugar

3 (12-ounce) packages chocolate chips or the equivalent amount of broken chocolate bars
1 (16-ounce) package pecans, chopped

Preheat oven to 350 degrees. Cover an 11x17-inch cookie sheet with parchment paper. Lay matzos in a single layer, breaking them into pieces to fit the cookie sheet.

In a saucepan, melt butter and add brown sugar. Cook for 4 minutes while stirring, being careful it does not boil over. Pour mixture over matzo layer, covering all the matzos. Bake 10 minutes. Remove from oven and sprinkle two packages of chocolate chips in an even layer over matzos. Place pan back in oven for about 5 minutes to soften chips.

Remove pan from oven. Add pecans and remaining chocolate chips. Use a spatula or knife to press nuts and chocolate into an even layer. If mixture is not soft enough to spread, place pan back into oven to melt chips.

Once chocolate layer is fairly smooth, allow mixture to cool 1 hour in refrigerator. Break or cut the "candy" into pieces. If the "candy" is too hard, allow it to stand at room temperature until it can be easily cut.

This is a very good "make ahead" recipe.

Yield: 2 dozen pieces

The Jewish Community Center

Plays, concerts, best-selling authors... whatever your interest, you can find something to do at the Jewish Community Center. With branches in both West Palm Beach and Boynton Beach there's always a class to be taken or a lecture to be heard. The annual Book Festival and renowned Center Stage Series will satisfy your "need to read" and will have you humming a Broadway tune. The JCC is a non-sectarian, community based organization that serves the cultural interests of everyone.

Tiramisu

How To Make Tiramisu, compliments of Café Chardonnay *in Palm Beach Gardens. Let's say Mom is having a dinner party tomorrow. The problem is she has no dessert. So while she's driving your sister to dance and your brother to baseball practice, you're going to stay home and make dessert to surprise her. So, you're thinking of what you can make in about 30 minutes to surprise your mom. "Ah hah!" you say, "Tiramisu would be great!" Making Tiramisu is fun and easy – here's how:*

1 cup Italian Mascarpone
   cheese mixed with
   ½ cup sugar
15 crumbled amaretto
   cookies, divided in half
1 cup pastry cream
1 cup sweetened whipped
   cream
1 cup brewed espresso

½ cup sugar
½ cup amaretto syrup
1 package Italian ladyfingers
1 small piece bittersweet
   chocolate
Mint leaves, for garnish
½ pint raspberries or
   blackberries
Confectioners' sugar or cocoa
   powder

Put Mascarpone cheese, half of the crumbled amaretto cookies, and pastry cream in mixing bowl; stir until blended, then fold in whipped cream. Refrigerate until needed again.

Put espresso, sugar, and amaretto syrup in a small pot and simmer 5 minutes, stirring often. Remove from heat and let cool. Completely layer the bottom of a shallow decorative bowl or pan with some ladyfingers; you may have to break some apart to fill in little gaps. Brush ladyfingers with cooled espresso mixture until they begin to soften. Remove cream filling from refrigerator and spread a layer of filling about ½-inch thick over ladyfingers. Top with another layer of ladyfingers. Again, brush ladyfingers with espresso until they begin to soften. Spread remaining cream filling over ladyfingers and smooth out with a spatula. Sprinkle with remaining crumbled amaretto cookies and grate bittersweet chocolate over the top. Refrigerate at least 8 hours before serving.

continued

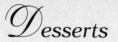

Tiramisu continued

When ready to serve, scoop a piece of tiramisu onto a plate and garnish with mint leaves and berries. Dust plate with confectioners' sugar or cocoa powder and top with pastry cream, if desired.

Pastry Cream:

1 cup milk
½ cup sugar
2 tablespoons cornstarch
2 egg yolks

½ vanilla bean
1 tablespoon unsalted butter
⅛ teaspoon salt

Combine milk, sugar, cornstarch, egg yolks, and seeds from vanilla bean in a medium saucepan. Cook over low heat until thick and lightly bubbling, stirring constantly. Remove from heat; add butter and salt. Transfer to a clean bowl and cover with plastic wrap, placing wrap on surface of cream. Cool to room temperature, then refrigerate at least 1 hour before using.

The Society of the Four Arts

The Society of the Four Arts is a nonprofit cultural center located in Palm Beach, along the Intracoastal Waterway. The four arts which constitute the Society's mission are music, drama, literature, and art. Every season - from November through April — The Four Arts presents notable speakers, concerts, films, educational programs, and art exhibitions to the public. The Gioconda and Joseph King Library and The Children's Library are open to the public year-round, showcasing guest authors in interactive discussions and book signings. The Four Arts Gardens and The Philip Hulitar Sculpture Garden provide beauty and enjoyment to visitors of this lakeside campus.

Peach and Pineapple Crisp

A tropical twist from the classic Apple Crisp.

4 cups sliced peaches
1 (8-ounce) can pineapple
  tidbits, undrained
2 tablespoons brown sugar
1 teaspoon quick cooking
  tapioca

½ cup quick cooking oats
¼ cup brown sugar
¼ cup all-purpose flour
1 teaspoon ground cinnamon
2 tablespoons butter

Preheat oven to 350 degrees. Combine peaches, pineapple, 2 tablespoons brown sugar, and tapioca in a medium bowl. Spoon mixture into an 8x8x2-inch baking pan; set aside.

Combine oats, ¼ cup brown sugar, flour, and cinnamon in another bowl. Cut in butter until mixture resembles coarse crumbs. Sprinkle over fruit mixture. Bake 35 to 40 minutes until hot and bubbly. Serve warm, with ice cream if desired.

The Pineapple

The pineapple plant stores starch in the stem rather than in the fruit itself. Just before the fruit ripens completely, the starch converts to sugar and enters the fruit. Once the fruit has been harvested, it won't get any sweeter, but it will get softer and juicier if left at room temperature for a day or two before serving. Harvested too green, the fruit will be fibrous and not very sweet.

Almond Cake

This cake is rich and great to serve on special occasions.

¾ cup sugar
1 stick unsalted butter, room temperature
1 (8-ounce) can almond paste
3 eggs
1 tablespoon Triple Sec (or Grand Marnier) liqueur
¼ teaspoon almond extract

¼ cup all-purpose flour
⅓ teaspoon baking powder
Confectioners' sugar
1 (4-ounce) package sliced almonds, toasted (optional garnish)
1 package frozen raspberries, thawed but still cold (optional garnish)

Preheat oven to 350 degrees. Generously grease an 8-inch round cake pan. Combine sugar, butter, and almond paste and blend well with electric mixer. Beat in eggs, liqueur, and almond extract. Add flour and baking powder, beating by hand until just mixed through. Do not overbeat. Pour into pan and bake until toothpick inserted into center comes out clean, 40 to 50 minutes. Cool 15 minutes in pan. Remove from pan and cool to room temperature on a cake rack. Slice into 6 to 8 servings. Pick optional garnish of your choice; either dust with confectioners' sugar and sprinkle with toasted almonds or top with puréed raspberries, strained to remove seeds. If using raspberries, place ¼ cup of the purée on each dessert plate, swirl to cover bottom, and place slice of cake on top. Dust with confectioners' sugar.

Yield: 6 to 8 servings

Boca Raton Agriculture

The construction of the Florida East Coast Canal (today's Intracoastal) and the Florida East Coast Railway in the 1890s made the Boca Raton region accessible to a group of resourceful pioneers. By the early 1900s, Boca Raton was a tiny agricultural community specializing in pineapple cultivation. A group of Japanese immigrants formed a community along today's Yamato Road. In the 1930s and 40s, Boca was known for its winter vegetable crop, particularly the green beans which commanded a premium in northern markets. In 1903 it was just a farming village of eighteen souls. Today it is home to 85,000 residents.

Buttermilk Cake

You might get your child to do chores for you in exchange for a piece of this Bundt cake.

2 sticks butter	1 cup buttermilk
2½ cups sugar	½ teaspoon baking soda
4 eggs	1 tablespoon hot water
3 cups flour	1 teaspoon vanilla
1 teaspoon salt	

Preheat oven to 350 degrees. Cream butter and sugar for 2 to 3 minutes. Add 1 egg at a time, beating well after adding each egg. Add flour and salt alternately with buttermilk; blend well. Stir baking soda until dissolved in hot water and add vanilla; add to batter. Pour into a greased Bundt pan. Bake approximately 1 hour.

Upside-Down Apple Cake

October is the month for fresh from the orchard apples. Here is a favorite recipe using McIntosh apples.

2 cups peeled and sliced McIntosh apples	3 tablespoons butter, melted
⅔ cup sugar	1 cup all-purpose flour
½ teaspoon cinnamon	½ cup sugar
Grated zest and juice of 1 lemon	1 teaspoon baking powder
1 tablespoon all-purpose flour	¼ teaspoon salt
	2 egg yolks
	1 tablespoon butter, melted
	¼ cup milk

Preheat oven to 425 degrees. Prepare an 8-inch deep pie pan by spraying with nonstick spray. Cover bottom of pie pan with apples. Sprinkle top with ⅔ cup sugar, cinnamon, lemon zest, and lemon juice. Stir in 1 tablespoon flour. Pour 3 tablespoons melted butter over apple mix.

Prepare batter by sifting together 1 cup flour, ½ cup sugar, baking powder, and salt. In a separate bowl, beat 2 egg yolks, 1 tablespoon melted butter, and milk. Add to dry mixture and mix until smooth. Cover apple mixture with batter. Bake 30 minutes. Remove cake from oven, reverse it on a serving platter or plate, and allow to cool. serve with vanilla bean ice cream or whipped cream.

Tropical Key Lime Cheesecake

Cool and tropical.

Crust:

½ cup graham crackers, crushed

1 cup lemonsnap cookies, crushed (or Key lime cookies, if you can find them)

6 tablespoons butter, melted

¼ cup sugar

Cheesecake:

1 envelope unflavored gelatin

½ cup sugar

⅓ cup light rum

½ cup Key lime juice

1 teaspoon grated Key lime zest

1 teaspoon grated lemon zest

4 large eggs, separated

2 (8-ounce) packages cream cheese

½ cup confectioners' sugar

1 cup heavy cream

To make the crust, place cracker and cookie crumbs in a bowl. Add butter and sugar; blend well. Press mixture onto bottom and partly up sides of a greased 9-inch springform pan. Chill 5 to 10 minutes in freezer until set, or bake 10 minutes in a preheated 350-degree oven.

To make the cheesecake, combine gelatin, sugar, rum, and lime juice in a medium saucepan. Stir in grated zest. Add egg yolks, mixing thoroughly. Cook over medium heat, stirring constantly until mixture thickens. Remove from heat and allow to cool.

In a large bowl, beat cream cheese until light and smooth. Add gelatin mixture to cream cheese and mix to blend thoroughly.

In a small bowl, beat egg whites to soft peaks, then slowly add sugar and continue beating until stiff peaks form. Fold egg whites into cream cheese mixture. Whip heavy cream until stiff. Fold whipped cream into the cream cheese mixture. Pour mixture into crust; chill 4 hours.

Jonathan Dickinson

The Jeaga Indians held Jonathan Dickinson and other passengers of the English ship, The Reformation, captive after they shipwrecked in 1696. After the Jeaga allowed the passengers to leave, the crew traveled 230 miles to St. Augustine.

Osterkuchen – Easter Cake

Frohe Ostern – *Happy Easter!*

Cake:

2 cups flour
1 dash salt
1 egg

3 tablespoons sweet cream
½ cup sugar
2 sticks unsalted butter

Filling:

2½ cups milk
1 dash salt
2 tablespoons unsalted
   butter
¾ cup semolina
¾ cup blanched almonds,
   chopped
Zest of 1 lemon

5 drops almond essence
1 handful raisins (optional)
½ cup sweet cream
4 egg yolks
½ cup sugar
4 egg whites
3 tablespoons sugar
Confectioners' sugar for
   dusting

Sift flour into large bowl. Add salt. Mix egg, cream, and sugar in separate bowl. Melt 2 sticks butter and let cool a bit, add to egg mixture, then add to flour. Form quickly into a dough (do not knead), cover, and refrigerate until filling is ready.

Preheat oven to 400 degrees. Bring milk, salt, and 2 tablespoons butter to boil in pan. Add semolina while stirring constantly; let simmer for 5 minutes, then remove from heat. Add almonds, lemon zest, almond essence, and raisins. Mix together and let cool. Mix cream, egg yolks, and sugar together, then add to batter. Beat egg whites and sugar in separate container until stiff. Fold beaten egg whites into batter.

Roll out dough and place in a buttered springform pan. Place filling onto rolled-out dough. Bake on lowest rack for 50 minutes or until done (dough should be light brown). Before serving, lightly dust with confectioners' sugar.

Cut out an Easter Bunny shape using parchment paper. Lay paper cut out on cake before dusting with confectioners' sugar. Remove paper before serving.

Jane's Pound Cake with Lemon Jelly Icing

This is a versatile cake. It can be served plain or made into many desserts such as strawberry shortcake, or it can be topped with ice cream and hot fudge sauce. It also can be sliced horizontally and iced with chocolate or lemon jelly icing and made into a torte, a rich cake. Seven layers are recommended for a torte.

Jane's Pound Cake:

¾ cup butter, softened
1 (16-ounce) package
   confectioners' sugar
6 eggs

3 cups and 2 tablespoons
   cake flour
½ teaspoon almond extract
½ teaspoon vanilla extract

Lemon Jelly Icing:

1 cup sugar
1 whole egg
2 tablespoons butter

Juice of 1 lemon
Grated zest of 1 lemon

Preheat oven to 325 degrees. Mix butter, confectioners' sugar, and eggs until creamy; gradually add flour and extracts. Pour into a loaf pan greased with vegetable oil. Bake approximately 1 hour or until a knife inserted in center comes out clean.

Beat all icing ingredients with a spoon until well mixed. Cook on medium heat in a heavy-bottom pot while stirring for approximately 5 minutes. Allow to cool, then beat a few more minutes.

Yield: Enough icing for a 2-layer cake or the 7-layer torte.

Museum of Lifestyle & Fashion History

This Delray Beach museum offers retrospective and anthropological exhibits showcasing lifestyle, history, cultures, people, places, fashion trends, architecture, furnishings, locomotives, and toys. Inspired by everything from the Barbie® Doll and Kate Spade handbags to the history of the local post office, the museum features an eclectic mix of exhibits. Also look for their narrated bus tour of historic Delray Beach, Florida.

Chocolate Roll Cake

An impressive presentation with moderate preparation. Can be made in advance. Makes a festive "yule log" for the holidays.

7 eggs, separated
1 cup sugar
8 ounces semi-sweet
    chocolate morsels
7 tablespoons brewed coffee

1 pinch salt
Cocoa powder, unsweetened
2 cups heavy cream
2 tablespoons rum

Preheat to 350 degrees. Beat egg yolks and sugar until fluffy and creamy. Set aside.

In a small saucepan, melt chocolate and coffee over low heat. Cool.

In a medium bowl, beat egg whites and salt until stiff. Set aside.

Combine yolk mixture, chocolate mixture, and beaten egg whites by folding gently. Oil a 10x15-inch jelly roll pan. Place a sheet of buttered wax paper (overlapping the ends of the pan) on the pan, butter-side up. (Spray butter is easier.) Spread mixture evenly in pan and bake 13 minutes.

Cool 5 minutes. Cover with a slightly damp cloth and cool completely at room temperature. Refrigerate for 1 hour. Remove cloth and sprinkle generously with cocoa powder. Turn out onto another sheet of waxed paper. Remove waxed paper from top.

Whip heavy cream with rum; spread over cake. Roll up very carefully and quickly like a jelly roll. This cake will crack as it rolls - it is supposed to resemble the bark of a tree.

Yield: 12 servings

Chocolate Cheesecake

This recipe must be made at least 24 hours ahead of time.

Crust:

1½ cups chocolate wafer crumb cookies

6 tablespoons butter, melted

Cake:

12 ounces semi-sweet chocolate chips

2 (8-ounce) packages cream cheese

⅔ cup sugar

1½ cups heavy cream

2 tablespoons butter, softened

1 teaspoon vanilla

3 large eggs

Cocoa powder, for dusting

Preheat oven to 375 degrees. Combine chocolate wafer crumb cookies and 6 tablespoons melted butter. Pat mixture into bottom of a 9-inch springform pan; bake 8 minutes. Set aside.

Reduce oven to 350 degrees. Melt chocolate and set aside. Beat cream cheese in food processor until smooth. Add sugar and beat until combined. Add heavy cream, 2 tablespoons butter, and vanilla. Add eggs, one at a time, beating well. When batter is smooth, add melted chocolate. Mix well and pour into pan. Bake 15 minutes, reduce heat to 325 degrees, and bake another 45 minutes. Cool and refrigerate at least 24 hours. Before serving, dust with cocoa powder.

Yield: 8 to 10 servings

Jack Nicklaus

Palm Beach County is home to countless celebrities, including legendary golfer Jack Nicklaus, who lives in North Palm Beach with his wife Barbara. Even though he hails from Columbus, Ohio, the Golden Bear has called the Palm Beaches home for years. Many consider Nicklaus to be the greatest golfer of the 20th century, winning 18 major titles during his career. Nicklaus is more than a great golfer. His grace and style on the golf course, whether in winning or in losing, have earned Nicklaus the reputation of being a true sportsman.

Tres Leches Cake

Tres Leches Cake is served at holiday celebrations such as Cinco de Mayo in Mexico and Central America. This cake is very rich and delicious and improves with time...it is even better a few days after it is made. This cake is worth every calorie.

1½ cups all-purpose flour
1 teaspoon baking powder
½ cup unsalted butter, softened
1 cup sugar
5 eggs
½ teaspoon vanilla extract

1 cup whipping cream
1 (14-ounce) can sweetened condensed milk
1 (14-ounce) can evaporated milk
1½ cups whipping cream
1 teaspoon vanilla extract
⅓ cup sugar

Preheat oven to 350 degrees. Grease and flour a 9x13-inch glass baking dish. Sift flour and baking powder together and set aside. Cream butter and 1 cup sugar together until fluffy. Add eggs and ½ teaspoon vanilla; beat well. Add flour mixture to butter mixture, 2 tablespoons at a time, mixing well until blended. Pour batter into prepared pan. Bake 30 minutes.

When cake has finished baking, pierce it in 8 or 10 places with a fork or skewer and allow to cool. Combine 1 cup whipping cream, evaporated milk, and condensed milk and pour over cooled cake. Refrigerate at least 2 hours before serving.

When ready to serve, combine remaining 1½ cups whipping cream, 1 teaspoon vanilla, and ⅓ cup sugar, whipping until thick. Spread over top of cake.

Because of the milk in the cake, it is very important the cake is kept refrigerated until ready to serve; serve chilled. Don't remove cake from baking dish – serve directly from the dish.

Vanilla Bean

Native to tropical America, the vanilla bean was cultivated by the Aztecs, who used it to flavor their chocolate drink. The seductively aromatic vanilla bean is the fruit of a fragrant orchid. Mature vanilla pods are green and have none of the familiar fragrance or flavor. For that they need curing, which is a labor intensive, time consuming process. Over a period of several months the beans dry in the sun by day, and sweat in blankets at night. Now fermented, they develop their wonderful flavor and turn their characteristic dark brown. Vanilla extract is made by macerating chopped beans in an alcohol-water solution to extract the flavor and aging the extract for several more months.

Pumpkin Roll

Something different to serve for dessert at your Thanksgiving dinner.

3 eggs
1 cup sugar
⅔ cup pumpkin
1 teaspoon lemon juice
¾ cup flour

1 teaspoon baking powder
2 teaspoons pumpkin
   pie spice
½ teaspoon salt
1 cup nuts

Filling:

½ cup confectioners' sugar
1 cup confectioners' sugar
6 ounces cream cheese

4 tablespoons butter
½ teaspoon vanilla

Preheat oven to 350 degrees. In a mixing bowl, beat eggs with a mixer on high speed for 5 minutes. Add sugar, pumpkin, and lemon juice. In a separate bowl, combine flour, baking powder, pumpkin pie spice, and salt; fold into pumpkin mixture. Pour mixture into a greased jellyroll pan and top with nuts. Bake 15 minutes.

Remove from oven and cool slightly. Carefully remove cake from pan and place on a tea towel. Sprinkle with ½ cup confectioners' sugar, roll up, and allow to cool.

To make the filling, mix 1 cup confectioners' sugar, cream cheese, butter, and vanilla. Unroll cake, spread with cream cheese mixture, and re-roll. Chill 6 to 8 hours.

Yield: 8 to 10 servings

The Seminole Nation

By 1690, many Florida natives had perished from imported European diseases and enslavement. The first English traders called the native Americans in Florida "Seminoles" after the Hitchiti phrase meaning free peoples. The tribes took in runaway slaves from the Spanish, English, and Americans and welcomed them into their lives.

Holiday Cranberry Orange Pound Cake

5 large eggs
1 teaspoon vanilla
1 teaspoon orange zest
Juice of 1 orange
2 sticks unsalted butter

1⅓ cups sugar
¼ teaspoon salt
2 cups sifted cake flour
½ bag fresh cranberries

Preheat oven to 325 degrees. Grease and flour a 9x5-inch loaf pan. Whisk together eggs, vanilla, orange zest, and orange juice. Beat butter in a mixing bowl until light and fluffy, about 1 minute. Gradually add sugar and salt; beat on high speed about 5 minutes. Reduce speed and slowly add egg mixture. Increase speed to medium and beat 3 to 4 minutes. Add flour in three parts, beating on low speed until smooth. Fold in cranberries. Pour batter into pan and bake 1 hour or until toothpick inserted in center comes out clean.

Yield: 8 to 12 servings, depending on how you cut slices

Uncle Dennis' U.S.S. Coral Sea Chocolate Chip Cookies

Need to feed a large crowd? This recipe serves the crew of an aircraft carrier or nuclear submarine or 1,000 of your closest friends!

62 pounds butter
62 pounds sugar
31 pounds brown sugar
250 eggs
3 cups vanilla extract

140 pounds flour
1 pound salt
1 pound baking soda
92 pounds chocolate chips
50 pounds chopped nuts

Preheat oven to 350 degrees. Combine butter, sugars, eggs, and vanilla. Add flour, salt, and baking soda. Stir in chocolate chips and nuts. Drop by spoonfuls onto baking sheets. Bake 10 minutes.

Chunky Chocolate Drops

These are great big decadent cookies.

6 ounces bittersweet or plain chocolate, chopped into small pieces
½ cup unsalted butter, diced
2 large eggs
½ cup granulated sugar
⅓ cup light brown sugar
6 tablespoons flour
¼ cup cocoa powder
1 teaspoon baking powder
2 teaspoons vanilla
1 pinch salt
1 cup pecans, toasted and coarsely chopped
1 cup (6-ounce package) plain chocolate chips
4 ounces fine quality white chocolate, chopped into small pieces
4 ounces fine quality milk chocolate, chopped into small pieces

Preheat oven to 325 degrees. Grease two large baking sheets. In a medium saucepan over low heat, melt bittersweet (or plain) chocolate and butter until smooth, stirring frequently. Remove from heat and leave to cool slightly.

In a large mixing bowl, beat eggs and sugars until pale and creamy. Gradually pour in melted chocolate mixture, beating well. Beat in flour, cocoa, baking powder, and vanilla. Stir in remaining ingredients.

Drop heaping tablespoons of mixture onto baking sheets, 4 inches apart. Flatten each to a 3-inch round; only 4 to 6 cookies will fit on each sheet. Bake 8 to 10 minutes, until tops are shiny and cracked and edges look crisp. Do not overbake or cookies will break when removed from baking sheets.

Remove baking sheets to wire racks to cool for 2 minutes until cookies are just set, then carefully transfer cookies to wire racks to cool completely.

Yield: 8 to 12 large cookies

Addison Mizner

It is hard to imagine that Mediterranean-style architecture did not exist in our area before Addison Mizner. He is renowned as the architect who brought that style here. An extraordinary promoter, he arrived here without any money of his own. His wealthy clients loved his elaborate, eclectic, old world touches. He had no formal architectural training yet he turned out one mansion after another. Legend has it that one mansion had a beautiful staircase leading to nowhere and another was designed without a kitchen.

White Chocolate Hazelnut Cookies

1 stick butter, softened
1¼ cups all-purpose flour
⅔ cup sugar
1 egg
½ teaspoon baking powder

1 (6-ounce) package white
    baking bar with cocoa
    butter, coarsely chopped
    (approximately 1 cup)
½ cup coarsely chopped
    hazelnuts, pecans, or
    macadamia nuts

Miami City Ballet

For twenty years, Miami City Ballet, under the direction of former New York City Ballet superstar Edward Villella, has been providing delectable fare for the cultural palates of Palm Beach residents and visitors. Among the nation's largest troupes, the Company brings five programs – from classical to contemporary to the Nutcracker – to the Kravis Center each year. This is usually the most Kravis shows presented by any local or regional arts company. Miami City Ballet performs in four Florida home counties and tours regularly to bring a taste of Florida culture to the rest of the nation.

Preheat oven to 375 degrees. In a large mixing bowl, beat butter with electric mixer on medium to high speed about 30 seconds or until softened. Add half the flour to the butter. Add sugar, egg, and baking powder. Beat until thoroughly combined. Beat or stir in the remaining flour. Stir in baking bar and nuts. Drop dough from rounded tablespoon 2 inches apart on ungreased cookie sheet. Bake approximately 8 minutes or until edges are slightly browned. Cool on wire rack.

Yield: About 30 cookies

Frosted Lemon Cookies

When zesting, be sure to get only the outermost colorful layer of the peel. The white pith below is bitter and should not be used.

Cookies:

2½ cups all-purpose flour
1½ cups sugar
2 sticks butter
2 eggs
1 tablespoon grated lemon
    zest

1 tablespoon lemon juice
1½ teaspoons cream of tartar
1 teaspoon baking soda
¼ teaspoon salt

Glaze:

2½ cups confectioners'
    sugar

¼ cup lemon juice
Lemon zest (optional)

Steamboats

Steamboats provided one of the earliest means of travel in our area. With no paved roads or rail service, steamboats were the best means of transportation around Lake Worth.

Heat oven to 400 degrees. Combine all ingredients in large bowl. Beat at low speed until well mixed, scraping bowl often. Drop dough by rounded teaspoonfuls 2 inches apart onto ungreased cookie sheet. Bake 6 to 8 minutes or until edges are lightly browned.

Combine glaze ingredients in small bowl and stir until smooth. Frost warm cookies with glaze. Sprinkle with lemon zest, if desired.

Yield: 5 dozen cookies

Lemon Cheesecake Bars

To easily remove bars from pan, line pan with foil before pressing crumb mixture onto bottom of pan.

Crust:

1½ cups soft coconut macaroon cookie crumbs

2 tablespoons butter, melted

Bars:

2 (8-ounce) packages cream cheese, softened

½ cup sugar

1 tablespoon fresh lemon juice

½ teaspoon vanilla

½ teaspoon grated lemon zest

2 eggs

Preheat oven to 350 degrees. Mix crumbs and butter. Press firmly onto bottom of greased 8-inch square baking pan.

Mix cream cheese, sugar, lemon juice, vanilla, and lemon zest with electric mixer on medium speed until well blended. Add eggs; mix just until blended. Pour over crust.

Bake 20 to 25 minutes or until center is almost set. Cool. Refrigerate 3 hours or overnight.

Yield: 12 servings

Coconut Macaroons

A favorite Passover treat, these are delicious anytime and so easy.

1 (14-ounce) package sweetened shredded coconut

1 (14-ounce) can sweetened condensed milk

1 teaspoon vanilla

Preheat oven to 350 degrees. Mix all ingredients in a bowl. Drop small teaspoonfuls onto nonstick cookie sheet. Bake 15 minutes or until golden brown. Cool on wax paper.

Grandma Rose's Mandel Brot

Mandel Brot, or mandel bread, is a traditional Jewish "biscotti." These cookies are very popular because they are not too sweet. They are great for dunking in coffee and they freeze well, assuming there are any left over! These cookies make visits with Grandma Rose a treat.

½ cup sugar
5 ounces vegetable oil
2 eggs
2 teaspoons vanilla extract
¾ cup chocolate chips or
    raisins

¾ cup chopped walnuts
2 cups unsifted flour
1 teaspoon baking powder
Cinnamon, for sprinkling on
    top of loaves

Preheat oven to 350 degrees. Beat together sugar, oil, eggs, and vanilla for approximately 1 minute. Add chocolate chips or raisins and walnuts to mixture. Add flour and baking powder and mix well. Divide dough into two elongated loaves, approximately rectangular in shape and about ¾-inches high. Place on a cookie sheet and sprinkle with cinnamon. Bake 22 minutes, then remove from oven. While still warm, slice each loaf into approximately 15 slices. Flip each slice on its side and bake an additional 4 to 5 minutes.

Yield: Approximately 30 slices

Mexican Churros

These fried pastry sticks with cinnamon and sugar are everywhere in Mexico and loved by everyone.

1 cup water
¾ cup sugar, divided into
    ¼ cup and ½ cup
½ teaspoon salt

2 tablespoons vegetable oil
1 cup all-purpose flour
2 quarts oil for frying
1 teaspoon ground cinnamon

In a small saucepan over medium heat, combine water, ¼ cup sugar, salt, and vegetable oil. Bring to a boil and remove from heat. Stir in flour until mixture forms a ball. Heat oil for frying to 375 degrees in a deep-fryer or deep skillet. Pipe strips of dough into hot oil using a pastry bag. Fry until golden; drain on paper towels.

Combine ½ cup sugar and cinnamon. Roll drained churros in cinnamon and sugar mixture.

Love

You're the cream in my coffee,

You're the salt in my stew

You will always be my necessity,

I'd be lost without you.

~B.G. De Sylva, Lew Brown, and Ray Henderson 1923

Rum Balls

Serve these chilled when it is not the holiday season for a different treat.

2 cups crushed vanilla wafers
1 cup chopped nuts
2 tablespoons unsweetened cocoa powder
2 tablespoons white corn syrup
¼ cup rum (or other liqueur)
1 cup confectioners' sugar
Additonal confectioners' sugar for rolling

Place all ingredients in a bowl and mix well. Shape into 1-inch balls and roll twice in confectioners' sugar. Store in plastic bags or tin can.

Yield: About 4 dozen

Irish Coffee Ice Cream Pie

Frozen perfection.

Crust:
1 (8½-ounce) package chocolate wafer cookies, crushed to crumbs
1 stick butter, melted
¼ cup finely chopped pecans
1 tablespoon coffee liqueur

Filling:
1 quart coffee ice cream, softened
1 cup heavy cream, chilled well
2 tablespoons sugar
1 tablespoon Irish whiskey
1 teaspoon instant espresso powder
Chocolate coffee bean candies for garnish

Preheat oven to 350 degrees. Mix cookie crumbs, butter, pecans, and coffee liqueur. Press into a 9-inch pie pan and bake until set, about 8 minutes. Cool completely, then freeze for 1 hour.

Spread ice cream into crust and freeze until set. Beat cream to soft peaks; add sugar, Irish whiskey, and espresso powder, then beat until stiff. Pipe decoratively over ice cream and garnish with candies. Freeze for at least 8 hours.

Yield: 6 to 8 servings

Mara Vaca Key Lime Pie

A non-traditional Key lime pie with lots of tanginess.

Crust:

1½ cups lemonsnap
    cookies, crushed
½ cup graham cracker
    crumbs

2 tablespoons confectioners'
    sugar
½ stick butter, melted

Key Lime Filling:

1 cup sugar
⅓ cup cornstarch
1½ cups cream
4 egg yolks
½ cup freshly squeezed Key
    lime juice

½ stick salted butter, cut up
1 tablespoon lime zest
5 ounces sweetened, flaked
    coconut, toasted

Bixa orellana

*Also called Annato
or lipstick tree, this
plant produces seeds
that are used in
cooking and making
dyes. The seeds are
ground to produce
a reddish-yellow dye
that is used to color
margarine and
cheese. It's also
used as a coloring-
flavoring ingredient
in Latin American
and Caribbean
cuisine. In some
cultures, the
pigment is used to
color lips and skin.*

Preheat oven to 350 degrees. To make the crust, combine crushed cookies, cracker crumbs, and sugar. Stir in melted butter. Press mixture into bottom of a square baking dish, coming up the sides only ¼ inch. Bake 10 minutes. Cool.

In a medium saucepan, mix together sugar and cornstarch. Add cream slowly, stirring until smooth. Cook mixture over medium-high heat, stirring constantly until nice and thick. Remove from heat.

In a small bowl, whisk egg yolks. Add 5 tablespoons of the hot mixture, 1 tablespoon at a time; whisk after each addition. Pour yolks back into saucepan of hot mixture and cook over medium-low heat for 3 minutes, stirring constantly. Remove from heat, add lime juice, and stir. Add butter and zest; stir until thoroughly mixed. Pour into crust and allow to cool in refrigerator until firm to the touch, approximately 6 hours. Sprinkle toasted coconut evenly across top.

Bottled Key lime juice may be substituted if fresh juice is not available.

Yield: 8 servings

Margarita Key Lime Pie

Gingersnap Crust:

¾ cup sweetened flaked
   coconut, toasted.
18 gingersnap cookies,
   crumbled

3 tablespoons unsalted
   butter, melted

Key Lime Filling:

4 large eggs
½ cup fresh Key lime juice
¼ cup orange liqueur
¼ cup tequila

2 (14-ounce) cans sweetened
   condensed milk
2 teaspoons shredded lime
   zest
2 cups whipping cream

Key Lime Vs. Persian Lime

*The Key lime is
Florida's own delicacy
which originated in
the Florida Keys. It is
smaller than your
average, supermarket
variety Persian lime,
and it has a yellower
skin and more seeds.
Each one yields only a
few teaspoons of juice.
Of course, we think
Key limes taste better,
but many pie bakers
find that the two
types of limes can be
interchangeable when
making Key lime pie.
Local Key limes are
available from April
through November.
When they are ripe,
the skin is yellow
and the tart juice
is almost sweet,
which is what
makes them
perfect for baking
pies.*

Preheat oven to 350 degrees. Combine coconut, gingersnap crumbs, and butter. Press into bottom and up sides of a 9-inch pie plate. Bake 8 minutes; cool.

Combine eggs, lime juice, orange liqueur, tequila, and condensed milk in a heavy saucepan over medium heat, stirring often, 20 minutes or until a candy thermometer registers 165 degrees. Remove from heat. Stir in lime zest; cool 2 hours or until completely cooled.

Beat whipping cream with an electric mixer at high speed until soft peaks form. Fold into cooled egg mixture. Spoon into crust.

Freeze 2 hours or until firm. Let stand 20 minutes before cutting.

Yield: 6 to 8 servings

Mango Pie

Fresh mangoes from your tree can be one of the great joys of South Florida living.

Crust:

2½ cups flour	1 stick butter
2 tablespoons confectioners' sugar	6 tablespoons shortening
	4-5 tablespoons water
2 teaspoons lemon zest	

Filling:

6 mangoes, chopped	¼-½ cup sugar
Cinnamon, to taste	2 tablespoons flour
1 teaspoon almond extract	1 tablespoon crushed almonds
1 teaspoon lemon juice	1 tablespoon flour

Mix together flour, confectioners' sugar, and lemon zest. Cut butter and shortening into flour mixture until mixture is crumbly. Sprinkle water 1 tablespoon at a time over dough. Stir with a fork until dry ingredients are moistened. Shape into a ball, cut in half, and chill for at least 30 minutes. Roll out one-half for bottom crust and line a 9-inch pie pan. Freeze for 2 hours. Leave other half of pastry covered in refrigerator until needed to be rolled and used for top crust.

Preheat oven to 350 degrees. Bake bottom crust 20 minutes.

Again, preheat oven to 350 degrees. In a bowl, mix together mangoes, cinnamon, almond extract, lemon juice, sugar, and 2 tablespoons flour; set aside. Sprinkle crushed almonds and 1 tablespoon flour over bottom of the baked bottom crust. Pour mango filling into crust. Roll out remaining pastry and transfer to top of pie. Cut slits in top crust to let steam escape. Brush pastry lightly with beaten egg yolk, if desired. Bake 30 to 45 minutes or until golden brown. Let pie cool before slicing.

Yield: 6 to 8 servings

The Morikami's Festivals & Public Programs

The thundering taiko drums of Fushu Daiko, the smoky jazz of Chicago artist Yoko Noge, the interactive storytelling of Kuniko Yamamoto, and the delicate creations of candy maker, Miyuki Sugimori are favorite features. On Children's Day, held in April, kids of all ages can make traditional Japanese art projects, while learning taiko drumming. At the Bon Festival, The Morikami welcomes back the spirits of loved ones who have passed away. Visitors can ring in the New Year during Oshogatsu celebration, a traditional time of new beginnings and hope in January.

Classic Key Lime Pie

Key lime pie recipes have topping and crust variations. The toppings are either a meringue or whipped cream. Meringue always makes a beautiful presentation, peaks broiled slightly to a golden brown. Traditionally, a pastry pie crust is used, but a graham cracker crust is more popular. Since a Key lime pie is kept and served cold, a pastry crust tends to get soggy, but a graham cracker crust does not.

3 egg yolks (if you are going to make meringue, reserve whites)

1 (14-ounce) can sweetened condensed milk

½ cup Key lime juice

2 teaspoons shredded lime zest

1 (9-inch) graham cracker pie crust

Meringue or whipped cream (fresh is preferred)

Meringue:

4 egg whites

1 pinch salt

1 cup sugar

Preheat oven to 350 degrees. Combine egg yolks and condensed milk in a mixing bowl. Beat with a mixer at high speed until light and fluffy, about 5 minutes. Gradually beat in lime juice and lime zest. Pour mixture into crust.

If topping with whipped cream, bake about 12 minutes (to cook eggs). Cool slightly and refrigerate. Serve with a dollop of whipped cream.

If using meringue, beat egg whites with salt until they hold soft peaks, add sugar, beating, 1 tablespoon at a time, until mixture holds stiff peaks. Spread meringue over filling. Bake on center rack 15 minutes or until meringue is just golden. Chill at least 2 hours before serving.

Yield: 8 servings

continued

Classic Key Lime Pie continued

Delicious variations from the usual graham cracker crust:

Almond Crumb Crust:

1 cup graham cracker crumbs
⅔ cup blanched almonds, lightly toasted, cooled, and finely ground in a food processor

4 tablespoons unsalted butter, melted and slightly cooled
¼ cup sugar

Preheat oven to 350 degrees. In a bowl, combine crumbs, almonds, butter, and sugar. Press mixture onto bottom and up sides of a 9-inch pie plate. Bake crust on center rack for 10 minutes or until lightly browned. Cool on cooling rack.

Pecan Crust:

⅔ cup pecans
4 tablespoons butter
1 cup graham cracker crumbs

1 teaspoon shredded lime zest
½ teaspoon cinnamon
¼ cup sugar

Preheat oven to 350 degrees. Sauté pecans in butter until lightly browned. Place nuts and butter in food processor or blender. Add graham cracker crumbs, lime zest, cinnamon, and sugar; mix until coarse. Press into a 9-inch pie plate, reserving some of the mixture for garnish. Bake crust on center rack for 10 minutes or until lightly browned. Cool on cooling rack.

Old-Fashioned Raspberry Pie

Sweet, tart, and full of flavor.

2 pie crusts, uncooked
½ cup sugar
2 tablespoons flour
1 teaspoon instant tapioca

2 cups fresh or frozen raspberries
1 teaspoon lemon juice
½ tablespoon melted butter

Preheat oven to 375 degrees. Place one of the pie crusts in a 9-inch pie plate. In a bowl, mix sugar, flour, and tapioca. Add raspberries, lemon juice, and butter. Pour mixture into crust, cover with second crust, and seal. Add decorative cuts to vent steam. Bake 30 minutes or until crust is golden.

Malpighia glabra

Barbados cherry is a large shrub or small tree that produces crabapple-sized, pretty red cherries that have more vitamin C than citrus. The tangy (some would say, sour) fruit tastes like a cross between crabapple and cherry, with a cherry-like texture. The fruits are eaten fresh (watch out for three small pits in each fruit) or used to make jellies.

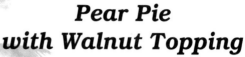

Pear Pie with Walnut Topping

You will need a fully baked 9-inch pastry crust for this recipe.

Filling:

¼ cup light brown sugar
¼ cup sugar
2 tablespoons cornstarch
1 teaspoon apple pie spice

5 large d'anjou pears, peeled, cored, and sliced
1 teaspoon lemon juice (optional)

Topping:

2 tablespoons light brown sugar
¼ cup granular sugar
½ cup flour

¼ teaspoon cinnamon
¼ teaspoon nutmeg
½ cup chopped walnuts
4 tablespoons butter, cut into slices

Preheat oven to 375 degrees. Combine sugars, cornstarch, and apple pie spice in a mixing bowl. Add pears and toss gently. If desired, add lemon juice to maintain pear color.

Combine all topping ingredients in a small mixing bowl. Cut mixture with a knife until very coarse and crumbly.

Fill pie crust with filling. Cover pie evenly and completely with topping, pressing down gently; this will prevent pears from burning. Bake 1 hour or until filling bubbles through topping. Serve warm or at room temperature.

Yield: 6 to 8 servings

Mom's Pumpkin Chiffon Pie

You will need a pre-baked pie crust for this recipe, but after that the pie itself requires no baking.

1 envelope unflavored
   gelatin
¾ cup brown sugar
½ teaspoon salt
1 teaspoon nutmeg
1 teaspoon cinnamon
½ cup evaporated milk
¼ cup water
3 eggs, separated

1 (15-ounce) can pumpkin
¼ cup sugar, and additional
   to taste
1 (9-inch) baked and cooled
   pastry crust
1 cup whipping cream
Nutmeg and roasted pecans
   or candied cherries, for
   garnish

Combine gelatin, brown sugar, salt, nutmeg, and cinnamon in a saucepan. Stir in milk, water, egg yolks, and pumpkin. Mix well and cook over medium heat until heated through and gelatin is dissolved. Remove from heat and chill approximately 30 minutes, until mixture mounds when dropped from a spoon.

Beat egg whites until stiff; add sugar to taste. Fold into gelatin mixture. Turn into pie crust and chill until firm.

Beat whipping cream with sugar until fairly stiff peaks form. Decorate top of pie with whipped cream. Dust with nutmeg and roasted pecans or candied cherries.

Yield: 8 to 10 servings

Palm Beach Dramaworks

Palm Beach Dramaworks calls home an intimate 84-seat black-box theatre in the heart of West Palm Beach on Banyan Boulevard. This award winning professional company plays a vital role in the cultural development of downtown West Palm Beach. Guided since 2000 by the artistic vision of its founding members and with the support of its dedicated Board of Directors, Dramaworks is committed to its mission of providing a home for South Florida actors, directors, designers, and playwrights, and presenting high-quality, seldom produced, classic and contemporary plays.

Black Bottom Pie

Crust:

25 gingersnaps, crushed   5 tablespoons butter, melted

Filling:

1¼ cups milk   1 teaspoon vanilla
2 eggs, beaten   1 tablespoon light rum
½ cup sugar   ¾ cup heavy cream
1 tablespoon cornstarch   ½ ounce bittersweet
1 ounce bittersweet   chocolate, shaved and
   chocolate, melted   grated

Preheat oven to 350 degrees. Combine gingersnap crumbs and butter. Press evenly into a 9-inch pie pan. Bake 10 minutes. Remove from oven and cool.

Scald milk in a double boiler. Slowly add eggs and blend. Combine sugar and cornstarch and stir into egg mixture. Cook, stirring occasionally, 10 minutes or until custard coats a spoon. Transfer ⅓ of custard into a bowl. Add melted chocolate to bowl and stir until smooth. Mix in vanilla. Stir remaining custard in double boiler until cool to avoid lumping. Mix in rum.

Whip cream until soft peaks form. Spoon chocolate custard into prepared crust. Spoon rum custard over chocolate custard and level off. Spread with whipped cream and sprinkle with shaved chocolate. Refrigerate until set, preferably overnight.

Yield: 6 to 8 servings

Traveler's Palm

This distinctive plant is not a true palm, but a cross between a banana and a palm. Its long green leaves extend out from the trunk, resembling a fan. The leaves can be 10 feet long and up to 20 inches wide. It blooms throughout the year and produces brown fruit containing pale blue seeds. They get their name from the reserve of water they hold in their leaf base ready for the thirsty soul who can handle such a large plant.

Contact List for Cultural Organizations

Armory Art Center
1703 Lake Ave., West Palm Beach
(561) 832-1776 www.armoryart.org
Page 36

Art Deco Society of the Palm Beaches
325 SW 29th Ave., Delray Beach
(561) 276-9925
Page 41

Arthur R. Marshall Foundation
525 S. Flagler Dr., #456, West Palm Beach
(561) 805-TREE www.artmarshall.org
Page 42

Artists Showcase of the Palm Beaches
815 Palm Beach Lakes Blvd., West Palm Beach
(561) 832-1323 www.artistshowcase.org
Page 81

Ballet Florida
500 Fern St., West Palm Beach
(561) 659-2000 www.balletflorida.com
Page 202

Boca Ballet Theatre
7630 NW 6th Ave., Boca Raton
(561) 995-8356 www.bocaballet.org
Page 86

Boca Raton Historical Society
71 N. Federal Hwy., Boca Raton
(561) 395-6766 www.bocahistory.org
Page 61

Boca Raton Museum of Art
501 Plaza Real, Boca Raton
(561) 392-2500 www.bocamuseum.org
Page 154

Boynton Womans Club
1010 S. Federal Hwy. Boynton Beach
(561) 369-2300
www.boyntonwomansclub.com
Page 208

Burt Reynolds Museum
100 N. US Hwy 1, Jupiter
(561) 743-9955
www.burtreynoldsmuseum.org
Page 130

Caldwell Theatre Company
7873 N. Federal Hwy., Boca Raton
(561) 241-7432 www.caldwelltheatre.com
Page 83

DuBois Pioneer House
See Loxahatchee River Historical Society
Page 155

Florida Atlantic University's School of the Arts
Boca Raton Campus
http://www.fau.edu/divdept/schmidt/
Page 167

Florida Stage
262 S. Ocean Blvd., Manalapan
(561) 585-3433 www.floridastage.org
Page 184

Henry Morrison Flagler Museum
One Whitehall Way, Palm Beach
(561) 655-2833 www.flaglermuseum.us
Page 126

Historical Society of Palm Beach
139 North County Road, Palm Beach
(561) 832-4164
www.historicalsocietypbc.org
Page 95

Jeannette Hare Art Gallery at Northwood University
2600 Military Trail, Turner Bldg.,
    West Palm Beach
561 478-5538 www.northwood.edu
Page 191

Jewish Community Center of the Greater Palm Beaches
Harold and Sylvia Kaplan JCC
3151 N. Military Trail, West Palm Beach
(561) 689-7700 www.kaplanjcc.org
Page 211

Jupiter Inlet Lighthouse
See Loxahatchee River Historical Society
Page 143

Klein Dance
811 Lake Avenue, Lake Worth
(561) 586-1889
Page 45

Lake Worth Playhouse
713 Lake Ave., Lake Worth
(561) 586-6169 www.lakeworthplayhouse.org
Page 133

Lighthouse Center for the Arts
Gallery Square North
373 Tequesta Drive, Tequesta
(561) 746-3101 www.lighthousearts.org
Page 199

Loggerhead Marinelife Center –
See Marinelife Center of Juno Beach
Page 159 *continued*

Loxahatchee River Historical Society
805 N. U.S. Hwy 1, Jupiter
(561) 747-6639 www.lrhs.org
Page 143

Lynn University
3601 N. Military Trail, Boca Raton
(800) 888-5966 www.lynn.edu
Page 157

Maltz Jupiter Theatre
1001 East Indiantown Rd., Jupiter
(561) 575-2223 www.jupitertheatre.org
Page 147

Marinelife Center of Juno Beach
14200 US Hwy 1, Juno Beach
(561) 627-8280 www.marinelife.org
Page 143

Miami City Ballet
at the Kravis Center for the Performing Arts
(877) 929-7010 www.miamicityballet.org
Page 226

Morikami Museum and Japanese Gardens
4000 Morikami Park Rd., Delray Beach
(561) 495-0233 www.morikami.org
Page 137, 172, 233

Mounts Botanical Garden
531 N. Military Trail, West Palm Beach
(561) 233-1757 www.mounts.org
Page 34

Museum of Lifestyle and Fashion History
322 NE 2nd Ave., Delray Beach
(561) 243-2662 www.mlfhmuseum.org
Page 219

Northwood University
2600 Military Trail, West Palm Beach
(561) 478-5500 www.northwood.edu
Page 21

Norton Museum of Art
1451 S. Olive Ave., West Palm Beach
(561) 832-5196 www.norton.org
Page 88

Old School Square
51 N. Swinton Ave., Delray Beach
(561) 243-7922 www.oldschool.org
Page 102

Palm Beach Dramaworks
322 Banyan Blvd., West Palm Beach
(561) 514-4042 www.palmbeachdramaworks.org
Page 237

Palm Beach Opera
415 S. Olive Ave., West Palm Beach
(561) 833-7888 www.pbopera.org
Page 58

Palm Beach Photographic Centre
55 NE 2nd Ave., Delray Beach
(561) 276-9797 www.workshop.org
Page 49

Palm Beach POPS
500 Australian Ave. S. #100, West Palm Beach
(561) 832-7677 www.palmbeachpops.com
Page 197

Palm Beach Zoo at Dreher Park
1301 Summit Blvd., West Palm Beach
(561) 547-9453 www.palmbeachzoo.org
Page 76

Raymond F. Kravis Center for the Performing Arts
701 Okeechobee Blvd., West Palm Beach
(561) 832-7469 www.kravis.org
Page 31, 111

S.D. Spady Cultural Arts Museum
170 NW 5th Ave., Delray Beach
(561) 279-8883
Page 143

Schoolhouse Children's Museum
129 E. Ocean Ave., Boynton Beach
(561) 742-6780
Page 53

The Society of the Four Arts
2 Four Arts Plaza, Palm Beach
(561) 659-8506 www.fourarts.org
Page 213

South Florida Science Museum
4801 Dreher Trail N., West Palm Beach
(561) 832-1988 www.sfsm.org
Page 139

Suncoast Community High School
600 West 28th Street, Riviera Beach
(561) 882-3400
www.suncoasths.palmbeach.k12.fl.us
page 74

Sunfest
525 Clematis Ave., West Palm Beach
(800) SUN-FEST www.sunfest.com
Page 198

Women in the Visual Arts
330 NE 2nd Ave., Delray Beach,
(561) 276-5579 www.witva.org
Page 204

Young Singers of the Palm Beaches
701 Okeechobee Blvd., #211, West Palm Beach
(561) 659-2332 www.yspb.com
Page 169

Index

A

A Spa in Your Refrigerator 43
Abuela's Puddin' 204
Aegean Seafood Salad 91
Aged Sherry Vinaigrette 70
Almond Cake 215
Almond-Crusted Grouper 172
Angel Hair Pasta with
  Sun-Dried Tomato Sauce 188

Appetizers *(also see Dips and Spreads)*
  Blinis 28
  Blue Crab and Sweet Corn Fritters 30
  Combo Pot Stickers 23
  Conch Fritters 29
  Crab and Artichoke Beignets 35
  Crab Cakes with Mango Salsa 32
  Crab Louie Martini 33
  Florentine Puffs 19
  Floribbean Ceviche
    of Yellowtail Snapper 37
  Grilled Bacon Wrapped Shrimp with
    Creole Rémoulade 38
  Grilled Margarita Shrimp 39
  Hot Artichoke-Lobster Flowers 27
  Jumbo Lump Crab Cakes 31
  Marshalls' Mussels 42
  Meat Samosas 22
  Mushroom Turnovers 20
  Mushrooms de Provence 19
  Pan Seared Scallops
    with Vegetable Aïoli 41
  Pierods – a Latvian Specialty 24
  Sazio Stuffed Portobello 25
  Smoked and Fresh Salmon Tartar 36
  Spanakopita – Greek Spinach Pie 26
  Steamed Corn Custard with Crab 34
  T-WA Shrimp 40
  Tom's Garlic Chicken Wings 21

Apples
  Apple Chutney 114
  Apple Pancake Café L'Europe 59
  Island Style Chutney 171
  Joy's Apple Bread 54
  Nantucket Island Salad 78
  Stuffed Leg of Lamb 153
  Upside-Down Apple Cake 216

Apricots
  Apricot Sweet Potatoes 124
  Granola Cereal 60
Armenian Broccoli Salad 82

Artichokes
  Artichoke Hazelnut Risotto 199
  Crab and Artichoke Beignets 35
  Hot Artichoke-Lobster Flowers 27
  Shrimp Dijonaise 182
  Spinach and Artichoke Casserole 126

Asparagus
  Summer Salad
    with Balsamic Vinaigrette 79
  Sunset Asparagus 120
  Veal Oscar from
    The Breakers, Palm Beach 148

Avocados
  Crab and Avocado Salad Louis 92
  Cucumber and Avocado Soup with
    Tomato and Basil Salad 104
  Floribbean Ceviche
    of Yellowtail Snapper 37
  Theory of Knowledge Bean Salad 74

B

Bacon *(see Pork)*
Baked Egg Frittata 62
Baked Gruyère Polenta 200
Baked Pompano 163
Balsamic Vinaigrette 79
Bammy Slices, Jamaican Golden 121
Barbecued Garlic Shrimp 181

Beans and Peas
  Aegean Seafood Salad 91
  Beef in Spicy Tomato Sauce
    with Black Beans 152
  Black Bean Sauce 148
  Black-Eyed Peas with Ham 122
  Curt's Tall Salad 81
  Easy Paella 140
  Green Bean and Tomato Salad 83
  Green Beans and Mushrooms
    in Garlic Sauce 120
  Moroccan Golden Split Pea
    and Butternut Squash Soup 99
  Moroccan Red Bean Dip 16
  Orecchiette Pasta
    with Broccoli and Chick Peas 195
  Pasta Fagioli 103
  Peruvian Chicken Stew 145
  Red Lentil Soup
    with Garlic and Cumin 98
  Theory of Knowledge Bean Salad 74
  Tia Mirta's Arroz con Pollo
    (Aunt Mirta's Chicken with Rice) 144
  Veal Oscar from
    The Breakers, Palm Beach 148
  White Bean Dip with Herbs 17
Béarnaise Sauce 148

Beef

Beef in Spicy Tomato Sauce
with Black Beans 152
Filet of Beef (Chateaubriand) 150
Grilled Steaks with Martini Twist 151
Meat Samosas 22
Ropa Vieja 150
Sazio Skirt Steak Sandwich 118

Bell Peppers

Roasted Red Pepper Aïoli 69
Roasted Red Pepper Sauce 167

Beverages

A Spa in Your Refrigerator 43
Hibiscus 43
Irish Cream Cordial 43
Kahlúa Martini 44
Painkiller 45
Simple Syrup 45
Singer Island Cosmopolitan 44
Sparkling Berry Punch 44
Sparkling Summer Tea 46
Strawberry Daiquiri 46
White Sangría 45
Bice Pesto 190
Black Bean Sauce 148
Black Bottom Pie 238
Black-Eyed Peas with Ham 122

Blackberries

Frozen Palm Beach Terrine
with Mango-Blackberry Sauce 209
Tiramisu 212
Blinis 28
Blue Crab and Sweet Corn Fritters 30

Blueberries

Blueberry Breakfast Popover 60
Blueberry Chutney 66
Blueberry Coffee Cake 61
Bouillabaisse Base 185
Brandied Pumpkin Soup 100

Breads

Flagler Museum's Pavilion Café
Traditional Scones 56
Irish Soda Bread 53
Joy's Apple Bread 54
Mango Bread 55
Pumpkin Bread 55
Southern Cornbread 58
Strawberry Bread 57

Broccoli

Armenian Broccoli Salad 82
Brown Rice Vegetable Casserole 197
Orecchiette Pasta with
Broccoli and Chick Peas 195
Rigatoni with Broccoli
Rabe and Sausage 196
Broiled Tomatoes 129

Brunch

Apple Pancake Café L'Europe 59
Baked Egg Frittata 62
Blueberry Breakfast Popover 60
Blueberry Coffee Cake 61
Crustless Spinach Quiche 48
Dutch Zucchini Carrot Pancake 52
Fruit Salad 62
Grandma's Lazy Day Coffee Cake 63
Granola Cereal 60
L'Opera Brasserie Quiche Lorraine 49
Overnight Orange French Toast 64
Smoked Salmon Cheesecake 50
Spicy Scrambled Eggs 48
Swedish Salmon Mousse 51
Buttermilk Cake 216

C

Cabbage

Currant Coleslaw 80
Red Cabbage and Walnut Salad 85

Cakes (see Desserts)

Candy (see Desserts)

Cantaloupe

Chicken Melon Salad 90
Fruit Salad 62

Carrots

Carrot and Sweet Potato Purée 125
Dutch Zucchini Carrot Pancake 52
Glazed Carrots 128
Saffron Carrots and Turnips 130
Casa de Leon House Salad 80

Casseroles

Apricot Sweet Potatoes 124
Baked Egg Frittata 62
Brown Rice Vegetable Casserole 197
Palm Beach Coconut Yams 123
Praline Sweet Potatoes 123
Seafood Casserole Supreme 177
Spinach and Artichoke Casserole 126
Squash and Rice Casserole 198

Cauliflower

Brown Rice Vegetable Casserole 197
Cauliflower and Potato Fry 127
Creamy Parmesan Cauliflower 124
Seasoned Cauliflower 128

Cereals and Grains (also see Rice)

Baked Gruyère Polenta 198
Chanterelles and
Pine Nut Couscous 202

Curried Chicken Salad 88
Granola Cereal 60
Tabouleh 85
Tomato Couscous 162

Cheese
Baked Egg Frittata 62
Florentine Puffs 19
Gorgonzola Pear Salad from
  The Breakers, Palm Beach 75
Ham, Brie, and Mango
  Chutney "Sidillas" 116
Sun-Dried Tomato and Goat Cheese
  Spread with Pita Chips 18
Cheney's Superb Barbecue Marinade 71

Chicken (see Poultry)
Chipotle Aïoli 69

Chocolate (also see Desserts)
Black Bottom Pie 238
Chocolate Chambord Truffle Torte 205
Chocolate Cheesecake 221
Chocolate Raspberry Pavlovas 206
Chocolate Roll Cake 220
Chunky Chocolate Drops 225
Irish Coffee Ice Cream Pie 230
Passover Pralines 211
Uncle Dennis' U.S.S. Coral Sea
  Chocolate Chip Cookies 224
White Chocolate Hazelnut Cookies 226
Cilantro Dressing 68
Citrus and Olives for Fish 72
Citrus Vinaigrette 93

Clams (see Seafood)
Classic Key Lime Pie 234
Clotted Cream 56

Coconut
Chicken Kurma 136
Coconut Chutney 66
Coconut Macaroons 228
Granola Cereal 60
Palm Beach Coconut Yams 123
Combo Pot Stickers 23

Conch (see Seafood)

Condiments and Sauces
  (also see Salad Dressings)
Aged Sherry Vinaigrette 70
Apple Chutney 114
Balsamic Vinaigrette 79
Béarnaise Sauce 148
Bice Pesto 190
Black Bean Sauce 148
Blueberry Chutney 66
Bouillabaisse Base 185

Cheney's Superb
  Barbecue Marinade 71
Chili Oil 40
Chipotle Aïoli 69
Cilantro Dressing 68
Citrus and Olives for Fish 72
Citrus Vinaigrette 93
Classic Aïoli 69
Clotted Cream 56
Coconut Chutney 66
Cranberry Sauce 67
Creole Rémoulade 38
Creole Sauce 170
Dijon Dressing 88
Dill Caper Sauce 67
Easy Rémoulade Sauce 71
Fresh Herb Aïoli 69
Ginger Glaze 166
Haden Mango Molasses
  Rum Sauce 166
Island Style Chutney 171
Lemon Aïoli 69
Lime Mayonnaise 29
Louie Sauce 33
Louis Dressing 92
Mango Chutney 68, 116
Mango Corn Salsa 168
Mango Salsa 32
Orange Dill Vinaigrette 162
Oriental Ginger Dressing 70
Papaya and Vidalia
  Onion Applesauce 158
Passion Fruit Beurre Blanc Sauce 175
Pineapple Mango Salsa 175
Pinot Grigio Vinaigrette 75
Roasted Red Pepper Aïoli 69
Roasted Red Pepper Sauce 167
Rosemary Aïoli 69
Saffron Aïoli 69
Sage Aïoli 69
Spice Rub 162
Spiced Pecans 79
Sun-Dried Tomato Pesto 190
Toasted Paprika Aïoli 69
Tropical Fruit Salsa 173
Tropical Fruit Sauce 183
Vegetable Aïoli 41
Wasabi Aïoli 69
Whiskey Barbecue Sauce 72
Zuppa de Pesce Sauce 186

Cookies and Bars (see Desserts)

Corn
Blue Crab and Sweet Corn Fritters 30
Conch Chowder 106
Lobster Chowder 107
Mango Corn Salsa 168
Steamed Corn Custard with Crab 34
Cornmeal-Crusted Soft Shell Crabs 179
Couscous *(see Cereals and Grains)*
Crab *(see Seafood)*
Cranberries
Cranberry Sauce 67
Flagler Museum's Pavilion Café
   Traditional Scones 56
Holiday Cranberry
   Orange Pound Cake 224
Red Cabbage and Walnut Salad 85
Cream of Poblano
   Chili Soup with Cheese 105
Creamy Parmesan Cauliflower 124
Creole Rémoulade 38
Crustless Spinach Quiche 48
Cucumbers
Cucumber and Avocado Soup
   with Tomato and Basil Salad 104
Seafood Bar Gazpacho
   from The Breakers 112
Smoked and Fresh Salmon Tartar 36
Cumin Roasted Potatoes 129
Currant Coleslaw 80
Curried Chicken Salad 88
Curt's Tall Salad 81

D

Dan's Tomato Basil Soup 102
Desserts
Cakes
Almond Cake 215
Buttermilk Cake 216
Chocolate Chambord
   Truffle Torte 205
Chocolate Cheesecake 221
Chocolate Roll Cake 220
Holiday Cranberry
   Orange Pound Cake 224
Jane's Pound Cake
   with Lemon Jelly Icing 219
Osterkuchen – Easter Cake 218
Pumpkin Roll 223
Tres Leches Cake 222
Tropical Key Lime Cheesecake 217
Upside-Down Apple Cake 216
Candy
Passover Pralines 211

Rum Balls 230
Cookies and Bars
Chunky Chocolate Drops 225
Coconut Macaroons 228
Frosted Lemon Cookies 227
Grandma Rose's Mandel Brot 229
Lemon Cheesecake Bars 228
Mexican Churros 229
Uncle Dennis' U.S.S. Coral Sea
   Chocolate Chip Cookies 224
White Chocolate
   Hazelnut Cookies 226
Frostings and Icings
Lemon Jelly Icing 219
Pies
Black Bottom Pie 238
Classic Key Lime Pie 234
Irish Coffee Ice Cream Pie 230
Mango Pie 233
Mara Vaca Key Lime Pie 231
Margarita Key Lime Pie 232
Mom's Pumpkin Chiffon Pie 237
Old-Fashioned Raspberry Pie 235
Pear Pie with Walnut Topping 236
Puddings and Desserts
Abuela's Puddin' 204
Chocolate Raspberry Pavlovas 206
Easy Flan 208
Frozen Palm Beach Terrine with
   Mango-Blackberry Sauce 209
Icebox Potica 210
Mango Ice Cream 207
Peach and Pineapple Crisp 214
Quebec Grand-Peres au Sirop D'erable
   (Dumplings in Maple Syrup) 205
Tiramisu 212
Dijon Dressing 88
Dill Caper Sauce 67
Dips and Spreads
Eggplant Caviar 15
Hearts of Palm Spread 18
Helen's Vidalia Onion Dip 14
Moroccan Red Bean Dip 16
Olive Tapenade 17
Smoked Salmon Cheesecake 50
Sun-Dried Tomato and Goat Cheese
   Spread with Pita Chips 18
Swedish Salmon Mousse 51
Tapenade with Sun-Dried Tomatoes 16
Toasted Almond Party Spread 14
White Bean Dip with Herbs 17
Duck *(see Poultry)*
Dutch Zucchini Carrot Pancake 52

E

Easy Flan 208
Easy Grilled Fish
    with Fresh Dill Sauce 161
Easy Paella 140
Easy Rémoulade Sauce 71
Eggplant Caviar 15
Eggs (also see Brunch)
    Baked Egg Frittata 62
    Crustless Spinach Quiche 48
    Egg Safety 43
    Irish Cream Cordial 43
    L'Opera Brasserie Quiche Lorraine 49
    Spicy Scrambled Eggs 48

F

Figs and Honey Balsamic Glaze over
    Polenta, Pan-Roasted Duck Breast
    with Mission 146
Filet of Beef (Chateaubriand) 150
Fish (also see Seafood)
    Almond-Crusted Grouper 172
    Baked Pompano 163
    Conch Salad 180
    Easy Grilled Fish
        with Fresh Dill Sauce 161
    Fish Pepper Delight 164
    Fish Picatta Shack Style 165
    Floribbean Ceviche
        of Yellowtail Snapper 37
    Gingered Chilean Sea Bass 166
    Grilled Dolphin
        with Mango Corn Salsa 168
    Island-Style Baked Snapper 176
    John's Trinidad Yellowtail 175
    Macadamia-Crusted
        Yellowtail Snapper 173
    Mango Nut Grouper 169
    Pan-Seared Mahi-Mahi and
        Shrimp with Creole Sauce 170
    Pecan-Encrusted Sea Bass
        with Red Pepper Sauce 167
    Seafood Casserole Supreme 177
    Smoked and Fresh Salmon Tartar 36
    Smoked Salmon Cheesecake 50
    Snapper Caprice with
        Island-Style Chutney 171
    Snapper with Shrimp Sauce 174
    Spice-Rubbed Atlantic Salmon 162
    Spicy Salmon Chowder 110
    Spoto's Bouillabaisse 185

Swedish Salmon Mousse 51
Swordfish with
    Tomato Vinaigrette 178
    Zuppa de Pesce 186
Flagler Museum's Pavilion
    Café Traditional Scones 56
Florentine Puffs 19
Floribbean Ceviche
    of Yellowtail Snapper 37
Fresh Herb Aïoli 69
Fried Rice with Cashews 201
Frosted Lemon Cookies 227
Frozen Palm Beach Terrine
    with Mango-Blackberry Sauce 209
Fruits (also see individual listings)
    Fruit Salad 62
    Island Style Chutney 171
    Melon Salad with
        Lemongrass Shrimp 94
    Tropical Fruit Salsa 173

G

Garlic Shrimp, Barbecued 181
Ginger Glaze 166
Gingered Chilean Sea Bass 166
Glazed Carrots 128
Gnocchi 188
Gorgonzola Pear Salad from
    The Breakers, Palm Beach 75
Grandma Rose's Mandel Brot 229
Grandma's Lazy Day Coffee Cake 63
Granola Cereal 60
Grapefruit
    Citrus and Olives for Fish 72
    Lobster and Pink Grapefruit Salad 93
Grapes
    Chicken à la Vineyard 138
    Fruit Salad 62
Green Bean and Tomato Salad 83
Green Beans and Mushrooms
    in Garlic Sauce 120
Greens
    Bacon Braised Greens 122
    Mustard Greens 121
Grilling
    Barbecued Garlic Shrimp 181
    Easy Grilled Fish with
        Fresh Dill Sauce 161
    Grill Marks 151
    Grilled Bacon Wrapped Shrimp
        with Creole Rémoulade 38

Grilled Dolphin with
  Mango Corn Salsa 168
Grilled Margarita Shrimp 39
Grilled Mongolian Pork Chops 160
Grilled Steaks with Martini Twist 151
Grilled Turkey Burger
  from The Breakers, Palm Beach 114
Grilling Temperature Control 168
Grilling Tips 115
Leila's Classic Lamb Kebab 155
Lemon-Honey Chicken 132
Marinated Grilled Fennel Salad 77
Swordfish with Tomato Vinaigrette 178

H

Haden Mango Molasses Rum Sauce 166
Ham *(see Pork)*
Hearts of Palm
Floribbean Ceviche of
  Yellowtail Snapper 37
Hearts of Palm Spread 18
Hibiscus 43
Holiday Cranberry Orange Pound Cake . 224
Hot and Creamy Turkey Sandwiches 117
Hot Artichoke-Lobster Flowers 27

I

Icebox Potica 210
Icing *(see Desserts)*
Indian Chicken Cutlets 135
Indonesian Rice Salad 86
Irish Coffee Ice Cream Pie 230
Irish Cream Cordial 43
Irish Soda Bread 53
Island Style Chutney 171
Island-Style Baked Snapper 176

J

Jamaican Golden Bammy Slices 121
Jane's Pound Cake with
  Lemon Jelly Icing 219
John's Trinidad Yellowtail 175
Joy's Apple Bread 54
Jumbo Lump Crab Cakes 31

K

Kahlúa Martini 44
Key Lime Broiled Chicken 134
Kohlrabi Salad 84

L

Lamb
Lamb Curry 154
Leila's Classic Lamb Kebab 155
Macadamia Crusted Rack of Lamb 158
Meat Samosas 22
Stuffed Leg of Lamb 153
Lemon
Frosted Lemon Cookies 227
Lemon Aïoli 69
Lemon Cheesecake Bars 228
Lemon Jelly Icing 219
Lemon-Honey Chicken 132
Lime
Classic Key Lime Pie 234
Key Lime Broiled Chicken 134
Lime Mayonnaise 29
Mara Vaca Key Lime Pie 231
Margarita Key Lime Pie 232
Tropical Key Lime Cheesecake 217
Linguine with Italian Sausage 192
Lobster *(see Seafood)*
L'Opera Brasserie Quiche Lorraine 49
Louie Sauce 33
Louis Dressing 92

M

Macadamia Crusted Rack of Lamb 158
Macadamia-Crusted
  Yellowtail Snapper 173
Mandarin Salad 96
Mangoes
Cornmeal-Crusted
  Soft Shell Crabs 179
Crab Cakes with Mango Salsa 32
Frozen Palm Beach Terrine
  with Mango-Blackberry Sauce 209
Haden Mango Molasses
  Rum Sauce 166
Ham, Brie, and Mango
  Chutney "Sidillas" 116
Island Style Chutney 171
Mango Bread 55
Mango Chutney 68, 116
Mango Corn Salsa 168
Mango Ice Cream 207
Mango Nut Grouper 169
Mango Pie 233
Mango Salsa 32
Pineapple Mango Salsa 175
Mara Vaca Key Lime Pie 231
Margarita Key Lime Pie 232

Marinated Grilled Fennel Salad 77
Marshalls' Mussels 42
Meat Samosas 22
Mediterranean Pasta with Shrimp 191
Melon Salad with Lemongrass Shrimp 94
Mexican Churros 229
Mom's Pumpkin Chiffon Pie 237
Moo Goo Gai Pan 142
Morikami Chicken Curry 137
Moroccan Golden Split Pea
    and Butternut Squash Soup 99
Moroccan Red Bean Dip 16

Mushrooms
    Chanterelles and
        Pine Nut Couscous 202
    Dutch Zucchini Carrot Pancake 52
    Green Beans and
        Mushrooms in Garlic Sauce 120
    Mushroom Turnovers 20
    Mushrooms de Provence 19
    Peruvian Chicken Stew 145
    Sazio Stuffed Portobello 25
    Washing Mushrooms 19
    Yakatori Chicken 143

Mussels *(see Seafood)*
Mustard Greens 121

N

Nantucket Island Salad 78
New Orleans Shrimp Rémoulade 180

Nuts
    Almond Cake 215
    Almond-Crusted Grouper 172
    Fried Rice with Cashews 201
    Icebox Potica 210
    Macadamia Crusted Rack of Lamb 158
    Macadamia-Crusted
        Yellowtail Snapper 173
    Mango Nut Grouper 169
    Passover Pralines 211
    Pear Pie with Walnut Topping 236
    Pecan-Encrusted Sea Bass with Red
        Pepper Sauce 167
    Red Cabbage and Walnut Salad 85
    Spiced Pecans 79
    Summer Salad
        with Balsamic Vinaigrette 79
    Toasted Almond Party Spread 14
    Uncle Dennis' U.S.S. Coral Sea
        Chocolate Chip Cookies 224
    Walnut and Pear Green Salad 76
    White Chocolate Hazelnut Cookies 226

O

Old-Fashioned Raspberry Pie 235
Olives
    Citrus and Olives for Fish 72
    Olive Tapenade 17
    Tapenade with
        Sun-Dried Tomatoes 16
Onions
    Helen's Vidalia Onion Dip 14
    Macadamia Crusted Rack of Lamb 158
Orange
    Casa de Leon House Salad 80
    Chicken Fruit Salad 87
    Citrus and Olives for Fish 72
    Holiday Cranberry
        Orange Pound Cake 224
    Mandarin Salad 96
    Orange Dill Vinaigrette 162
    Overnight Orange French Toast 64
Orecchiette Pasta with
    Broccoli and Chick Peas 195
Oriental Ginger Dressing 70

P

Painkiller 45
Palm Beach Coconut Yams 123
Pan Roasted Pork Chop 156
Pan Seared Scallops
    with Vegetable Aïoli 41
Pan-Roasted Duck Breast 146
Pan-Seared Mahi-Mahi and
    Shrimp with Creole Sauce 170
Papaya
    Macadamia Crusted Rack of Lamb 158
    Papaya and Vidalia
        Onion Applesauce 158
Passion Fruit Beurre Blanc Sauce 175
Passover Pralines 211
Pasta
    Angel Hair Pasta with
        Sun-Dried Tomato Sauce 188
    Chicken Fruit Salad 87
    Chicken with Cold Sesame Noodles ... 141
    Gnocchi 188
    Linguine with Italian Sausage 192
    Lobster Penne 190
    Mediterranean Pasta with Shrimp 191
    Orecchiette Pasta with
        Broccoli and Chick Peas 195
    Pasta Fagioli 103

Rigatoni with Broccoli
Rabe and Sausage 196
Rigatoni with Grilled Vegetables 193
Seafood Casserole Supreme 177
Spaghetti Primavera
with Shrimp and Crabmeat 194
Spinach Gnocchi (Gnocchi Verde) 189

Peaches
Chicken Fruit Salad 87
Peach and Pineapple Crisp 214

Pears
Gorgonzola Pear Salad from
The Breakers, Palm Beach 75
Pear Pie with Walnut Topping 236
Walnut and Pear Green Salad 76

Peas (see Beans and Peas)

Pecans (see Nuts)
Peruvian Chicken Stew 145
Pierods – a Latvian Specialty 24

Pies (see Desserts)

Pineapple
A Spa in Your Refrigerator 43
Chicken Fruit Salad 87
Painkiller 45
Peach and Pineapple Crisp 214
Pineapple Mango Salsa 175
Pinot Grigio Vinaigrette 75
Polynesian Prawns with
Tropical Fruit Sauce 183

Pork
Bacon Braised Greens 122
Black-Eyed Peas with Ham 122
Combo Pot Stickers 23
Grilled Bacon Wrapped Shrimp
with Creole Rémoulade 38
Grilled Mongolian Pork Chops 160
Ham, Brie, and Mango
Chutney "Sidillas" 116
Linguine with Italian Sausage 192
Pan Roasted Pork Chop with
Garlic Smashed Potatoes 156
Pierods – a Latvian Specialty 24
Rigatoni with Broccoli
Rabe and Sausage 196
Ropa Vieja 150
Schinkengipfeli
(Croissants Filled with Ham) 113

Potatoes
Cauliflower and Potato Fry 127
Cumin Roasted Potatoes 129
Gnocchi 188
Pan Roasted Pork Chop with
Garlic Smashed Potatoes 156

Poultry
Chicken
Chicken à la Vineyard 138
Chicken Fruit Salad 87
Chicken Kurma 136
Chicken Marbella 134
Chicken Melon Salad 90
Chicken with
Cold Sesame Noodles 141
Chicken with
Sun-Dried Tomatoes 139
Chicken with Wine Sauce 133
Combo Pot Stickers 23
Curried Chicken Salad 88
Easy Paella 140
Indian Chicken Cutlets 135
Key Lime Broiled Chicken 134
Lemon-Honey Chicken 132
Moo Goo Gai Pan 142
Morikami Chicken Curry 137
Peruvian Chicken Stew 145
Sesame Chicken 132
Tia Mirta's Arroz con Pollo (Aunt
Mirta's Chicken with Rice) 144
Tom's Garlic Chicken Wings 21
Yakatori Chicken 143
Duck
Pan-Roasted Duck Breast 146
Turkey
Grilled Turkey Burger from
The Breakers, Palm Beach 114
Hot and Creamy
Turkey Sandwiches 117
Praline Sweet Potatoes 123

Puddings (see Desserts)

Pumpkin
Brandied Pumpkin Soup 100
Mom's Pumpkin Chiffon Pie 237
Pumpkin Bread 55
Pumpkin Roll 223

Q

Quebec Grand-Peres au Sirop D'erable
(Dumplings in Maple Syrup) 205

R

Raspberries
A Spa in Your Refrigerator 43
Chocolate Chambord Truffle Torte 205
Chocolate Raspberry Pavlovas 206
Old-Fashioned Raspberry Pie 235
Sparkling Berry Punch 44
Tiramisu 212

Red Cabbage and Walnut Salad 85
Red Lentil Soup
   with Garlic and Cumin 98

Restaurants
  Bice Restaurant
    Bice Pesto 190
    Tartara di due Salmon
      con Gazpacho 36
  Café Boulud
    Melon Salad
      with Lemongrass Shrimp 94
  Breakers Hotel, The
    Gorgonzola Pear Salad 75
    Grilled Turkey Burger 114
    Seafood Bar Gazpacho 112
    Veal Oscar 148
  Café 1451 at the Norton
    Curried Chicken Salad 88
  Café Chardonnay
    Blue Crab and
      Sweet Corn Fritters 30
    Cornmeal-Crusted
      Soft Shell Crabs 179
    Macadamia-Crusted
      Yellowtail Snapper 173
    Pan-Roasted Duck Breast 146
    Pan-Seared Mahi-Mahi and
      Shrimp with Creole Sauce 170
    Pasta Fagioli 103
    Rigatoni with Grilled Vegetables 193
    Shrimp Dijonaise 182
    Spaghetti Primavera
      with Shrimp and Crabmeat 194
    Tiramisu 212
    Zuppa de Pesce 186
  Café Du Parc
    Blini Appetizers 28
  Café L'Europe
    Apple Pancakes 59
  Carmine's Ocean Grill
    Crab Cakes 31
  City Cellar
    Spice Rubbed Atlantic Salmon 162
  Cornell Café at the Morikami Museum
    Almond-Crusted Grouper 172
    Morikami Chicken Curry 137
  E.R. Bradley's
    Crab Louie Martini 33
  Finton's Landing Bed and Breakfast,
   Keuka Lake, NY
    Cranberry Sauce 67
  Food Shack, The
    Fish Picatta Shack Style 165

  Nirvana Restaurant
    Gingered Chilean Sea Bass 166
  No Anchovies!
    Linguine with Italian Sausage 192
  Off The Vine
    Marinated Grilled Fennel Salad 77
  One Thai Restaurant
    Combo Pot Stickers 23
  Palm Beach Yacht Club, The
    John's Trinidad
      Yellowtail Snapper 175
  Pavilion Café at Whitehall
    Traditional Scones with
      Cranberries and Clotted Cream 56
  PGA National Resort & Spa
    Floribbean Ceviche of
      Yellowtail Snapper 37
    Macadamia Crusted
      Rack of Lamb 158
  Reef Grill
    T-WA Shrimp 40
  Ritz Carlton
    Pan-Roasted Pork Chop with
      Garlic Smashed Potatoes 156
  River House, The
    Island Style Baked Snapper 176
  Sazio Restaurant
    Skirt Steak Sandwich 118
    Stuffed Portobello Appetizer 25
  Spoto's Oyster Bar
    Spoto's Bouillabaisse 185
  Tabica Grill
    Mango Nut Grouper 169
  Zaza's Cucina, Ithaca, NY
    White Wine Sangría 45

Rice
Artichoke Hazelnut Risotto 199
Brown Rice Vegetable Casserole 197
Chicken with Wine Sauce 133
Easy Paella 140
Fried Rice with Cashews 201
Indonesian Rice Salad 86
Morikami Chicken Curry 137
Pan-Seared Mahi-Mahi and
  Shrimp with Creole Sauce 170
Polynesian Prawns with
  Tropical Fruit Sauce 183
Squash and Rice Casserole 198
Tia Mirta's Arroz con Pollo (Aunt
  Mirta's Chicken with Rice) 144
Rigatoni with Broccoli
  Rabe and Sausage 196
Rigatoni with Grilled Vegetables 193

Roasted Red Pepper Aïoli 69
Roasted Red Pepper Sauce 167
Ropa Vieja 150
Rosemary Aïoli 69
Rum Balls 230

S

Saffron Aïoli 69
Saffron Carrots and Turnips 130
Sage Aïoli 69

Salad Dressings
  Aged Sherry Vinaigrette 70
  Balsamic Vinaigrette 79
  Citrus Vinaigrette 93
  Dijon Dressing 88
  Louis Dressing 92
  Orange Dill Vinaigrette 162
  Oriental Ginger Dressing..................... 70
  Pinot Grigio Vinaigrette 75

Salads
  Aegean Seafood Salad 91
  Armenian Broccoli Salad 82
  Casa de Leon House Salad 80
  Chicken Fruit Salad 87
  Chicken Melon Salad 90
  Conch Salad 180
  Crab and Avocado Salad Louis 92
  Currant Coleslaw 80
  Curried Chicken Salad 88
  Curt's Tall Salad 81
  Fruit Salad 62
  Gorgonzola Pear Salad from
    The Breakers, Palm Beach 75
  Green Bean and Tomato Salad 83
  Indonesian Rice Salad 86
  Kohlrabi Salad 84
  Lobster and Pink Grapefruit Salad 93
  Mandarin Salad 96
  Marinated Grilled Fennel Salad 77
  Melon Salad with
    Lemongrass Shrimp 94
  Nantucket Island Salad 78
  Red Cabbage and Walnut Salad 85
  Summer Salad with
    Balsamic Vinaigrette 79
  Tabouleh 85
  Theory of Knowledge Bean Salad 74
  Tomato and Basil Salad 104
  Walnut and Pear Green Salad 76

Sandwiches
  Grilled Turkey Burger from
    The Breakers, Palm Beach 114

Ham, Brie, and Mango
  Chutney "Sidillas" 116
Hot and Creamy
  Turkey Sandwiches 117
Lobster Roll 115
Sazio Skirt Steak Sandwich 118
Schinkengipfeli
  (Croissants Filled with Ham) 113
Sazio Skirt Steak Sandwich 118
Sazio Stuffed Portobello 25
Scallops (see Seafood)
Scalloped Florida Lobster 184
Seafood
  Clams
    Aegean Seafood Salad 91
    Easy Paella 140
    Linguine with Italian Sausage 192
    Spoto's Bouillabaisse 185
    Zuppa de Pesce 186
  Conch
    Conch Chowder 106
    Conch Fritters 29
    Conch Salad 180
  Crab
    Blue Crab and
      Sweet Corn Fritters 30
    Cornmeal-Crusted
      Soft Shell Crabs 179
    Crab and Artichoke Beignets 35
    Crab and Avocado Salad Louis 92
    Crab Cakes with Mango Salsa 32
    Crab Louie Martini 33
    Jumbo Lump Crab Cakes 31
    Seafood Casserole Supreme 177
    She-Crab Soup 109
    Spaghetti Primavera with
      Shrimp and Crabmeat 194
    Steamed Corn Custard
      with Crab 34
  Lobster
    Hot Artichoke-Lobster Flowers 27
    Lobster and Pink
      Grapefruit Salad 93
    Lobster Bisque 108
    Lobster Chowder 107
    Lobster Penne 190
    Lobster Roll 115
    Scalloped Florida Lobster 184
    Seafood Bar Gazpacho from
      The Breakers 112
    Spoto's Bouillabaisse 185
    Zuppa de Pesce 186

Mussels
Marshalls' Mussels 42
Spoto's Bouillabaisse 185
Zuppa de Pesce 186
Scallops
Pan Seared Scallops
with Vegetable Aïoli 41
Seafood Casserole Supreme 177
Shrimp
Aegean Seafood Salad 91
Barbecued Garlic Shrimp 181
Casa de Leon House Salad 80
Combo Pot Stickers 23
Easy Paella 140
Grilled Bacon Wrapped Shrimp
with Creole Rémoulade 38
Grilled Margarita Shrimp 39
Mediterranean Pasta
with Shrimp 191
Melon Salad with
Lemongrass Shrimp 94
New Orleans
Shrimp Rémoulade 180
Pan-Seared Mahi-Mahi and
Shrimp with Creole Sauce 170
Polynesian Prawns
with Tropical Fruit Sauce 183
Seafood Casserole Supreme 177
Shrimp Chowder 111
Shrimp Dijonaise 182
Snapper with Shrimp Sauce 174
Spaghetti Primavera with
Shrimp and Crabmeat 194
T-WA Shrimp 40
Squid
Aegean Seafood Salad 91
Seasoned Cauliflower 128
Sesame Chicken 132
Singer Island Cosmopolitan 44
Smoked and Fresh Salmon Tartar 36
Smoked Salmon Cheesecake 50
Snapper Caprice
with Island-Style Chutney 171
Soups
Brandied Pumpkin Soup 100
Conch Chowder 106
Cream of Poblano Chili Soup
with Cheese 105
Cucumber and Avocado Soup with
Tomato and Basil Salad 104
Dan's Tomato Basil Soup 102
Lobster Bisque 108
Lobster Chowder 107

Moroccan Golden Split Pea
and Butternut Squash Soup 99
Pasta Fagioli 103
Peruvian Chicken Stew 145
Red Lentil Soup
with Garlic and Cumin 98
Ropa Vieja 150
Seafood Bar Gazpacho from
The Breakers 112
She-Crab Soup 109
Shrimp Chowder 111
Spicy Salmon Chowder 110
Sweet Potato Soup 101
Southern Cornbread 58
Spaghetti Primavera
with Shrimp and Crabmeat 194
Sparkling Berry Punch 44
Sparkling Summer Tea 46
Spice Rub 162
Spice-Rubbed Atlantic Salmon 162
Spiced Pecans 79
Spicy Salmon Chowder 110
Spicy Scrambled Eggs 48
Spinach
Crustless Spinach Quiche 48
Florentine Puffs 19
Sazio Stuffed Portobello 25
Shrimp Dijonaise 182
Spanakopita – Greek Spinach Pie 26
Spinach and Artichoke Casserole 126
Spinach Gnocchi (Gnocchi Verde) 189
Spoto's Bouillabaisse 185
Squash (also see Zucchini)
Baked Egg Frittata 62
Moroccan Golden Split Pea
and Butternut Squash Soup 99
Squash and Rice Casserole 198
Squid (see Seafood)
Steamed Corn Custard with Crab 34
Strawberries
A Spa in Your Refrigerator 43
Chicken Fruit Salad 87
Fruit Salad 62
Sparkling Berry Punch 44
Strawberry Bread 57
Strawberry Daiquiri 46
Summer Salad with
Balsamic Vinaigrette 79
Stuffed Leg of Lamb 153
Sun-Dried Tomato and Goat
Cheese Spread with Pita Chips 18
Sun-Dried Tomato Pesto 190
Sunset Asparagus 120

Swedish Salmon Mousse 51
Sweet Potatoes
   Apricot Sweet Potatoes 124
   Carrot and Sweet Potato Purée 125
   Macadamia Crusted Rack of Lamb 158
   Praline Sweet Potatoes 123
   Sweet Potato Soup 101
Swordfish with Tomato Vinaigrette 178

T

T-WA Shrimp 40
Tabouleh 85
Tapenade with Sun-Dried Tomatoes 16
Theory of Knowledge Bean Salad 74
Tia Mirta's Arroz con Pollo
   (Aunt Mirta's Chicken with Rice) 144
Tiramisu 212
Toasted Almond Party Spread 14
Toasted Paprika Aïoli 69
Tomatoes
   Angel Hair Pasta with
      Sun-Dried Tomato Sauce 188
   Broiled Tomatoes 129
   Chicken with Sun-Dried Tomatoes 139
   Conch Chowder 106
   Dan's Tomato Basil Soup 102
   Floribbean Ceviche
      of Yellowtail Snapper 37
   Green Bean and Tomato Salad 83
   Linguine with Italian Sausage 192
   Sun-Dried Tomato and Goat Cheese
      Spread with Pita Chips 18
   Sun-Dried Tomato Pesto 190
   Swordfish with Tomato Vinaigrette 178
   Tapenade with Sun-Dried Tomatoes 16
   Tomato and Basil Salad 104
   Tomato Couscous 162
Tom's Garlic Chicken Wings 21
Tres Leches Cake 222
Tropical Fruit Salsa 173
Tropical Fruit Sauce 183
Tropical Key Lime Cheesecake 217

Turkey *(see Poultry)*
Turnips, Saffron Carrots and 130

U

Uncle Dennis' U.S.S. Coral
   Sea Chocolate Chip Cookies 224
Upside-Down Apple Cake 216

V

Veal
   Veal Oscar from The Breakers,
      Palm Beach 148
Vegetables *(also see individual listings)*
   Vegetable Aïoli 41

W

Walnut and Pear Green Salad 76
Wasabi Aïoli 69
Watermelon
   Fruit Salad 62
   Melon Salad with
      Lemongrass Shrimp 94
Whiskey Barbecue Sauce 72
White Bean Dip with Herbs 17
White Chocolate Hazelnut Cookies 226
White Sangría 45

Y

Yakatori Chicken 143

Z

Zucchini *(also see Squash)*
   Baked Egg Frittata 62
   Dutch Zucchini Carrot Pancake 52
   Linguine with Italian Sausage 192
   Pan Roasted Pork Chop with
      Garlic Smashed Potatoes 156
   Squash and Rice Casserole 198
   Yakatori Chicken 143
Zuppa de Pesce 186
Zuppa de Pesce Sauce 186

$\mathcal{I}$llustrations

Cover Art, all Section Dividers, and art accompanying Sue Archer's bio on page 183 are copyrighted by Sue Archer.

Images that accompany our area's organizations are courtesy of the individual organizations: pages 21, 31, 34, 42, 36, 53, 58, 81, 83, 86, 89, 95, 102, 111, 112, 114, 127, 130, 133, 137, 139, 143, 145, 147, 149, 155, 157, 167, 174, 191, 197, 202, 208, 213, 219, 226.

Images from Jupiter Images and its Licensors: pages 64, 67, 70, 76, 84, 92, 107, 117, 159, 198, 201, 214, 232, 238.

Images from Corel: pages 135,164, 221.

Florida Photographic Collection, State Archives of Florida: pages 33, 54, 101, 118, 152, 176, 178, 225, 227.

Marjory Stonemam Douglas courtesy of Arthur R. Marshall Foundation: page 40.

Flagler Museum archives: pages 22, 57, 78, 165.

Additional photo credits:
  Bill Antalek: page 49
  Bruce Bennett: page 184
  Robert Brantley: page 61
  Janice Cohen: page 204
  Robert James Photo and Video: page 154
  Irwin Spivak: page 237

$\mathcal{I}$nformation

Write ups for area cultural organizations are courtesy of the organizations themselves or the Palm Beach County Cultural Council.

Information on animals courtesy of Palm Beach Zoo: pages 77, 84, 200.

Information on plants courtesy of Mounts Botanical Garden: pages 34, 117, 231, 235.

Information courtesy of the Boca Raton Historical Society: pages 85, 215.

Information courtesy of the Loxahatchee River Historical Society: pages 143, 150, 155.